Strindberg—Other Sides

Seven Plays

Translated and introduced
by Joe Martin

with a Foreword by
Björn Meidal

PETER LANG
New York • Washington, D.C./Baltimore • Boston
Bern • Frankfurt am Main • Berlin • Vienna • Paris

Library of Congress Cataloging-in-Publication Data

Strindberg, August, 1849–1912.
[Plays. English. Selections]
Strindberg—other sides: seven plays / Joe Martin (Translator).
p.   cm.
Includes bibliographical references.
1. Strindberg, August, 1849–1912—Translations into English.
I. Martin, Joe. II. Title.
PT9811.A3S635   839.72'6—dc21   96-54508
ISBN 0-8204-3691-7

Die Deutsche Bibliothek-CIP-Einheitsaufnahme

Strindberg—other sides: seven plays / Joe Martin (transl.).
–New York; Washington, D.C./Baltimore; Boston; Bern;
Frankfurt am Main; Berlin; Vienna; Paris: Lang.
ISBN 0-8204-3691-7

The photo on the front cover is Strindberg at Värmdö-Brevik, 1891. The back cover depicts "Strindberg's last walk" from 1912. Photos courtesy of Strindbergsmuseét. Author photo by Patricia Barrow.

This translation of *The Ghost Sonata* was first published by IE Clark, Copyright © Joe Martin, 1991.

The paper in this book meets the guidelines for permanence and durability
of the Committee on Production Guidelines for Book Longevity
of the Council of Library Resources.

© 1997 Peter Lang Publishing, Inc., New York

Printed in the United States of America.

CONTENTS

▪ ▪ ▪

▪ ▪ ▪

FOREWORD

by Björn Meidal

AUGUST STRINDBERG has been a presence in the United States for more than a hundred years. In 1893 Gustaf Steffen authored the first introduction to his work. In 1899 Nelly Erichsen's translation of *The Father* appeared. It took until 1905 before Strindberg was presented on an American stage. In that production silent film star Alla Nazimova played *Miss Julie*—in Russian!—in New York. James Huneker, Strindberg's first champion in America, published *Iconoclasts*, a study of ten modern dramatists. Strindberg, with whom he was familiar through Emil Schering's German translations, is praised as Sweden's Shakespeare and is commended for drawing splendid characters. He describes Strindberg's dramatic technique as being as revolutionary as Wagner's innovative music-drama. Huneker maintains additionally that Strindberg is "a good hater." Such work is "rare and stimulating." He considers *Miss Julie, Creditors* and *A Dream Play* his best works. The study concludes with the assertion that Strindberg might very easily come to surpass Ibsen, but that the so-called "woman-hater Strindberg" would still have difficulties becoming popular in the United States, "the promised land of woman-worshippers."

Huneker's prophecy would be borne out. This, despite the fact that even before Strindberg's death in 1912 Swedish-speaking American translators were in full progress transforming Strindberg's drama to American English. Strindberg wrote to one of them, as a conclusion to a letter: "And so: good luck on your undertaking! which will certainly be long and trying!" After the American premiere of *The Father* at the Berkeley Lyceum Theatre in New York in 1912, a triumphant telegram was sent to Strindberg. "[The] performance of father in newyork is tremendously gripping growing in power with the public." But the reviewers were of another opinion: "Nothing is to be hoped for from Sweden. The New York production of *The Father* was powerful but to the point of being repellant when considered as realism. It is hardly likely that our lack of playable drama will be filled by import from Sweden." The critic George Jean Nathan summed up the reception ironically:

> Strindberg, as my readers know, is a curious admixture and psychiatric synthesis of Nietzsche, Shaw, Ibsen, Balzac, Brieux, Renan, Rousseau, Hauptman, Gorky, Tolstoy, Poe and Harry Thorn. He is a supernormal alienist utilizing himself as his subject, a neurasthenic genius, with a pen of moral aconite, a sorehead, a romantic business man, a practical poet of the deadly prosaic, a leper in the ball room who lays hands on the whitest pair of shoulders, a dramatist of the shudder that to him is but a hollow and awful giggle, a vice president of the board of directors of Hell, a madman who cuts the elevator cable, a cocktail made entirely of bitters, a trusting clod pâté and a suspicious sage, a sourball, a reporter of hangover psychopathia sexualis, a master of words, a cannoneer of the moor buzzards called women, a martyr in his own eyes, a mistaker of the teapot for the open sea, an atheist with a four days' growth leering from his window at passing school children, a safety razor with the safety attachment broken, a man who expectorates on the counterpane of the bed chamber, a calm, cool statistician, a sex anarchist, a dramatist for vast wonder.

Unfortunately it turns out that Nathan's amusing exaggerations have sunk deep roots. F.L. Lucas, in his *The Drama of Ibsen and Strindberg* (1962) speaks of "the unbalanced, neurotic, daemonic" Strindberg as "the world's wildest misogynist" and "one of the craziest geniuses." John Gassner insisted at the end of the 1950s that Strindberg had not had a single artistic or commercial success on an American stage. And Eric Bentley pointed out in *The Playwright as Thinker,* that of the great figures in theatre Strindberg was almost unknown in America. This, despite the productions of *The Ghost Sonata* (1924) and *A Dream Play* (1926) by Kenneth McGowan,

Robert Edmond Jones and Eugene O'Neill at the Provincetown Playhouse in New York. In their collective protest against the commercial theatre, they claimed Strindberg to be "the most modern of moderns, the greatest interpreter in the theatre of the characteristic spiritual conflicts which constitute the drama—the blood—of our lives today."

Perhaps Strindberg has himself partly to blame for the entrenched image of the "madman" and "misogynist." In the first place, it seems as if the exciting story of August Strindberg's life, from his birth in 1849 until his death in 1912, has always competed with all the narratives, plays, novels and stories he himself produced. An English Strindberg biographer makes a comparison with Ibsen on this point: "But though Ibsen is an interesting character, his plays are more interesting still; whereas Strindberg, often, I think, overrated as a writer, remains a personality far more extraordinary than any of his works."

In the second place, at the end of the 1880s the old sets of contradictions in Strindberg's thinking—idealism vs. compromise, nature vs. culture, and overclass vs. underclass—are replaced by the new antithesis man vs. woman. In *A Madman's Defence* (in which the title was intended ironically) he published a self-exposé of his own subjective picture of his first marriage. Influenced by the contemporary interest in hypnosis and suggestion, Darwinism and Nietzsche's superior man, in the naturalistic tragedies *The Father* and *Miss Julie* the emphasis is placed on the struggle between the sexes. From a purely formal point of view the dramatist is clearly objectively impartial, as the woman wins in the one and the man in the other. But in the reality of the theatre it is of course the director and the actors who will decide in which direction the sympathies of the public will go.

Third, it is tempting to confuse the rhetorician, the theorist and the propagandist Strindberg with the author of the same name. In his plays opposing characters are always supplied with equally strong arguments. The "half-woman" that the foreword to *Miss Julie* mentions, in the play becomes a dream role for any actress, a portrayal of an independent woman that has no equal in the drama of the nineteenth century. In his draft for his play about the seventeenth-century Swedish monarch *Queen Christina*, Strindberg writes that she "was so much a real woman that she was a woman-hater." And when he was planning his play about the eighteenth-century King Carl XII his objective was to present a portrait that polemicized against him. In both cases, however, it was the dramatist that won out over the propagandist. The theoretical types are transformed on the stage into living and complex characters.

In the older critical work on Strindberg the emphasis was placed upon biographical material: Strindberg as a man possessed by his obsessions. More recent work stresses instead the way the artist Strindberg has supreme control in the way he handles and transforms his material. In this area recent important contributions have been made by American commentators. Evert Sprinchorn underscores in *Strindberg as Dramatist* (1982) Strindberg's central place in literary modernism and draws a portrait of a consciously experimenting artist who exploits his own experience to create drama. And Harry G. Carlson in *Strindberg and the Poetry of Myth* (1982) lays bare ingeniously a mythopoetic pattern in Strindberg's dramatic oeuvre. Robert Brustein summarized in the *New York Review of Books*: "Strindberg is at last beginning to exist—not for his influence on others but by virtue of his own achievements, not as a biographical curiosity but in recognition of his own unique gifts."

And the American revaluation of Strindberg continues! In 1988 I had the pleasure of meeting Joe Martin in connection with my teaching Strindberg courses at the University of Pennsylvania and University of Maryland. To my delight I found that Martin, as proficient as he is enthusiastic, was in the midst running an ambitious Strindberg Festival in Washington D.C. He had translated *Carl XII* for a reading, and had both translated and directed *The Ghost Sonata*. Three Strindberg one-acts, meanwhile, were running at another off-broadway theatre. Strindberg was, as he himself put it, "a man who knew a thousand arts." Beside a torrent of literary works, he devoted himself to expressionistic painting, experimental photography (without lens and sometimes even without a camera), history, chemistry and alchemy and also ventured into linguistics. His translator Joe Martin is not far behind him in his versatility. Martin's experience as a scholar, playwright, novelist, poet, essayist, theatre director and producer is a perfect fit, as he presents "other sides" of Strindberg to a North American public.

These "other sides" have not only to do with the selection of plays, but also with the generous commentaries concerning the background, form, content and reception of the works that Martin includes here. At the heart of this effort lies the intention to understand and explain the remarkable synthesis of the later Strindberg's work: the dialectic between religious mysticism and political radicalism. Furthermore, those who served as inspirations for Strindberg are discussed, such as Swedenborg and Schopenhauer, as well as those inspired *by* Strindberg, like O'Neill, Brecht and Ingmar Bergman. Martin's translations are based upon the new Swedish critical edition of Strindberg's *Collected Works*. The objective in this respect has been twofold: to be as loyal as possible to the text—including punctuation—and to produce stageworthy scripts for actors. In the present book Martin introduces in his own translation seven of Strindberg's plays—well, actually eight, as the American public will have the opportunity for the first time to make the acquaintance of the remarkable dramatic fragment *Toten-Insel.*

Strindberg is internationally known above all for his naturalistic and pre-expressionist dramas. It is therefore a welcome feature of this anthology that space has been set aside for two of Strindberg's other contributions to world theatre: his series of one-acts, and his sequence of Swedish historical dramas. Martin surprisingly turns the Strindbergean chronology on its head, but with good reason. The volume opens with *The Ghost Sonata* (1907)—about which Dürrenmatt, a modern fellow playwright, asserted: "Modern drama has come out of Strindberg: we have never gone beyond the second scene of *The Ghost Sonata*"—and works its way backward to three one-acts which Strindberg wrote in the years 1888–89. The thought here, of course, is that this will help free the reader from the simplistic attempts of the textbooks to label Strindberg's plays in the form of "isms." Provided with the penetrating lens of the "pre-expressionist" or "absurdist" *Ghost Sonata*, we shall discover new things even in the "naturalistic" play *The Stronger* and in the "history" play *Carl XII.*

Strindberg is not only a historic force as the father figure of the modern theatre—expressionism, theatre of cruelty, absurdism—but remains a potent force to this day. Or in the words of Franz Kafka: "We are Strindberg's contemporaries and successors."

University of Uppsala
1997

PREFACE

WITH the publication of this new volume of translations of Strindberg plays, it is my hope that more will be accomplished than simply providing stageworthy English versions, that accurately reflect the intentions of the Swedish master playwright. There has been a steady and ongoing revaluation of his works taking place over recent decades, perhaps beginning with Eric Bentley's seminal *The Playwright as Thinker*; followed by publication in English of some of Strindberg's many novels; biographies such as that of Olof Lagercrantz; collections on Strindberg's socially engaged work in Swedish by, among others, Jan Myrdal; and the release in a facsimile edition of his huge *Occult Diary (Ockulta Dagboken)*. There have been increasingly successful attempts to stage his so-called dream plays throughout the world, and in Sweden there has been a return to that same material as well as his dozen or so little-known history plays, which run the gamut from Shakespearean-style chronicle to expressionistic epic. Nevertheless, a rather garish image of Strindberg still lingers in North America and England—very different from the understanding of Strindberg the man and the artist which one finds in Germany, France and of course the Scandinavian countries.

If I were to summarize this distorted image of Strindberg as found among American and some British intellectuals—thereby perhaps distorting it further—it would sound something like this: "Strindberg. Yes of course we know him: The misogynist who went mad—but wrote three great plays about the battle of the sexes for therapy." Others are aware of his most innovative and productive later period, roughly from 1898 to 1912, but explain away the power and innovation in these works by labeling them "symbolist," which puts him in the wake of other less radical experimenters with theatrical form, instead of crediting him as a founder of the expressionist movement in the theatre—and of truly modern drama as well. The new national edition of Strindberg's extraordinary multifaceted writings will comprise seventy-five volumes when the process is finished, and will contain seventy-two plays: far more than Bentley seemed to be aware of when he tried to impress upon his American readers the scope of Strindberg's work. The vast majority of Strindberg's oeuvre is "underplayed," and this volume hopes to add one more turn of the knob to retune our image of the man and his writing.

The reference to "other sides" in the title does point, partly, to Strindberg's later philosophical concerns—referring both to the spiritual realm which he saw existing on the other side of everyday existence, but also to the strange mix of his social and political criticism and his hard fought-for mystic philosophy, influenced by Schopenhauer, Buddhism and Swedenborg.   To that end, this collection attempts to steer away from *The Father* and *Miss Julie*, which have been the two supposedly "marketable" Strindberg classics, in favor of showing a broad range of work from the rest of his seventy-two plays—now finally being brought out in a reliable Swedish National Edition, upon which these renderings are based. In addition to attempting to restore editorial deletions and making corrections based upon the national edition, and examinations of the final handwritten or typed drafts, I have hewn as closely as possible to Strindberg's use of punctuation: taking a cue from Ingmar Bergman's instructions to actors to begin with the cues Strindberg provides through his detailed "coding" of the text. Strindberg, perhaps a bit like Pinter in our own time, tended to code his text with pauses, silences—but also ellipses, double, triple and quadruple hyphens, and in his later work he even breaks the plays down into units by using asterisks, each marking a new *turn-of-idea.* That the vast majority of English editions, British and American, delete important elements of Strindberg's "score" has always been unsettling—especially inasmuch as we are dealing with a writer whose stage instincts were extremely acute, and who at times consciously structured his works by principles of music.[1]

That said, it has certainly been my goal to provide readable and actor-friendly translations that work well for American theatre artists, in order to make these "other" highly innovative works by Strindberg available to audiences. I have taken some time in the introductory "Revaluation of Strindberg" and the discussion of the plays that follows it, to try to illuminate these strange hybrid works with some of the newer thinking on Strindberg not available to English readers. Not just Lagercrantz's book, but Björn Meidal's work on Strindberg's spiritual ideas and social engagement, *From Prophet to People's Tribune: Strindberg and the Strindberg Feud*, and yet a few more, have prepared the ground for a new understanding of his work among North American theatre aficionados and artists.

*

Once again, I must thank the American Scandinavian foundation for two separate fellowships, and the Strindberg Museum in Stockholm for a research residency which enabled this project to come to fruition. The staff in the manuscript section of the Royal Library in Stockholm were ever helpful, as was Anita Persson, then at the Strindberg Museum, and Göran Rossholm at Stockholm University. I am especially grateful to Olof Lagercrantz and Björn Meidal, both for their books and their personal cues and guidance on exploring the labyrinth that is Strindberg. Among the innovative "Strindberg directors" who spent time with me poring over their sets and models, I include Per Verner-Carlsson, who certainly helped to put *The Pelican* back on the map as one of the major European dramas of the first decade of this century. Stefan Johansson of Teater 9 in Stockholm was a trove of information and imagination in our long talks about his approach to Strindberg; and Martha Vestin of Friteatern taught me something highly interesting when, despite her ambivalent relationship to Strindberg's works, she invited me to her company's eye-opening comic staging of *The Dance of Death*. I am obliged to mention the theatres in Washington which gave encouragement to this project by presenting these translations in performance for an American public for the first time: Michael Kahn, Artistic Director of the Shakespeare Theatre; Pat Murphy Sheehy, Artistic

Producer of Source Theatre; Robert McNamara, now Artistic Director of Scena Theatre; Carolyn Griffen, Producing Director of Metro Stage (known as American Showcase Theatre at the time of the productions). Others who helped bring these translations to fruition include Dr. Rose-Marie Oster at University of Maryland, one of the first to raise her voice in support of the somewhat off-beat concept of a "Strindberg Festival" back in 1988; and Lisa Wormser, whose superb efforts as Production Coordinator of the Strindberg Festival and Open Theatre in Washington helped to put five of these translations on stage in their first productions. As always, personal and professional thanks go to Lisa Lias, not the least for her assistance with the book manuscript. On this particular project, there is no one who deserves more appreciation than Beate Sydhoff, whose moral support and proactive engagement as Cultural Counselor of Sweden was invaluable in producing and polishing these translations, and whose hospitality in Sweden, along with that of her late husband, the artist Lars Millhagen, will not be forgotten in this lifetime.

Joe Martin
Washington, D.C.
July 1997

INTRODUCTION:
STRINDBERG—A REVALUATION

1.

MOST every devotee of the theatre knows August Strindberg as an unbalanced Swede who, driven by problems with his mother, and women in general, wrote two brilliant plays—*The Father* and *Miss Julie*. They might even be aware that Henrik Ibsen—the dramatist whom Strindberg found himself reacting *against* more often than not—kept Strindberg's portrait on the wall above his desk because of the power of his "mad eyes." Although on the one hand his plays are considered a *sine qua non* in any library of dramatic literature, the works of this "madman and misogynist" are not often cracked open, but are left standing on the shelf for fear of the sulphur fumes which might inundate the atmosphere of "correct" intellectual discourse.

How many are aware that George Bernard Shaw left a portion of his estate to ensure that translations of Strindberg's works would be produced in English? Or that Eugene O'Neill and Tennessee Williams later claimed Strindberg as their single most important influence? O'Neill in fact was partly responsible for the introduction of Strindberg's work to an American public, and dedicated much of his Nobel Prize acceptance speech to his literary mentor. In the late 1940s Eric Bentley, in his classic work *The Playwright as Thinker*, made Strindberg the pillar sustaining his discussion of modern playwrights, remarking, "If it be asked how a major modern writer can be so little known, I can only reply that I do not know. . . . The distribution of fame is capricious . . ."[1] Although Bentley tended to extend the myth, promoted somewhat by Strindberg himself, that he wrote for therapy—which resulted in an "outer circle" of confessional prose works, which then generated an inner circle of refined dramatic works[2]—he drew clear lines from Strindberg to modernity. He employed chapter titles such as "From Strindberg to Jean-Paul Sartre," and "From Strindberg to Bertolt Brecht." Even some of the early works of Brecht echo Strindberg's expressionist period (as is the case with the battle of husband and wife at the end of *The Wedding*), and Brecht's *Mother Courage* might not have come to be had he not seen a production of Strindberg's work on the Thirty Years War, *Gustav Adolf*. Theatre artists throughout the world continue to pay tribute to Strindberg as a writer still capable of "renewing" the theatre. An award-winning Norwegian playwright of the 1980s and 90s, Cecilie Løveid, confirmed that Strindberg helped to make her work possible, much more so than Ibsen: "He was ahead of the others. He thought more like us, today."[3] And of course Ingmar Bergman has repeatedly affirmed Strindberg's massive influence on his work, both on stage and in his films. Beyond his public assertions to that effect, Bergman's achievements as one of the world's great Strindberg directors also bear witness to this.

Today, when a revaluation of Strindberg's work has been underway for several decades, we can see that those earlier savvy students of world theatre did their homework well. The recent biography by Olof Lagercrantz, the dean of Swedish letters, shows Strindberg not as a hysteric or latent schizophrenic whose turbulent mind, delusions and hallucinations, drove him to write—but rather as an artist, methodical and disciplined in the extreme, who did not hesitate to inject turbulence into his life and mind in order to generate material to write. In the U.S., Evert Sprinchhorn has come up with similar conclusions.[4] That is, his writing didn't emerge from the chaos in his life: he injected chaos into things to fill his mental inkwell. There is a not-so-subtle distinction here. Life was his palette. (It should be mentioned that Strindberg has received increasing recognition for his painting and photography, in books by Harry Carlson and others, as well as from curators throughout Europe.) He made a necessary mess of it, until he got the blends he wanted. This makes him appear quite ruthless at times. He comes to resemble Kierkegaard's experimental and destructive "Esthetic Man" in *Either/Or*. Meanwhile there were also long periods of social and political commitment in his life—for better or for worse. Jan

Myrdal's anthology of Strindberg's prose, *The Word in My Power: A Reader for the Underclass* (*Ordet i min makt: En läsebok för underklassen*) reveals another Strindberg: Strindberg the advocate for the underprivileged and exploited, who—despite a conviction that there exists a spiritual and intellectual elite—in social and economic matters was democratic and even egalitarian, almost stridently so.[5] On top of all this, extensive works have been written on Strindberg's peculiar brand of religion, a sort of Christian mysticism inspired partly by the Theosophical movement in Europe and Buddhism, but even more by his 18th-century countryman Emanuel Swedenborg. Björn Meidal's book *Från profet till folktribun: Strindberg och Strindbergsfeiden: 1910-12. (From Prophet to People's Tribune: Strindberg and the Strindberg Feud)* deals superbly with these two passions of his later life.

The register and range of Strindberg's writing, as Lagercrantz has underscored repeatedly, is so much broader than the run-of-the-mill classic playwright, that this one quality alone might cause us to designate his work as "great." The theatre naturalism which he did not "father," but at whose birth he certainly served as midwife (along with Zola, less successfully, in France) is just one of the styles and subgenres in which he worked. There are epic plays, chronicle plays of wars, politics and kings, fairy tales, morality plays, world religious dramas (less successful), political tragedies, as well as the works which many consider to be the first expressionist dramas—*A Dream Play, The Ghost Sonata, The Great Highway,* and the trilogy *To Damascus*—and even strange proto-absurdist hybrids like *The Dance of Death.* Though it may be no indicator of true greatness by itself, the sheer quantity of his work cannot be overlooked. The new Swedish national edition of his works, still unfinished after more than a decade, will consist of 75 volumes: fiction, drama, poetry, scientific (and pseudoscientific) treatises, linguistic studies (on such topics as "The Evolution of the Hebrew Language" and "The Evolution of the Chinese Language"), social commentaries, political polemics and more. Recent exhibitions of his oil paintings and photography in Europe have cast light on yet another facet of this bottomless source of creative mass. Strindberg stands now as one of history's most restless and productive artists. Among his most extraordinary and

revolutionary contributions are the many works for the theatre which
he wrote during the last fifteen years of his life. These later works,
I am convinced, cannot be understood without a grasp of Strindberg's
broader output as a writer and artist. Reflecting on his other literary
or artistic ventures, in order to throw light on his theatre, may seem
to risk getting sidetracked. It seems to me, nonetheless, that to
understand *this* unique playwright's dramaturgy and formal experiments, we need to look at the imagination at work in his fiction, the
politics behind his sense of the *theatrum mundi*—and in addition, we
must examine his spiritual vision in order to understand such wide-
ranging experiments in theatrical form. That is, therefore, what I
propose to do in this revaluation of Strindberg. The intention is to
make some "other sides" of this classic-modern dramatist somewhat
better understood.

2.

Born in 1849, the son of a steamship company owner and his working
class wife, Strindberg was educated to join the Swedish professional
class as a teacher or physician. An early fascination with literature
drew him in other directions. Schiller's works, among others, fired his
imagination. His failed attempts to become a professional actor were
fueled by an early ambition to play Karl Moor in Schiller's "jacobin"
play, *The Robbers*.

In his younger years Strindberg mixed in constantly with the
cultural and political movements in Sweden. He was obsessed by
revolution, social change, reform of education, and was in constant
rebellion against received bourgeois values. His radical democratic
ideals—in his youth fostered by his readings of Rousseau, which in
turn led him in the direction of socialism, Bakunin and the anarchist
view of things—these ideals found their way into his first major play:
the now famous work about the Swedish Reformation of the sixteenth
century, *Master Olof*. In that play, Olaus Petri (Olof), as theologian
and philosopher, is unable to follow through with a democratic and
egalitarian revolution, when King Gustav Vasa puts a bloody halt to
social change once he has achieved the union of the Swedish nation

state under the new Lutheran Church. Olof abandons his rabble-rousing social radical friend Gert Bokpräntare, when they are facing death, and must choose compromise. His longtime friend and companion is dragged off to death crying out "Apostate!" and the democratic/egalitarian ideal is crushed by the *realpolitik* of the times. The play was written in prose originally, but during the ten years that it lay unproduced and consistently rejected by the institutional theatres supported by King Oscar II, the young playwright slowly transformed it, in three separate drafts, into a verse work, in which the message was much more chastening for hotheaded revolutionaries.[6] The form and message of the original prose version was unheard of at a time when the verse history drama *à la* Shakespeare and Schiller was in vogue. It was an earthier, more revolutionary epic text. His early radicalism can also be found in his first major fiction works, such as the satirical and very Dickensian novel *The Red Room.* His radical and pacifist views can be found in his works well into the 1880s. In 1884 he wrote a pacifist novella *Pangs of Conscience (Samvetskval)* for the Stockholm Peace Association, which would be revived and published in many European languages after the outbreak of the First World War. In the 1880s, converting rapidly to the new and progressive literary movement of Naturalism, Strindberg began a four-volume work of autobiographical fiction. He claimed to be using literature as a "scientific" tool to probe a society and an era.[7] The sequence was to be named after the first of its volumes, *Son of a Servant (Tjänstekvinnans son).* His opinions, in terms of society and politics, would undergo some strange permutations in the 1880s, as would his personality, which would cause some of his old political and artistic friends to revile him. But it did not happen all at once. And in any case, there were many who reviled him even before these "transformations" took place.

Strindberg's pamphlets, essays and prose pieces criticizing the monarchy, the Church, the state, as well as the sexual moralists, earned him something much worse than notoriety. Notable among these was the collection *The Swedish People (Svenska folket)* and *The New Kingdom (Det nya riket).* He became for some "the enemy." A campaign against "Strindbergian literature" emerged in the early 80s in Sweden. During his first self-imposed exile in France, Switzerland and Germany, court actions were begun against him in Sweden for his short story collection *Getting Married, Part I* (*Giftas, I*, 1884) which probed rather too deeply into both the Church and the bedroom for those times. The fact that certain well-situated advocates of women's rights joined with the highly moralistic pietist movement in the campaign to have him arraigned may have been the catalyst for the famous and increasingly virulent attacks against the "blue-stockings"—who he claimed were an idle class cooking up a middle class feminism. His assault on blue-stockings and a variety of feminists would continue for years to come. Strangely, the author's preface to the ill-fated *Getting Married* included a manifesto on the future "Women's Rights" which "the laws of nature would grant her, but of which, thanks to our perverse social system (and not as a result of male tyranny), she has been deprived."[8] In a nine-point program, Strindberg suggested: "The right to the same education as men"—although he lambastes the utility of the learning available in the school system and calls for a single examination for everyone; co-educational institutions; that a girl of school age "will have the same opportunity to 'run wild' and choose what company she pleases"; "complete equality between the sexes" in which false gallantry will disappear, and a man will learn "to make his bed, or sew on his shirt buttons"; "women shall have the vote"; that women "shall be eligible for all occupations"—where he adds, "Is anyone wiser or better suited to govern than an old mother, who has learnt through motherhood and running a household both how to rule and how to administrate? (Our forefathers had such a veneration for the wisdom of older women that they believed them to possess supernatural knowledge.)" Strindberg further suggests: that the code of morality will be less rigid with women in the system, for "no one knows better than she how patient and unexacting you must be with the erring children of man"; that women will be exempt from military service, due to the duties motherhood brings upon them—adding that in the future military service will not be viewed as particularly glorious, but a duty; and finally he calls for a more just distribution of society's wealth "to ensure that all who are born receive sustenance and instruction" which will ensure that marriage will not be an agreement of necessity, but made in freedom—"the female will be the one to choose" and women's position and that of society will improve thereby.[9]

Strindberg followed his "ideal" list of changes with a list of fifteen practical social reforms which could be put in place *immediately*, including: the right to vote; the introduction of civil marriage; the rescinding of a husband's rights as his wife's guardian; a legal age of adulthood for women of 18; mandatory deeds of settlement between couples in all marriages; and that "a woman shall keep her own name" in marriage. Additionally, he recommends separate bed chambers for married couples to avoid "satiety," and to give a woman "the right to possess her own body." Women who have no other occupation than that of responsibility for household and children must receive a fixed allowance for clothes and recreation. A woman should not be given money or clothes "for which she has to say thank you." She must have enough money to pay for entertainment herself "and thus be spared from always being *treated*." A woman who works and maintains the house shall keep all her money, but a woman who works and does not take care of the household should contribute as much financially as the man.

Of course, having put himself on firmer ground on issues at that time associated with Ibsen, he then feels ready to resume his old attack upon him. Strindberg complains of "a fixed code of conduct" which is implied in *A Doll's House (Et Dukkehjem,* 1879). Perhaps he is alluding to the approach in which a woman abandons her children when her husband's dealings with her are too patronizing. He adds: "In *Brand* he protested against Christianity, but his readers turned it into a Christian code. . . . In *Ghosts* he protested against immorality, and the moralists turned it into a code for immorality. In *An Enemy of the People* he protested about society, and the worst enemies of society pelted him with stones. That's what happens when you are Moses upon the mountain, and speak with tongues, and cover your head with a blue veil."[10] Strindberg suggested Ibsen needed to stop writing like a prophet and join humanity. In a mock interview with himself which ensues, Strindberg is told by his interviewer that he must be a socialist. "Of course. All enlightened people are today."

The essay ends with the assertion: "Woman does not need me to defend her." This relinquishing of responsibility will pale beside the invective against the aspirations of "liberated women" that would follow in the ensuing decade.

The collusion of pietists and the moralist strand of the women's movement to stigmatize *Getting Married* took on force, and a trial would soon be scheduled—the charges carrying a jail sentence of a year or more if he was found guilty. At this time Strindberg began his first period of self-imposed exile. Joining him was his wife, of Finnish-Swedish aristocratic extraction, Siri von Essen. Strindberg had spirited Siri out of a relationship with a Swedish military officer, the young Baron Carl Gustaf Wrangel. It is now generally agreed that before their other children were born, there was another bond between them apart from their mutual passion for art and theatre (She was an actress). Siri was seven months pregnant at their wedding on December 30, 1877. As was the case with the fictional couple who had a child out of wedlock in *The Red Room* (Struve and the woman he kept in secret), they had a premature baby which they left with a mid-wife the day it was born, and which died two days later under her care.[11] The tragedy occurred as they were planning complex maneuvers to adopt the baby, after registering the birth without using their names. Strindberg had married *up* in society, where appearances were everything—a phenomenon that would obsess him even at the end of his life.

The couple were mutually supportive in terms of their careers as well, and they both had a taste for a certain amount of bohemian existence. Yet this was to become one of the most famous of all turbulent marriages, wracked with mutual ruthless attempts at self-assertion, heightened by Strindberg's demanding combative intellect and his constant financial difficulty. It would be brought to the boiling point by his consistent use of the most painful personal matter from his own life, and thus Siri's too, as raw material for his writing—all of which is why the pairing of Siri von Essen and Strindberg has come to be seen as the artistic "marriage in hell" *par excellence*. Their relationship and marriage lasted officially from 1877 to 1892, which spans several transitions in Strindberg's *Weltanschauung* and his work. The marriage with Siri will supply the palette, paints and canvas for all his later, better known explorations of relations between the sexes. For this, Siri von Essen would pay a price—something for which the better classes of Östermalm in Stockholm did not forgive him, and it is said they still haven't to this day.

During this period of absence from his native land—from the later 1880s through the early 90s—Strindberg was increasingly influenced by Nietzsche, whose idea of the *superior man* was absorbed and adapted by him with his own unique twists in his fiction and plays. (It should be noted that Nietzsche, perhaps more than Marx, was for George Bernard Shaw too the most influential of the philosophers from the late 19th century.) Strindberg and Nietzsche carried on a correspondence, partly in Latin, in which they praised each other's work and thinking. Strindberg cut off this correspondence when it became clear that the grandiose tone of Nietzsche's letters was beginning to go over the deep end, becoming delusional. He had no way of knowing that the probable paresis of the brain, which was to turn Nietzsche into a howling patient, tied to his bed in his own home, was now approaching its sad climax. Still, it is clear from his fiction, his plays and letters that during much of this decade Strindberg felt himself, increasingly, to be part of an intellectual aristocracy, persecuted by a mob of small minds. During the 1880s he wrote a stream of arrogant and often stinging letters to or about—not only his enemies, but some of his most ardent and loyal supporters as well. This includes his well known anti-Semitic remarks in letters about his primary publishers, the Bonniers (Albert and Karl Otto)—who were not cooperative about publishing his work when it took its controversial turns in the 80s—as well as off-handed negative observations on the European Jews in general primarily in his correspondence, some articles and a satirical sketch.[12] There was also his defensiveness on the issue with the great Danish and Jewish journalist, Edvard Brandes, who early on had supported and helped disseminate his work throughout Europe.[13] (The Brandes brothers Georg and Edvard would return again to champion his works and his political campaigns at the beginning of the twentieth century.) By the mid-80s, his anti-Semitic remarks were public knowledge. By the early 1890s his anti-Semitic utterances will cease, fitting with a pattern of radical changes in his thinking and perspective.

At the same time Strindberg's attacks against the "bluestockings" transformed into attacks on the women's movement in general, and a sort of biological theory of conflicting needs between the genders that cause them to engage in absurd battles, which he managed with astounding success to incorporate into the most famous plays of his "naturalist" period *The Father, Miss Julie, Creditors*—and in some lesser plays such as *Comrades (Kamraterna)*. His best naturalism was driven by psychology, and a theory of conflict which he called *hjärnornas kamp,* a "battle of brains" or "battle of souls." (Plays like *Comrades*, ironically, suffer from the very *programmatic* form of realism which he accused Ibsen of exploiting.) In fact, the chemistry of ideas which allowed him to put his psychological naturalism on the map of the world stage was an imaginative combin-ation of three sorts of conflict: 1) the defeat of an inferior soul by a superior one, the Nietzschean idea, as for example in his 1888 piece for a silent woman and a verbose woman, *The Stronger (Den starkare)*; 2) the inherent conflict between the sexes due to a paradox of biological determinism ("The mother was your friend, you see, but the woman was your enemy, and love between the sexes is strife" says Laura in *The Father*);[14] and 3) class conflict.

This last type of conflict unites in a thrilling hybrid with the other two in *Miss Julie*. There the aristocratic Julie, every bit a match in intellect and power with her virile and savvy servant and lover Jean, is doomed to lose as a member of the decaying aristocracy, while Jean—as a representative of the laboring class that knows how to make the world work—is striving to rise and become the future. This view makes the working class the source for the superior man of the future—a rather un-Nietzschean application of the master's ideas of class, caste and nobility. In the novella *Tschandala*, meanwhile, Nietzsche's notions of an aristocrat of the soul winning out over an "outcast" is more closely applied. For Strindberg the actual under-class sometimes served as a model for the superior man, but ironically he perceived a sort of dangerous "untouchable" underclass of the mind. He found a model for *both* sorts of underclass in the figure of

Ludvig Hansen, caretaker at the Danish estate in Skovlyst in Denmark, where the Strindbergs resided in 1888. (Siri and he lived on the estate with their children, but were sleeping and lodging separately by now.) Skovlyst was owned by a Danish countess who had gone mad, but roamed the estates leaving matters in the hands of her long-time employee. Strindberg was at first fast friends and drinking partners with the robust man of the working class. However, after Hansen accused him of sexual involvement with his half-sister—correctly, as Strindberg admitted in a letter to Siri—and Strindberg reported Hansen to the police as a thief they were hunting, Hansen went to the press with his *scandal*, and life at Skovlyst became a frightening stand-off.[15] The relationship moved from solidarity, between two "superior" sorts, to conflict—a battle of souls in which the superior man must summon all his vital force to overcome the *sly* survival instincts of the inferior man (who maintained a pack of vicious great danes). Hansen may have inspired both the virile figure of Jean in *Miss Julie* and the criminal pariah in *Tschandala*. And so these conflicting world-views—the superiority of the underclass in the art of living, and the superiority of the aristocracy of spirit—lived side by side in Strindberg's writing in the 80s. His tortuous work on his sociological book, *Among French Peasants (Bland franska bönder)* was to be his last proletarian undertaking for many years. But in less than a decade he would begin writing of these years with loathing, describing his attitude as that of *hubris*.

3.

Needless to say, Strindberg's old liberal and radical friends were becoming estranged from his work at this time. Swedish socialist leader Hjalmar Branting was no longer his defender, and the Brandes brothers were much less likely to come to his defense in the world of letters. Despite a brief return to Sweden in 1884 to face the conclusion of the trial—where he was given the welcome of a working class hero, and one of the longest standing ovations in European history at the opening of his fantasy epic play *The Travels of Lucky Per (Lycko-Pers resa)*—he had gone off again to Switzerland with his

family, still feeling very much the scourge of Swedish society. The
turn his work had taken, the "depravity" the critics found in his
naturalism as well as his pronouncements on the women's movement
and Swedish national culture, his aristocratic demeanor in discussing
his enemies—all this seriously alienated him from former defenders.

Eventually, the time came for final prolonged and difficult
divorce proceedings with Siri—but not before Strindberg's art-drawn-
from-life threw an effective monkey wrench into that life. His book
written in French while they were living in France, between September 1887 and March 1888, *Le Plaidoyer d'un fou (A Madman's
Defense)* seemed to many to chronicle his struggles with Siri in
heightened and detailed fashion. Like so many of Strindberg's works,
it has often been brought down a few pegs by critics for its being
autobiography rather than fiction. As is the case with his plays, this
criticism is simplistic when applied to these so-called "confessional"
works of fiction. For they are fiction. The character Axel in *A
Madman's Defense* can easily be seen by the perceptive critic to be an
unreliable narrator, at times comically so: for Axel, the abused
husband/writer, is portrayed as hovering at the brink of paranoia—before taking a full-fledged dive into it. Of course, one of his problems
is that every time he tries to recover his composure, his wife commits
another act of psychological horror which confirms his suspicions.
The macabre atmosphere he creates around the wife's apparent affair
with a masculinized "liberated" woman is, to be sure, based upon
incidents that occurred when Siri's friend Marie David—who laid
claim to being Georg Brandes's illegitimate daughter—came to stay
with the family, and as a sort of uninvited guest (from Strindberg's
point of view) stayed on—and could not be dislodged when her
friendship with Siri grew intimate. Also apparently true is the story
that Strindberg pushed Siri into a river during a walk in the woods.
But at all times, the narrator is in the throes of florid doubts and an
angst-colored world. The material is being used by Strindberg to shift
out of the naturalist mode. It is taking him in the direction of his
fellow Scandinavian, the painter Edvard Munch—whom he knew, and
with whom he would become comrades in the bohême that gathered
in the early 90s in the Berlin café known as the *Kloster*, which he

dubbed "Zum Schwarzen Ferkel" (The Black Pig).

This is another landmark moment in our revised survey of Strindberg's career. Strindberg was using his own life, and Siri's, at a cost of great pain to both of them to be sure, to create material. Increasingly he was stirring up life, to generate *Stoff* as the Germans would say—more material for his quest to plumb the human psyche. Some may protest this assertion. As mentioned earlier, even as astute a commentator as Eric Bentley has suggested that the therapeutic impulse drives his work. In the case of this novel, this thinking is reinforced by the final lines of the protagonist Axel: "The story is now terminated, my Adored one. I have avenged myself; we are quits . . ."[16] The image of Strindberg as continuously mad, raging with bullish hatred toward women, arrogant, elitist—this is all a lasting and perversely beloved image of the man: more so in America and England than elsewhere. It is part of a set of mythologies that indeed make Strindberg a character to amaze us, but which for a long time have caused misunderstanding and a lessened appreciation for his own fictional and theatrical characters. In a preface to the American translation of *Le Plaidoyer d'un fou* by Anthony Swerling, Børge Gedsø Madsen looks to the *Getting Married* trial and suggests: "the strain of the trial and a morbid fear of being imprisoned left him badly upset emotionally; the second volume of [*Getting Married*] . . . is clearly the work of a gravely disturbed and unbalanced mind." He adds that "critics should not suppose that the novel . . . is a true-to-life account of actual first marriage, or accept the one-sided portrayal of Maria as an authentic representation of the real Siri von Essen."[17] To his credit Madsen too perceives the beginnings of the new forms Strindberg was going to forge in the coming decades, a "technique of distortion and exaggeration" as he will use "so often in his dramas (especially in his late 'expressionistic' period)."[18] Many commentators don't see even this much method (or style) in Strindberg's "madness." If the madness comes first, and forces the work into existence, out of a sort of need for therapy, then the craftsman cannot come first. The artist is just a finely tuned receiver and sender for the disturbances in his psyche. He cannot help himself.

How can it be then, that during the same precise time period,

Strindberg had been writing one of his most popular fiction works: tightly structured, classic in terms of its narrative, written in the third person—and stylistically a cross between Dickens, Brontë and Poe: *The People of Hemsö (Hemsöborna)*? This novel of outrageous intrigue on an island farm estate in the Stockholm archipelago, is still considered one of the splendid yarns in all of Scandinavian literature. It is facts like this that have led writers of the stature of Olof Lagercrantz, recently, to suggest that Strindberg created turmoil and troubles in his life in his constant artistic obsession with *material*, to explore new content or create new forms, rather than to find an artistic outlet for his obsessions. Strindberg the madman, misogynist, bigot, elitist, however much fun he may be for our critical pen-lashings and cultural amusement in England and America, may not be so smugly pinned down.

In his decade of "hubris"—a term he will later use to describe his attitude during the 1880s and early 90s—Strindberg could still temper his arrogance in his fiction and plays. But in his massive correspondence and public remarks he vented spleen. In his December 1885 essay "On My Anti-Semitism" Strindberg tries to address his recently acquired reputation as an anti-Semite head on, and publicly (in a manner the activist literary anti-Semites like Daudet in France—who published antisemitic political pamphlets and would not associate with Jews—would never do). He suggests that his anti-Semitic statements of the past had been based upon his dashed expectations of Europe's main community of "outsiders," who originally brought other, healthy cultural values with them. He sees greed, materialism, and petty shopkeepers' mentality as a native European phenomenon. He portrays his "anti-Semitism" as ironic, based upon disappointment that the Jews of Europe conformed to Europe. His anti-Semitism, he says, boils down to this: "The Jews are not Jewish enough."[19]

This description—patronizing and in tune with his style in the 80s—can be substantiated to an extent by re-examining Strindberg's work from the radical 1870s and even the 80s. Lagercrantz has written a small book of *Afterthoughts on Strindberg (Eftertankar om Strindberg)*. He recalls the story from *The Red Room*, mentioned above, in which a couple lose their baby, conceived out of wedlock, and before it is baptized. The Church will not allow a service for such a child, it is simply to be put into the earth. At the funeral are the young bohemian band of students and artists who are the focus of Strindberg's first major novel. No one knows what to do. It is the Jewish member of the band, Levi, who removes his hat on the cold winter day (though Jewish custom is actually to keep the hat on), looks up into the empty winter sky, and recites aloud among the silent group and before the forlorn parents, the Kaddish.[20]

In the *Son of A Servant 2: Time of Ferment (Jäsningstiden)*, also based on autobiographical material, the young protagonist Johan leaves teaching in the public school to live in the home of a physician who convinces him that he should train in medicine. The physician's family is Jewish: the well-stocked book shelves, the interest in art, the high priority placed on education make the place a house of culture typical of "the children of Israel," which the protagonist experiences as a relief from the pretensions to culture he has seen in his country.[21] In personal letters, Strindberg found an outlet for a great deal of bile—much of it connected with his frustrations with publishers and, in some cases, producers. The letters can be coarse, salted with violent epithets that arise uncensored and in knee-jerk fashion. It is there that Strindberg's anti-Semitic remarks of the 1880s are found, never in his plays. Portrayals of Jews in his literary works, with the exception of one satirical sketch, do not accord with the slanderous tone of his self-indulgent letters—which found all sorts of other targets as well. Notably, the *Occult Diary* for which he forbade publication, contains none.

4.

In the early 90s Strindberg will move away from writing fiction, and will write almost no drama at all, as he enters upon a series of relationships and personal projects leading to the "Inferno period"—which refers to the famous "autobiographical" novel which he produced at the end of it all. One might say it begins with the dissolution of his marriage with Siri, who moved away from Stockholm with the children, and his alienation from his family. In Berlin he becomes involved with the circle at the pub he called "Zum Schwarzen Ferkel" now known to posterity as the "Ferkel Circle." Perhaps it was there the expressionist painter Edvard Munch becomes an influence on his sense of esthetics. He meets the Polish iconoclast poet Stanislaw Przybyszewski and the charismatic Norwegian woman Dagny Juel—introduced to the group by Munch—and who soon became the Polish poet's fiancée. Strindberg too succumbed to her energy and vitality, after her engagement with Przybyszewski, and in the penitential rain that fell upon him during the later events described in *Inferno*, guilt over this incident plagued him. In that book he would continue to hear or hallucinate a poet named "Popoffsky" playing on piano, near his Paris apartment, the *Aufschwung* by Schumann: the same piece with which Przybyszewski liked to rouse the Ferkel Circle. Munch rendered a famous portrait of Strindberg during this period, and included his back in his sequence of lithographs on "Jealousy": Przybyszewski's face, in them, is prominent. (Dagny would be found dead in Georgia in 1901, shot by a Russian lover, who then killed himself. Przybyszewski in 1896 was arrested for the murder of an ex-mistress and one of their children—until it was proven she had taken her own life.) He felt increasingly at sea as a dramatist and writer during this time. Though his reputation in France had grown with André Antoine's staging of *Miss Julie*, and various publications, in Sweden he was still a pariah.

It was while he was among the artists and literati in this circle in Berlin that Strindberg met the Austrian journalist Frida Uhl, who was, for a few years beginning in 1893, to become his second wife. Their brief marriage and their difficult parting are described in the appropriately slim, sadly toned novel *The Cloister* (*Klostret* 1898). This relationship seems to have provided some material for the mysterious play *There Are Crimes and Crimes* (*Brott och brott*, 1899). More importantly, Frida Uhl— whom Strindberg came to feel he had met on a path through repentance to illumination—is the indirect model for the character of the Lady in his trilogy of pilgrimage, *To Damascus*. It is a play that will change the history of the drama, and blaze a new path for a modern theatre in Europe. Uhl insisted later in life that Strindberg's stormy relationships arose because, despite his temper, he could not bear to be with a woman who was not his intellectual equal.[22] It was a set-up for drama and conflict that few women would have tolerated as long as Siri, or treated as philosophically as did Frida.

After Strindberg's marriage with Frida went into dissolution, she left him and went abroad. In his novel *Inferno* the author Strindberg uses a great deal of compression to tell of his existence alone in Paris: of his published scientific experiments, leading to alchemical investigations, done in his own apartments with a small portable lab and a stove. While his hands are blackening from his experiments and a bad case of psoriasis—from which the real Strindberg would suffer till the end of his life—he hears the piano playing of Przybyszewski (here called Popoffsky). Though he changes apartments, the piano playing follows him. At one point in the narrative he believes that repairmen in the apartment above him are converting wires and bedsprings into an electric device with which to radiate his room. He places himself under the care of a doctor at a sanitorium who can help him with his hands, and, it is implied, with his psychological decline. Though he makes progress there, he flees. He accepts the invitation of his wife's family to stay with them in a mountainous region of Austria, near a valley called Klam. (Interestingly, the name Kafka chose for the elusive bureaucrat who is the object of K's quest in *The Castle* was "Klamm." Kafka was a devoted reader of Strindberg's works.[23]) In the novel he is trapped in the alpine valleys, and in the home dominated by religious relatives of his wife—toward whom he felt extreme ambivalence. They are alternately portrayed as suffocating him, and offering him a path to liberation with their suggestions that he has ignored his spiritual side. In the novel *Inferno* the central character is indeed named "Strindberg." The protagonist wanders the countryside, begins seeing shapes and meanings—personal meanings and shapes, to be sure—in the sculpted landscape around him. That landscape is dotted with roadside shrines commemorating lives, losses and faith. He begins to describe a sense that he is being pursued by "powers." In that regard, it is interesting that to this day, one can read wry comments in Swedish literary publications about Strindberg and "the powers." By the time he wrote *The*

Ghost Sonata in 1907, Strindberg himself seemed to see occasional humor in these matters. When he comes upon a noisy blacksmith's workshop, full of blazing coal fires and glowing instruments, he reads it as an external representation of his internal state. In fact, he is reading signs everywhere in human relations and his environment. The world has become a semiotic field, like a book, revealing his internal world—or alternately, a place where he can read the judgment that falls on his own acts and life.

In a chapter of *Inferno* called "Swedenborg," the narrator (Strindberg) writes of the debt he owes his "fellow countryman": the 18th-century scientist and engineer turned mystic, whose thinking, together with that of Schopenhauer's, will lead Strindberg to investigate the philosophical systems of Hinduism and Buddhism at the turn of the century. He is in particular struck by Swedenborg's teaching in his work the *Arcana Coelestia* of *correspondences*: of forms in nature which reflect one other—the moth that takes on the colors of the rocks and moss where it lives—or things in nature that reflect back cosmic phenomena—as flowers reaching for the sky resemble the shape of light radiating from the stars and sun.[24] He also begins to differentiate between *exoteric* experience, in which one lives one's daily life, and *esoteric* experience, which contains events in the world of the spirit. He returns to the southern coast of Sweden meditate on his new insights.

In the end the book's protagonist, "Strindberg," discovers the meaning of "resignation." The *powers*, which resemble the Greek furies as much as they do elements of Divine will, seem willing to release him. Even so, he continues to see what he calls "the finger of God" in events in the world that seem to have particular meaning for him.

The novel about the *Inferno* period, certainly purports to recount an all-consuming spiritual crisis resulting in mental breakdown, stemming from revulsion against his previous arrogance and pride. Strindberg is combining a Christian mysticism—he contemplates conversion to Catholicism—Swedenborgianism, and the Greek notions of hubris and nemesis. The road to resignation for Strindberg, however, either the character or the author, did not come easily.

Neither would it be the last stop on his long path. This transitional period leads directly to the enormous stream of plays that he would pen at the turn of the twentieth century. He would now, in the last fourteen years of his life, write about half of his seventy-two plays. The "pilgrimage plays," which he will write in the years to come, are among the first true expressionist dramas—though one might look back to Büchner's *Woyzeck*, and also to Strindberg's contemporary, the sometime romantic companion of his second wife Frida: Frank Wedekind. *To Damascus*, not just part one, but all three parts, recounts the *Inferno* events in a highly stylized dramatic form. In his visual concept for the play as a performance event, Strindberg drew upon the design of the stage for the massive passion play at Oberammergau.[25] Thus, Strindberg's pilgrimage play has elements of the medieval passion in it, as much as elements of the Morality—with that genre's depiction of a soul's pilgrimage. The Strindberg plays that we now call expressionist show the wandering and destiny of a soul toward his final end or illumination, with every scene representing a "station" as it were: a form with clear links to the medieval Moralities.

Strindberg was responsible for casting the 22-year-old Harriet Bosse in the role of the Lady, after seeing her as Puck in *A Midsummer Night's Dream*. And the bond between them brought about his third marriage. In this case—though they had a child together—the gap in age, Strindberg's demanding nature, and issues of sexual incompatibility between them caused them to drift apart. She had already taken an extended trip away to the Stockholm Archipelago, after the run of *To Damascus (I)*. When she was cast in the role of Indra's Daughter in the first production of *A Dream Play* in 1907, they had been divorced for more than three years.

His final play, *The Great Highway (Stora landsvägen)* written in 1909, also has this structure, and the scenes are even designated as "stations." A play with a related structure—but so radical in its break with previous forms that it remains one of the pivotal works of the twentieth-century theatre revolution—is *A Dream Play*. Ostensibly it portrays the descent of Indra's Daughter to earth to discover the state of human beings in this existence. In fact the play has no central consciousness, no central character, but a constantly shifting perspective, unanchored by everything except what Strindberg called "the logic of the dream."

Strindberg also wrote seven history or chronicle plays about Swedish monarchs between late 1899 and 1902. Some like *The Saga of the Folkungs (Folkungasagan)* have dreamlike qualities. That play deals with themes of repentance and resignation in a king. *Gustav Vasa*, meanwhile, shows the politics of the nation-state with the sharpness of a bayonet and halberd—and allowed him to return to his compromised revolutionary, Master Olaus Petri. Other of the history plays walked a middle line between a mystic apprehension of life, and the ironies and injustice of the political world. *Gustav Adolf* is a massive epic of the Thirty Years War, and the absurd Protestant-Catholic schism that was cynically manipulated in that great European catastrophe. It employs various scenes from the people's perspective instead of that of the nobility. A few decades later this play is said to have had an impact on Bertolt Brecht, who would later write perhaps his greatest play based upon that war: *Mother Courage*.[26] *Carl XII* is a play of war and economics, a return to Strindberg's previous dissections of a national sacred cow in Swedish history. This time, however, he shows a strange sympathy with Carl's resignation to his fate, and some scenes have expressionist elements—or dream play elements, if you will—in which Carl tries to interpret signs in the world around him: the plague that wracks Sweden after his defeat in Russia; the massive inflation he causes to build and army for new foreign adventures; the parade of aggrieved women who pass before his bed as petitioners as he lies in a delirium. *Gustav III* tells the story of the final year of Sweden's paradoxical "theatre king"—who built Sweden's "Versailles" at Drottningholm, while claiming he would lead the "French Revolution" in Sweden against the aristocracy—who wrote his own plays, acted in them, and was shot while in costume at a masked ball in his own opera house. This is a work which combines the Shakespearean form with elements we now call postmodern. *Queen Kristina* too, about a monarch-actor who abdicated when she converted to Catholicism, displays some tendencies of "meta-theatre."

The Dance of Death, completed in 1900 at the pivot of the century, presents a strange hybrid in which Strindberg brings some of his old form and content—a living room setting and a battle of brains and genders—together with expressionist elements. The result is neither naturalism nor expressionism. It lacks a clear linear plot. It is more of a circular plot, which has been cited by Martin Esslin and others as a forerunner of the theatre of the Absurd.[27] The five chamber plays written between 1907 and 1909, meanwhile, also walk a tightrope between the two tendencies in Strindberg's dramatic works. Of those plays, *The Ghost Sonata (Spöksonaten)* leans in the direction of pure expressionism, putting the world of the mind on stage, while in *The Pelican (Pelikanen)*, despite its initial realism, the tensions between the exploitative mother and her two children rise to a level that causes the play to burst into the realm of nightmare: it paints a middle-class life which is a hell, from which the characters seek liberation. *The Burned House (Brända tomten)* and *Storm (Oväder)* show the world of mind and phenomena existing in terrible tension: the realities, like those of one of Strindberg's artistic heirs, Harold Pinter, are hard to interpret. Yet unlike Pinter—who with Edward Albee goes further along the path forged by *The Dance of Death*—there is a sense of resignation which colors these plays, and gives them poetic power. *The Black Glove (Svarta handsken)* is a mystic verse play set at Christmas, obviously with a broader audience in mind. All these pieces are inspired by the many hours that Strindberg's brother Axel spent playing piano for him when he lived in the "Red House," a grand building on Karlavägen in Stockholm, after 1901 (He moved to the "Blue Tower" on Drottninggatan in 1908). Axel's forte was sonatas, and it was the three-movement sonata form that Strindberg employed to shape his dramatic works during this period. It is a structure the chamber plays have in common.

From 1907 to 1910, Strindberg worked closely with the young director August Falk and the company at the Intimate Theatre in Stockholm, dedicated to producing his works. His *Open Letters to the Intimate Theatre (Öppna brev till Intima teatern)* present a remarkable exposition of his theories of dramaturgy, acting, production and theatre esthetics—and testify to the tremendous debt that Strindberg felt he owed to Shakespeare.

5.

Interestingly, during this period, in his fiction Strindberg turned back
to a literary form that brought him renown as a young author—that
of *The Red Room*. He began combining the razor-edged social satire
with his spiritual concerns in novels like *The Gothic Rooms* (*Götiska
rummen*, 1904)—and more particularly in 1907 with *Black Banners*
(Svarta fanor, actually written in 1904). *Black Banners* returns to the
cast of characters from his youthful best-seller in their retirement. It
is a strange and fascinating amalgam. But what these books reveal
is a slow turning, in Strindberg, back to the combative impulse of his
youth. This transition in his last fifteen years, from an overriding
spiritual quest, to a point where it begins to combine with his
previous strong sense of justice and injustice, has been recounted and
explored with ample space and documentation by Björn Meidal in his
book *Från profet till folktribun (From Prophet to People's Tribune)*. In
particular, Meidal traces a transition in Strindberg's later thought
from St. Paul's position—after his illumination and penitence on the
road to Damascus—that "everything serves" the Divine will, both
suffering and joy—to St. John's more dualist idea of the autonomy of
evil and the need for struggle if human beings are to progress.[28]
These novels look forward to the exploration of the psyche and
society in the work of the German expressionists.

In 1910 Strindberg approached several influential left-wing
papers in Stockholm, including *Social-Demokraten,* and offered to
begin a series of articles in them attacking the state's attitude toward
workers' issues, the growing nationalism, the threat of war—but
insisted that these socialist periodicals would not be able to censor his
views in any way. He asked for no pay in return. (His financial
situation was more comfortable now, and in 1911 the advance on his
collected works would give him complete security, allowing him to
divide sums with Siri von Essen—who was living in Finland—and
their children.) Even the radical left Socialist paper *Stormklockan*
agreed to his terms. That journal together with the liberal *Afton-*

Tidningen and *Social-Demokraten* became the conduit for the opinions of Sweden's literary patriarch from that day forward. From that point, between 1910 and his death in 1912, he unleashed what has gone down in history as the "Strindberg Feud" (*Strindbergsfejden*). In his barrage of articles he attacked, among other things, the trend toward militarism and war—which tended to forge Swedish alignment with Germany and enmity with Russia—and he accused a number of his former liberal colleagues, who were now successful pillars of media and literature, of selling out the national culture. His greatest disdain was reserved for Verner von Heidenstam the poet, whose work *The Carolinians* called up the idealism of the nation again in the spirit of Carl XII, Strindberg's historical bête noire, and Sven Hedin, the explorer, whose bellicose attitude toward Russia he excoriated. Earlier in *Black Banners* he had raked Gustaf af Geijerstam over the coals: a fellow radical writer in the 70s and 80s, whom he accused of opportunism in his capacity as a publisher, and of purveying shallow national ideology through a sort of yellow journalism. It might be said, in a sense, that the feud began three years earlier, with that controversial work of fiction, before the first newspaper article appeared. The salvos fired back at Strindberg in the press were even more relentless, and they came from several corners, printed in the most powerful publications. In this particular "culture war" Strindberg's position seems to have been vindicated by history. A first world war did eventually come about, but Sweden remained neutral and did not join the German fight against Russia. Sven Hedin, his nemesis for much of the lengthy debate, later became one of Sweden's best known and intellectually influential Nazis. It is also impossible to ignore the fact that Sweden soon would become the first country in Europe to begin the experiment with Social Democracy. Though the debate often focused on a writer's role in the world and society, and the issue of militarism, Strindberg's allies had been the socialist press—and the issues of worker's rights and social justice had emerged during various phases of the "feud".

In 1909, Strindberg had been bypassed, conspicuously, for the Nobel Prize which was awarded to the extraordinary but lesser known Selma Lagerlöf, with the result that his admirers—then growing in number—awarded him an "anti-Nobel prize." In both 1909 and 1912, on his sixtieth and sixty-third birthdays, there were city-wide tributes to Strindberg by cultural and political organizations. His attack on Heidenstam, who had sided against the general strike of 1909, won Strindberg the avid support of the labor movement. In 1912, the Stockholm Worker's Commune held a torch-light march to the Blue Tower. He waved with his hat from the balcony, his daughter Greta beside him, to the cheering crowd and union banners below.

Strindberg died of stomach cancer on the 14th of May, 1912. He maintained a daily writing schedule close to the end. There is a photo of him taking his long daily walk in Stockholm in freezing snow only a month before his death. (In this extraordinary photograph, now labeled "Last Walk," the contours of the city around the writer, in his black top hat and frockcoat, begin to vanish into the white backdrop of falling snow.) Although Strindberg had requested explicitly that his funeral not be a public event, it was not only the actors and artists of his Intima Teatern that followed the casket, but many thousands of workers and other members of Sweden's cultural community. Among the crowd were innovative political figures who had taken his side in the historic press debate: like the socialist activist and feminist Kata Dahlström,[29] and the re-found compatriot of his youth, Hjalmar Branting, the first leader of Sweden's Social Democratic party. This was perhaps a fitting last scene for the man who liked to call himself "Son of a Servant"—perhaps too fitting. For like every other description of Strindberg, or interpretation of his "philosophy," or his style, or his métier, or his main passions, or his politics or his religious thought, it captures only a phase in a life of rapid transformation: a process of transformation like fire, destroying and creating simultaneously.

The same can be said of Strindberg's literary output, of which the works for the theatre have proven to be the most lasting achievement. An exploration of his plays beyond the works of naturalism such as *The Father* and *Miss Julie*—which have stuck Strindberg with a label that is too narrow—is now the task for anyone who wants a more complete picture of his achievement. In his novel—or volume of literary reflections—*Days of Loneliness (Ensam,* 1903), which emerged from the period after his breakup with Harriet Bosse, in a passage of unusual tranquility, our "narrow-minded" and "obsessive" author perhaps reveals the secret of his broad register as a playwright:

> When I . . . have arrived home and am sitting at my writing table, then I live again. . . . I am living, and I live over and over again the human lives I depict; I am happy with those who are happy, irate with those who are irate, and those who are good make me feel good. I creep out of my own personality and speak out of the mouths of children—of women—of old men; I am king and I am beggar; I am the highly placed one, the tyrant, and the most despised among men, the oppressed hater of tyrants; I have a multitude of opinions, and confess to all religions; I dwell in all ages and have ceased to exist as myself. And all this is a state of mind which gives me an indescribable joy.[30]

THE PLAYS

6.
The Ghost Sonata, of all the plays from this period, provides perhaps the best example Strindberg's striking attempts to create a synthesis of his social thought and his spiritual concerns. It is a play which provides the key to his late innovations. A close probing of just this play—which demanded such a radical new approach to theatre performance at the dawn of the twentieth century—and an understanding of the context in which it was written, can give us an excellent lens through which we can see the modern Strindberg emerging. Here we find the Strindberg who helped to change drama and theatre for good. Those who have worked closely with this controversial play know that it contains, in kernel form, most everything Strindberg was trying to say in terms of metaphysics, religion, social commentary and satire at the turn of the century.

The Ghost Sonata is included in Strindberg's collected works as one of the "chamber plays," which Strindberg labeled as "opus" 1 through 5. The first four were completed in 1907: *Storm, The Burned House, The Ghost Sonata* and *The Pelican. The Black Glove* was completed in 1909. *The Ghost Sonata* was designated "Opus 3." Music in fact provided a structuring element in all the chamber plays. In this case it was Beethoven's Piano Sonata in D minor. The key of D minor is one which Strindberg had indicated before in works with a streak of melancholy in them. The play was written in a brief span of time between February and March 1907.

The Ghost Sonata acquired, during the first half of the twentieth century, a worldwide reputation as a dark and gloomy play, which is true enough in some ways, but the reputation leads us to ignore some of its most alluring features. If we resort to Strindberg's biography, we certainly find plenty of things which motivate the play's famous "darkness" in his own life. He was living alone in his Karlavägen apartment (in "the Red House"), where his brother Axel would visit to play piano for him, between daily work sessions at his desk. His hands were again bleeding and discolored from psoriasis, from which he had first suffered in the 90s. He was probably also experiencing the first symptoms of the stomach cancer which would bring on his death in 1912. *The Ghost Sonata*, however, is also a play to which Strindberg applied the fantasy that produced surprising and colorful works like *The Keys to Heaven (Himmelrikets nycklar), The Travels of Lucky Per, To Damascus* and *A Dream Play*. This does not mean that *The Ghost Sonata* should be too easily categorized as a "dream play," even though it has become common practice to refer to Strindberg's use of "dream play techniques" in this play and in such other stylistically diverse plays as *Carl XII* and *To Damascus*. Strindberg himself described his approach rather differently: "A fairy-tale fantasy play in the present, with a modern household, was what I was aiming at."[31] It was not the first time in his career that Strindberg had come up with a formula for something new. It is this play, in fact, more than *A Dream Play*, or perhaps even *To Damascus*, which has come to be associated with the birth of European expressionism—after a long gestation period seeded by works of Strindberg and the other authors mentioned previously. This is in part due to its first truly successful production in 1916 by Max Reinhardt—which was also one of Reinhardt's own breakthrough successes as a world class director.

Strindberg's fantasy plays are not primarily motivated by *psychology.* That is, they are not set up as nightmares, or products of fevered brains. Perhaps this is what he means when he discusses his preference for E.T.A. Hoffman over Poe in a letter to Hennig Berger in August 1906: "That's how Edgar Poe ruined his stories with so-called natural explanations, while Hoffman took the supernatural as entirely natural, and thereby saved the poetry (the atmosphere)."[32] Göran Lindström has suggested that some of Strindberg's ideas for his play of a modern "household" came directly from Hoffman's story "Das öde Haus."[33] Additionally, Wagner was the rage at the time, and *Die Walküre* played in Stockholm in 1906: another work involving the collapse of old idols and illusions.

Outside of Sweden, and sometimes inside as well, *The Ghost Sonata* has been regarded as a work that demonstrates exclusively religious or spiritual concerns. Gunnar Ollén, who has written the most comprehensive work on Strindberg's complete dramatic *oeuvre* (*Strindbergs dramatik*) is convinced that "*The Ghost Sonata* presents a dark view, in the spirit of Schopenhauer, of a writer whose social criticism is only secondary."[34] At least the first half of this statement is irrefutable. Strindberg's semi-Christian mysticism, which kept him at loggerheads with the organized Church right up to his last days, is actually half Buddhism and Hindu philosophy, as received through Schopenhauer and Theosophy. The other half is inspired by the works of the Swedish mystic Emanuel Swedenborg.[35] As we've seen, a chapter of *Inferno*—Strindberg's novelization of the experiences which brought him to a spiritual perspective—is titled "Swedenborg." Swedenborg turns up as a character in his history play about Sweden's doomed militarist king, *Carl XII.* There, as a young architect and engineer, he is an intellect with a budding seer's gift. The debt to Swedenborg is implicitly acknowledged in the name Strindberg gives to the clairvoyant student in *The Ghost Sonata*, for Johan Arkenholz is a name that appears in Swedenborg's diary in spring, 1744: one of the mystic's disciples in fact. The "student" therefore may be seen as on the path of more than one kind of knowledge.

It is Swedenborg's teaching that *correspondences* exist between

things in the natural world and things in the world of the spirit, which
lie behind the remarkable word-play between the Student and the
Daughter in the last section of the play. To their growing enchant-
ment, the pair discover together that stars, snowflakes, snow crystals
and flowers such as hyacinths, shallots, snowflakes and snowdrops all
seem to share the same form. As stars shine from the heavens, so do
flowers reach for the heavens. This scene, taken by itself, veers
toward a spiritual ecstasy rather than the pessimism for which this
play and its author are famous. In Strindberg's later thought, both
happiness and sorrow exist, but each contains the seed of its opposite.
In the scene mentioned above, the veil is torn away from the couple's
momentary happiness. Here, and throughout the play, the ruling
motif is the tearing away of the mask of illusion, or the "veil of
Maya" as Schopenhauer—in line with Buddhist philosophy and
Vedanta—would refer to it. For Schopenhauer, and Strindberg—and
perhaps the Western mind in general—there is a trepidation. Rather
than a liberation, this "truth" beyond the purely rational is fraught
with danger.   The revelation is so frightening (*"schauderhaft"*) that
for many people only death could liberate them from what their more
open perceptions have shown them. Or so thought these Western
writers who made the first serious attempts to digest Eastern thought.
Strindberg wrote to his German translator, Emil Schering, on March
28, 1907:

> With today's mail I'm sending off another chamber play
> (Opus 3) called *A Ghost Sonata* [sic]— — —It is *schauderhaft*
> just as life is, when the veil falls from your eyes and you see *Das
> Ding an Sich*— — —so many secrets exist in every household—
> — —The one thing which did not darken my soul during the
> work is my religion (=*Anschluss mit Jenseits*) the hope of
> something better; and the firm conviction that we live in the
> world of lunacy and delusions (illusions), from which we must
> fight our way forth.[36]

Strindberg's metaphysical concerns, surprisingly, don't contribute
to making the dialogue or structure murky. This is the play's great

achievement. He makes all of his metaphysical concepts concrete: in the form of IOUs (i.e., "debt" or "guilt"), or the false teeth, false mustaches, and a worthless signet ring in which the Colonel is "costumed"—or the food coloring employed by the monstrous Cook in part three of the play, which replaces the nutrients in the food. True to the art of theatre, everything is made concrete. The "invisible is made visible," to borrow a phrase from Peter Brook. On the other hand, this is all helped by the fact that Strindberg the social critic and satirist—the perspectives which dominated the works from his younger years, and which will return with a vengeance during the "Strindberg feud" of 1910 in Sweden—is very much alive in *The Ghost Sonata*. The bite of his first major play, *Master Olof*, and the barbs and irony of his early fiction like *The Red Room* and *The Isle of Happiness (Lycksalighetens ö)*, and of his satirical sketches in *The New Kingdom (Det nya riket)*, reemerge in this drama from the last decade of his productivity. Still, one can argue, as Ollén does convincingly, that Strindberg no longer focuses his attack on one social class or group, but on the lie which all individuals in the world must live. Strindberg feels obliged, says Ollén, "on the basis of the scope of the moral degeneration to regard the entire social structure, not simply certain social classes, as rotten."[37]

Nevertheless, in terms of his spiritual and social views, Strindberg cannot be said to be concerned with solely one to the exclusion of the other during this period. He is, in fact, casting about for a synthesis of these things. In the decade following his Inferno period and its attendant philosophy of resignation, he had written a long sequence of historical dramas which ran the gamut from the religious play of redemption, *The Saga of the Folkungs*—to ice-clear social epics, replete with semicomic jabs at revered historical figures, employing a class analysis of historical events, as in the play on Sweden's "jacobin" theatre-king *Gustav III*. He also returned to writing social-satirical novels, which first brought him renown with *The Red Room* in 1879. His late novels such as *Gothic Rooms* and *Black Banners* revived the form, to an extent, and even some of his old characters reappeared in them. Onto this he began to graft his spiritual vision. The result, in fact, was a clash between two literary objectives. In

Black Banners—written in 1904 but not published until 1907, the year of *The Ghost Sonata*—the open collision between the story of a spiritual quest and the savage satire on a corrupted liberal bourgeoisie, produces a rare and extraordinary work. The target of Strindberg's satire in this book was his old artistic and literary colleagues from the liberal and radical movements of the 1870s and 80s. They were now owners of publishing houses and newspapers, had gained control of both capital and political power. Even so, they maintained a facade of being exposers of injustice and hypocrisy when, conveniently—in Strindberg's view—they could profit by it. In *Black Banners* this group is represented by the publisher Zachris (among others) who is portrayed as a subtle exploiter with the habits of a vampire. Strindberg describes him with a flair for the grotesque which runs through the entire book. Zachris himself, self-declared champion of truth, is described in terms virtually the same as those which are used to describe the sinister Director Hummel in *The Ghost Sonata*:

> Everything he owned he had stolen. He stole people and thoughts, words and expressions, he could steal the expression of a person he admired; he could steal another person's fame and talent, substitute himself in another person's life. . . .[38]

As to the group which Zachris represents, we are given the judgment of Strindberg's skeptic Dr. Borg—now grown old since he was first seen in *The Red Room*—who finally breaks with this web of hypocrisy. He loses the balanced irony which characterized him, something cracks and gives way to wrath:

> You liberal royalists, liberal bureaucrats, liberal reactionaries, liberal summer soldiers! You are liberal liars . . . I'm going over to the socialists—they are the people of the future, while you belong to the past, the passing excrement. You're going to rot to the roots, you are without substance, and the ax is too good for you—you really deserve a rope. There aren't enough prisons for you all, and the prisoners would be ashamed of your com-

pany. You have falsified public opinion, poisoned the wells, and brought up an entire generation on lies and delusion. You call me conservative because I'm not a sodomite, because I am a republican, a citizen of the world, because I love justice and fight against bigotry, violence, and roguery. From now on, you can regard me as your open enemy; I will treat you as thieves and murderers.[39]

Björn Meidal, in *From Prophet to People's Tribune,* has outlined how Strindberg's religion after the Inferno period passed through two distinct phases. In his first phase he took a position which can be associated with St. Paul, "everything serves" (*"allt tjänar"*)—a view of life imbued with resignation in which even the pain inflicted upon us is there to serve a higher purpose. Later, he moves to a Christianity of St. John, with whom Strindberg associated the quest for justice, for revelation, and which assumes the possibility of a divine power that struggles—and the possibility of fighting injustice on earth. In Dr. Borg's speech, the wrath being expressed surpasses the individual character, who seems suddenly to become a channel for—if not a higher power, at least Strindberg. But it is an indication that Strindberg has made the transition that Meidal suggests. Two years after writing *The Ghost Sonata* the transition will be complete, and so will Strindberg's process of bringing his politics and religion together.

In the "Strindberg feud," the great debate which ran in the national press from 1910 to 1912, Strindberg will launch an assault upon some of Sweden's supposedly liberal cultural elite who, he warned, were coming to embrace militarism and nationalism. He saw them singing paeans to the kings and warriors of the past, while dressing themselves in the robes of a new national nobility.

Of all the chamber plays, *The Ghost Sonata* is the one which shows the most evidence of these tensions, just as *Black Banners* is the prose work which reveals most in terms of these conflicts between social views and spiritual quest: between spiritual resignation and the discontent of the social critic and satirist. In the play, both pessimism and a mystic sense of wonder at existence are aired in the final scene in the hyacinth room. In Strindberg's *Black Banners*, the publisher

Zachris is juxtaposed to the writer Falkenström, who abandons Stockholm's elite as a gang of thieves, and goes to live at a sort of cloister or lodge (run by no identified Church or order) where the members are obliged to produce Platonic (Socratic) dialogues on subjects of their choice. Falkenström's discourse is on the remarkable correspondences of things of the world and things of the spirit. Max, the founder of this cloister, gives his on "matter as living essence," a discussion of the sensitivity of inanimate objects (pianos, violins, works of art) and a variety of plants and flowers to their environment. The flowers, in particular, reflect the world around them in their color, shape or posture, and even respond to human speech. He goes through the specific cases of tulips, roses, phoenix palms and aspidistras. ("This furtive, secretive aspect of the aspidistra makes it resemble cryptograms; but its leaves may look even more like a reptile. . . ."[40]) Swedenborg's teachings about the presence of signs in nature and day-to-day life fit well with Strindberg's own reflections based upon his frequently derided scientific experiments in the 90s. He developed his scientific hypotheses into philosophic reflection, which in the end took literary form in *Sylva sylvarum* (1896). Olof Lagercrantz, in his biography, is among the first to point out this connecting point between Strindberg's experiments and his literary and dramatic works. It shows up again in the sprawling work of "global" thinking on nature, science, philosophy, spirituality, called *A Blue Book (En blå bok)*, completed two years prior to the first four chamber plays. The premise in these works is that of *monism*: that there is an essential unity between all things in the cosmos, and a single substance or essence from which all things emerge.

This lengthy digression to the subject of *Black Banners* and other works from the same period can be justified if we now turn to the opening sentence of the novel itself: "There was to be a ghost supper at Professor Stenkåhl's. . . ."[41] The ghost supper turns out to be a grotesque event, dominated by lies and charades of every sort. When the writer Falkenström enters, he is sure to insert his false teeth which he removes from a tin, the guests bare their teeth when they meet each other, and at the meal they roll their bread into little balls "with their hands so that the table looked like a beach at low tide covered with crabs." And when the soup was served, "one could observe sixteen bowed craniums, most of them quite dolichocephal-ic. . . . The soup eaters all seemed to be watching their reflections in the deep soup bowls or hiding their faces to avoid showing the mirrors of their souls. They were perhaps praying for the ruin of the others present. . . ."[42]

The parallels with *The Ghost Sonata* can not be made clearer than through this central motif: the ghost supper. In the play, the servant Bengtsson describes similar events which take place in the household where he works:

> It is the usual ghost supé, as we call it. They drink tea, speak not a word, unless the Colonel talks by himself, and they munch their biscuits all at once, so it sounds like rats in a storage room.[43]

It should by now be obvious that *The Ghost Sonata* is not a play about ghosts (with two exceptions), but is peopled by living dead, spiritual and social vampires. Its characters have grotesque traits, and the various depictions of people as animals underscores this element of the grotesque. The Mummy begins as a parrot, and Hummel ends up reduced to a cuckoo. Animalistic and grotesque as these portraits may be, the drama is meant to portray the living. The house harbors many phantoms, it is true, and the Dead Man and the Milk Maid can walk through the play, giving form to the crimes and guilt of the inhabitants. It is not a dream play in which time and space are in no way fixed, as is the case with *A Dream Play* itself. It is a play about our world at the point where the veil of illusion is torn. Its genius is that it represents a balancing act, in which the characters move in and out of their *real* selves (their facades in the "real world") and their *true* selves (their corrupt essences)—and it is the latter that appear to us to be fantastic. Both of these selves, actually, are based on fundamental dishonesty. The possibility of a higher or better "self" is only hinted at and never appears in this play—other than in the sequence when the Mummy stops the clock, and begins speaking the truth with a strangely different, authentic and humane voice.

It is Hummel who—posing as the champion of truth in his "chariot" wheelchair—first exposes the lie which everyone lives in this microcosm of the "house of man" to the Student. But like Zachris in the novel, he uses his exposés of others to his own profit. He shows the student the corrupt, entangled relationships and the false foundations upon which this "house" is built. People are not what they seem. Wives are not wives, for they are other men's lovers. Nor are husbands the husbands they seem to be. Daughters are not daughters, for they may be the offspring of seducers, and inherit from them rather than their *apparent* fathers. Happiness too is illusory. Hummel reveals all of this. In fact, though, he is a Strindbergian vampire because he uses the truth—a selective and therefore equally illusory truth—to bleed and exploit others. (More than fifty years later Ingmar Bergman will use this same correlative, exploiter as vampire, in his film about scandal-mongering bourgeois types in *The Hour of the Wolf [Vargtimmen].)*

Hummel claims the role of ruthless unmasker in a world of lies. If there is a story in the play it is precisely this: one of unmasking. But it is a labyrinthine story, in which unmasking becomes a vicious cycle until, like Peer Gynt in the famous onion peeling scene in Ibsen's play, we come down to the terrible fact of the nothing in the center.

Hummel unmasks the Colonel, a figure representing aristocracy, authority and the "best" values in society, in five steps. After he gets him in his power by paying off his debts, he strips him first of his material possessions. The second layer to go is his aristocratic name, which proves to belong to an extinct family. The third layer he takes from him is his rank as colonel—which proves to have been abolished along with the American volunteer army which fought in Cuba. The fourth layer he loses is his appearance—his teeth, his mustache, his corset—"and then we shall see," says Hummel, "if a certain servant XYZ doesn't recognize himself: the one who used to sponge food in a certain kitchen. . . ."[44] So the illusion is broken in this case by a class reversal, and the aristocrat is shown to be a man of a lower order. When Hummel offers proof that the Colonel is not the father of his own daughter—Hummel is—the unmasking is complete.

Hummel claims to have unmasked the deceit in the house so ruthlessly, so that his sickly daughter will be able to breathe in a healthier atmosphere. Then the Mummy "stops the clock," and gets the servant Bengtsson to testify to Hummel's own murderous usury and other past crimes, and that Hummel had in fact once been a sponger who had worked as a servant for Bengtsson himself. Once again there is a class reversal, and the unmasker himself has been unmasked. The "story" of the play now takes on a labyrinthine quality. All the more so when in part three the student tells the story of how his own father was carted off to a madhouse after unmasking a group of phonies at a gathering. *"Allt går igen"*: "Everything comes back," or "everything repeats itself," or "all things walk again," are among the various connotations of the phrase. This is the refrain which appears in Strindberg's *Dance of Death* and in other works. Interestingly, it is also the meaning behind the title Ibsen gave his own play known as *Ghosts* in English: *Gengangere* (or things which walk again or come back). Nowhere has Strindberg staged and illustrated the meaning of this phrase better than in *The Ghost Sonata*.

The final part of the play portrays the destructive nature of the naked truth in another way. The Student explains:

> Sometimes a furious desire comes over me to say everything that I think; but I know that the world would come crashing down if there were nothing but complete honesty.[45]

He proceeds, nonetheless, to batter the fragile hyacinth girl with so many truths, so much unmasking, that she is herself left stripped of illusions which have served as her final protection, and dies. The ambiguous outburst, "Why won't you be my bride? Because the source of life in you is sick . . ." can certainly be read to mean that he realizes that she has inherited venereal disease from her real father: the invalid former Don Juan, Hummel. This literal interpretation of the phrase would be consistent with Strindberg's working method in the chamber plays—in which something in the literal and natural world reveals a *correspondence* with something on the metaphysical plane. The literal reading of this line, which once again has echoes of Ibsen's *Ghosts*, has been to some extent underscored by Swedish commentators like Gunnar Ollén, and by perhaps the foremost of living Strindberg directors—Ingmar Bergman. Bergman made the Student's remark a fatal one, for the fragile Daughter, in his 1973 production at the Royal Dramatic Theatre in Stockholm. (He has directed the play three times, as he has done with the *Dream Play* as well.) There, the Student dragged the Daughter from her chair in a fury, tearing her clothes to reveal blood-flecked undergarments: giving emphasis to the idea of a deadly physical disease to go with the idea that "the source of life is sick" in her soul as well. This, together with some restructuring and cuts, provided one possible solution to the supposedly difficult final scene. It is arguable whether such literalness is needed, and given his other stagings of the play, Bergman might not disagree.

Strindberg's own idea was in fact that the Daughter is quite literally sick, but he had not intended to resolve the question of who had responsibility for the sickness (termed "inherited or acquired" in lines he cut). Whether it is a case of "the guilt of the fathers," or whether the daughter herself is responsible for the lie she has been living is left open. In addition: it is an open question whether the Student means to emphasize her physical sickness, or the malaise of helpless, self-indulgent resignation into which the girl has descended. In either case, it is the truth which kills the Daughter, whose life has been protected by a web of lies. Even though the destructive force that truth brings with it is amply demonstrated in all that comes before, it is still an imperative in our existence. "By keeping still too long," says the Student, defying the Daughter's fear, "we let decay set in on the stagnant waters . . ." If the veil of illusion is allowed to go undisturbed, the result is rot.

The Daughter's death comes at the moment of her revelation. She dies a sacrifice to the knife of Truth. This in turn provokes the Student's final revelation, and his radical change in tone from that of an intolerant and impatient assault to one of a striking, sudden compassion. This is no petty compassion—but a compassion cued by the presence of the Buddha in the scene. Yet the logic of the play seems to imply that sacrifice is required in order that truth and compassion can live. Something must die.

Strindberg does not moralize here. He simply sets about to dramatize a terrible paradox. Human beings cannot acquiesce to illusions and lies or their lives will fall into decay, and their every action will become destructive. At the same time, human beings cannot live entirely without illusions as that is part of being human. Ruthless and inhumane unmaskers can produce destruction as well. The theme was portrayed with less metaphysical overtones in Ibsen's *The Wild Duck (Vildanden)*. It is no coincidence that it was a central theme in the works of the avowed Strindberg disciple Eugene O'Neill—most notably in *The Iceman Cometh*.

Not satisfied with one contradiction of this magnitude, Strindberg leaves us with another to ponder. The resignation of the hyacinth girl and the destructive idealism of the student are both qualities which make life impossible: they have become destructive. Still, though they are opposites, they might have come together in a mutually nurturing unity had they not been taken to their extremes.

This tension between resignation and struggle gives a peculiar quality to most of Strindberg's later plays: it is a key dilemma for characters in *A Dream Play*, and it stands out in the chamber plays —including the *Pelican* in this collection—and many of his late history plays: especially *Carl XII*. Strindberg wrote in his *Occult Diary*—which he kept from 1896 to 1908:

> The fact that I have revealed the relative nothingness of life (Buddhism), its insane contradictions, its wickedness and unruliness, may be regarded as praiseworthy if it imbues people with resignation. (15 April 1907)

He also wrote the following in the same *Occult Diary*:

> Resignation! Yes indeed. But if you put up with everything, in the end you have to endure filth and humiliation, and *that* is what you have no right to do! (6 September 1901)[46]

7.

The Pelican (Pelikanen), also completed in 1907, was to become "Opus 4" of the chamber play sequence, but not until Strindberg had started on two other planned but aborted chamber plays. The first was to have been called *The Bleeding Hand (Den blödande handen)*, which he called "more horrible than the others," but the day after announcing this new work in a letter to Schering on April 4, he wrote another note saying "today I burned up Opus IV. . . ."[47] Later that April he began work on another chamber play, named for the final image he suggested for the end of *The Ghost Sonata*: *Toten-Insel*, or the *Isle of the Dead* inspired by Böcklin's painting. "I'm working, at the moment, on 'Toteninsel' [*sic*] in which I am portraying the reawakening after death, and that which follows after, but doubt and shrink from laying bare life's bottomless misery."[48] He wrote that he wanted to use the painting *Toteninsel* this time as the basis for the scenography for the play, but that he lost interest after a good start. *The Pelican*, a very different work, was the result of his third attempt. On the 19th of June he wrote to Schering: "Now I have finished the fourth chamber play; it's *schauderhaft*, but good!"

A clue to the remarkable heat one finds in this play might be found in an alleged account by August Falck of Strindberg's writing method. The incident took place at a time when Strindberg was at work on *The Pelican*:

> I sat in the room outside and now and then crept in on my tiptoes to retrieve some pages of the manuscript. He wrote at full throttle, pushed aside the sheets as he finished them, and tossed them, before they were dry, on the floor, where I was able to pick them up, carry them out and sit down to read."[49]

Contrary to any notion that Strindberg was unaware of new and innovative staging and directing around Europe (which Ibsen biographer Michael Meyer contends was the case in his relentlessly negative biography of Strindberg) he was highly attuned to the new directions taking place in performance and wanted badly to be part of it. Max Reinhardt accepted *Storm Weather* at his Kammerspielhaus (which Strindberg was following closely and was in fact targeting with his *Kammarspel* plays). He was greatly excited about this link-up, as he reported in the *Occult Diary* (20 June 1907). He had hoped that the selection would be *The Ghost Sonata*, but he felt encouraged nonetheless. He felt that it was by this route, via Reinhardt, that he might be able to introduce his new genre—or "moderne Kunst"—of theatre to Europe at large. In fact, in the ensuing decades, and after his death, this hope would be realized.

The Pelican, aside from *The Ghost Sonata*, has been the most frequently performed of the chamber plays in Europe. It has a ferocious tempo and terse structure—and drives toward a classical purgation of emotions—bile, hatred, anger, despair—and in fact Strindberg made the comparison with the story of Medea, who brings on the death of her guiltless children.[50] Yet, the play has such a heightened intensity, while appearing to take its style from earlier naturalism or realism of the Ibsen type, that it begins to tip over into a psychological grotesque style which in turn veers toward expressionism. All of this makes the play either a potential fiasco or an event full of fascinating surprises.

The possible real-life models which gave rise to the play are several. In March 1907 Strindberg's once close sister Anna moved in with him at Karlavägen. Her husband Hugo Philp had recently died.[51] The story of the Philps and Strindberg's attitude towards the couple is of interest because of the manner in which Strindberg reverses his perspective on where to lay the blame for their troubles. The Inferno period brought something new into his thinking: relativism. There may be more than one possible understanding of people's actions, even opposite understandings—what we might call today a *Rashomon* perspective. The couple had been long-time companions to Strindberg, but he began to suspect Hugo Philp of a lust for power and a will to dominate that made him the model for Edgar in *The Dance of Death*—a play in which the husband is described as an exploiter with qualities of a "vampire": a character who far outdoes the wife in his ability to do evil. Strindberg's relationship with Anna soured rapidly during her stay with him. She arrived on the 19th of March and moved out on the 26th. On an earlier visit from Anna in 1904, while Hugo was still sick, Strindberg wrote in his *Occult Diary*: "Anna moved in with me. In the evening I heard urgent cries down at the gate, like there was a drunk in the ditch. Thought it was Philp, but he was in Uppsala."[52] Strindberg increasingly perceived her as an irresponsible bohemian, who went in for entertainment, frills, going out, who preferred playing the piano to getting involved in any kind of work—including house work. On this last visit in 1907 the strain must have been felt on both sides, since she left without warning, which only fed Strindberg's feelings of resentment. The two never saw one another again.

Strindberg felt compelled to reexamine his evaluation of Hugo—especially now that he was dead. Philp's last words were: "It's summer outside—I want to sleep," which seems to link up with the ending of *The Pelican*.[53] Strindberg seems to have felt repentant now—especially since he himself had encouraged his sister to try to leave Hugo a few years before. This is what moved him to start work on the long fragment, *Toten-Insel*, which warrants further examination in connection with the *Pelican*—the chamber play which he did finish. *Toten-Insel* bore the subtitle "Hades." In accordance with Theosophy and Swedenborg's thought, he used this to portray the first station of the human soul on its journey after death. There, the threads of a soul's lifetime and suffering would all come together. Bitterness would depart. "This was the rest station, or the summer holiday after the first death," he wrote in *A Blue Book, III*.[54] In the play fragment a man referred to as a teacher has died and arrived at the isle of the dead. He rises to speak several monologues, unaware that he has crossed to the "other side." They include a long speech to his wife (named Anna) about what it is like to have to get up early to teach class, and how to cook eggs properly, and one in which he attempts to get a certain "Hummel" to be guarantor for a loan. In the second scene the deceased has been given a new name, "Assir" (Earth man). He now has a "teacher" on the isle of the dead, who leads him through a Socratic/Buddhistic dialogue in which he demonstrates to the dead man that life can be a dream and that dreams have as much to teach as reality. He teaches how the dead man's perceptions of himself and others had always been distortions and illusion. He is confronted with his wife and daughter and son, as well as a colleague, from the world of the living, who evaluate him. The teacher invites Assir to see a play in order to reflect further, since theatre was what he loved most in his worldly existence. "[B]ut if life is a dream, then a play is a dream of a dream, even though you treat it as reality."[55] He sits to watch a play at this point. That play-within-a-play, according to Strindberg researchers as reliable as Gunnar Ollén, was to have been *The Pelican*.[56] After the play is over, the teacher asks Assir:

> TEACHER   Did you find it true to life?
> ASSIR   Yes, more than true. But it was so heavy, it was
>   horrifying.
> TEACHER   Can you give a summary of what it contained?
> ASSIR   No. It was so dreadful that I've struck it from my
>   memory . . .[57]

Strindberg left off work on *Toten-Insel*. Perhaps the mood of the play was too much one of reconciliation. His thoughts seem to have turned to the dead man's wife, this "Anna," and this was the dramatic material which drew him.

"Opus 4" of the chamber plays, *The Pelican*, was written during a period of several weeks in late spring of 1907, and was finished on June 19. It may be that it was only then that he began to see *Toten-Insel* as a framing device for *The Pelican*—in which the characters in the dreamlike realm of the "stations of death" would view a more conventional play casting light on the type of life the dead man had left behind. The styles would have created an absolute contrast. *The Pelican*, however, was never published together with *Toten-Insel* as a frame-play. With a very few exceptions it has always stood on its own in production.

The action of *The Pelican* begins after the funeral of the family father. Simply to read a short synopsis of *The Pelican* gives one the feeling of entering the realm of the absurd, or even the insane. A mother has deprived her children of proper nourishment and winter heating as they've grown up, in order to have extra funds to enjoy the finer things in life herself. The result is that the children have grown up mentally and physically fragile. When their father, whom she has tried to turn them against, dies, the daughter gets married and the mother proceeds to steal her daughter's husband. After discovering a letter from their deceased father revealing the truth about the past, the children go into a protracted revolt to slay the ego of the mother who claimed to feed them with her life blood—as the pelican does in the myth—but in fact had sucked the blood out of them. It culminates in a fire in the house, from which the self-absorbed mother flees by leaping from a window, and which engulfs the children who have given up on this existence of suffering—yet share a last vision of a loving family on a summer voyage.

Here as in other Strindberg plays, the truth is too much. "I'm walking in my sleep, I know that," says Gerda, the daughter, "but I don't want to be wakened! Then I wouldn't be able to go on living!" Her brother responds to this key paradox with, "Don't you think we're all walking in our sleep." Thus the play begins its movement from a realistic, if grotesque, depiction of the household tyranny of an obsessive-compulsive, to a statement with broader ramifications about human existence, about the nature of truth, the denial of truth, and the suffering that is built into life by the very nature of the human ego: *self-ishness*. There is also the hint that human existence is often based upon a symbiosis of exploiter and exploited.

The revelation that her mother has taken even her love from her, in the form of her husband, is the blow that brings Gerda to her painfully clear vision. The formerly calculating son-in-law too begins to realize he has been seduced into someone else's corrupt world, and bows out of the action of the play in a scene fraught with ambiguity. The two siblings have already begun to go to work—ruthlessly—not to kill their mother in a literal sense, but to kill off, brutally if necessary, the "evil" which possesses her: her rampant ego. The children are attempting to slay a dragon. This is the veiled "late Strindberg" message behind the more familiar psychological combat typical of his earlier plays. They are fighting to break down this woman's destructive and sclerotic delusions which have reduced her to a miserly creature dominated only by compulsions that go far beyond penny-pinching. Without this understanding, the play might seem to some a misanthropic orgy.

After they unmask her, the mother says to her son, "Don't you feel any compassion for me?" Fredrik responds, "Of course I do! How often have I said of you: She is so sick she should be pitied."[58]

As the house burns at the end all seems hopeless in this world, but the dialogue between Gerda and Fredrik seems to be leading toward some greater reconciliation: in their memories of a hopeful childhood, of "summer vacation," of the memories of the steamships that would carry them out over the waters. Such an ending, with flames or smoke rolling over this tormented family and their household, is also reminiscent of the nihilist pronouncements of the young Strindberg, which always tended to have an apocalyptic side to them. He once wrote to Norwegian novelist Jonas Lie, "I think Armageddon will come about when we'll all be annihilated in one single great fire, which we ourselves will light."[59] In the poem "The Wolves Are Howling" ("Vargarne tjuta") from as late as 1903, he describes a great city consumed by a cloud of smoke from a massive fire, while the caged animals of the town howl for their freedom.[60]

Because *The Pelican* stretches the boundaries of stage realism beyond the point to which they actually can go, the effect is that the allegory or greater message is heightened. The latter half of the play might well lead a director, designer and actors to find solutions that drop the realistic trappings altogether, especially in the final scene. One particularly interesting design solution was used in a Polish production, in which sheets which had been covering the walls and furniture began to lift as if the flames were burning them up toward the ceiling, revealing darkness and emptiness behind them.[61] Meanwhile a Swedish Television Theatre version had the memories of the children and the glowing white steamships and water of "summer vacation" wipe out the image of the fire.[62]

8.

Carl XII is unique among Strindberg's works, and yet it also represents a genre in which he loved to work: his historical plays which are

unfortunately not yet well known outside of Scandinavia and central
Europe. Strindberg wrote a dozen epic history plays—eight of which
were completed shortly before and after the turn of the century, from
1898 to 1903. Written in 1901, the year after *The Dance of Death*,
Carl XII confronts the issues of militarism, economics and the human
soul. The historical Carl XII has been alternately worshiped and
reviled as Sweden's last warrior king—whose death also represented
the end of Sweden's role as a great power in Europe. During his
invasion of Russia, Carl came closer to Moscow than any invader
before or after him (the "after" period being most significant, as it
includes both Napoleon's and Hitler's invasions). After being routed
at the battle of Poltava in 1709—defeated by the forces of Peter the
Great—his army retreated to Turkey, where it remained for years.
There he and his men were sometimes referred to as hostages and
other times as "honored guests" of the Sultanate.

Upon his return to Sweden, Carl found a country devastated by
its war economy as well as an outbreak of the plague, not to mention
a rebellious parliament which had been preparing to unseat him.
Living like a renegade in his own kingdom at the coastal city of Lund,
he began to consolidate his power once again in 1715. On the advice
of his finance minister Görtz he began printing more money to raise
a new army for yet another military campaign—creating massive and
uncontrollable inflation. Without apparent motivation or provoca-
tion, he planned his ill-fated invasion of Norway. There, during the
siege of Fredriksten fortress—which still sits above the town of
Halden, formerly Fredrikshalden—he was killed by a bullet which
may have come from the troops behind him: that is, his own side.

All of this is part of Strindberg's version of Carl's story. Yet for
Strindberg, Carl's story, like that of Antigone, is that of a soul
compelled to move irresistibly toward its doom. He is fascinated by
the militarist's sense of masculinity—and confronts his character Carl
with a sort of chorus of aggrieved and bereaved women, from both
the disenfranchised classes and from the powerful families of Europe.
Carl XII—like the Elizabethan drama, and like the epic theatre of
Brecht—shows society from top to bottom, and makes free use of
poetic and epic devices to tackle large and universal themes.

If it may be said that Strindberg created a new hybrid form of drama with *Dance of Death*, blending his expressionist and naturalist modes, there is a similar dramaturgical alchemy going on in *Carl XII*—though with very different results. Although Shakespeare and Schiller had served as Strindberg's models in shaping his own history plays, and he makes his debt to Shakespeare unmistakably clear in his outline of theatre craft to his actors in *Open Letters to the Intimate Theatre*,[63] the tone and timbre and even structure of his pilgrimage plays like *To Damascus* are in evidence in various places. Carl's existence seems as if he were in the clutches of a dream. Here the illusory existence is a very particular one: the world of political and military power. Carl is not a simple fatalist. His sense of resignation, paradoxically, leads him to conduct massive war campaigns. He is being carried along by a force which seems to be greater than he. Perhaps one might say it is "the powers" (*makterna*) as is the case with the Stranger (*Den Okände*) in *To Damascus*. The play may also be interpreted as a study in the way the forces of history make and break rulers—a more materialist interpretation. It may be seen as a psychological study of a man blinded by ambition, the child of a great power which could not last. It may also be interpreted as classical tragedy, in which a clear and obsessive *hubris* brings about the protagonist's final and strange downfall: a burning-out, like a flare on the parapets of Fredrikstens fortress, into oblivion (I refer here to the final image: he is in fact shot). In the end, its peculiar qualities emerge because there seem to be two reasons for all that happens to Carl: an inner reason and an external reason. It is Swedenborg's dichotomy of the exoteric man versus the esoteric man at work.

The presence of the figure of the young Emanuel Swedenborg in the cast of characters, signals clearly that Strindberg's interest in the story goes beyond the parable about militarism and economics. Strindberg, like Shakespeare, is using historical compression here. In 1715 Swedenborg was a young scientist and engineer in the service of the crown. Together with the great Polhem (whose daughter is Swedenborg's desperate and jilted almost-fiancée in the play), Swedenborg helped design the advanced mechanized mine-works in Dalarna, and was a prodigy in the technologies of the time. It was later in life that his consciousness experienced a radical "turning," and he became one of Europe's best known philosopher-mystics.[64] During the period of the play, he was not yet the figure sought out by religious thinkers, tacitly condemned by the state Church, who claimed to "converse" with the divine in different forms—one interesting manifestation of which was a flaming dream image of the figure of doomed glory, Carl himself. So in drawing a bond between these two figures, and in allowing Swedenborg his esoteric pronouncements on the movements of fate and history, Strindberg turns Swedenborg, the inspiration for his own later ideas on spirituality and poetry, into a striking character and theatrical device.

So the historical chronicle bears traits of Strindberg's pilgrimage plays and expressionist dramas. Yet there are elements of the epic theatre in the play. The opening tableau on the coast of Scania clearly sets out the nature of the political situation, outlines the parliamentary power of the estates representing the different classes; reveals the economic devastation wrought by the King's foreign adventures; and does so with a deeply ironic series of scenes and dialogue which foreshadow Brecht. It is also quite uncommon for playwrights to successfully put economics on the stage. Brecht and his collaborators would later make several fairly successful attempts in that direction. Strindberg not only outlines the deleterious effects of overspending on the military when other industry is not in order, but simultaneously turns the worthless treasury and inflated economy into a metaphor for the emptiness of Carl's undertakings—one more comment on the illusory nature of the value which human beings attribute to just about anything. Yet, the just complaints which have the Swedish commoners at the brink of revolt, the inflamed class antagonisms, also seem to foreshadow the Brechtian epic theatre.

Throughout Strindberg's career as a writer, Carl XII was a Swedish national hero whose history he sought to revise. He was one of the subjects of the two-year "Strindberg feud" in the press between 1910 and 1912—for Strindberg saw the so-called "Carolinian" movement, inspired by the nationalist work *The Carolinians* by Verner von Heidenstam, and Sven Hedin's pamphlet *A Word of Warning*, as a new rally for war with Russia.[65] Indeed, the first world war was fast approaching. It must be said, however, that in the play there is plenty of evidence of points of identification between Strindberg and his antihero. It is simply one more example of the committed dramatist stepping into the shoes of even the characters toward which he feels antipathy. His essays on Carl would never reflect such understanding of his fate.

A much later manifestation of Carl's legacy gives Strindberg's perspective on the king he called "the crook" added interest. In the 1990s it began to become popular for Sweden's right wing skinheads and neo-Nazis to have large congregations around the downtown statue of Carl XII—whose arm points heroically eastward—followed from time to time by fighting and rioting against foreigners. This is the same statue at the unveiling of which, in 1868—according to some sources—the young Strindberg took part in riots *against* what this national hero symbolized.[66] The play has been frequently produced in Europe: it fared particularly well in neutral Sweden during the second world war, and has had notable productions in Germany, expecially immediately after both world wars.

9.
The Dance of Death is a strange hybrid of a play. As if a harbinger of things to come in the new century, it was completed in 1900: coming after *To Damascus*, parts I and II, but before *A Dream Play* and the chamber plays. Not a few commentators have noted that it has the same basic framework, the dramatic "unities" and the use of psychological combat found in Strindberg's naturalistic drama—yet it contains some entirely new ingredients. "It is my strongest and simplest play . . ." he wrote in 1902 and 1903 in his letters to Schering, his German translator, seeking a production by Max Reinhardt in Germany. "It is my deepest play, with a fair number of new discoveries in it . . ."[67] Coming after his first forays into expressionism with the *To Damascus* trilogy, it is riddled with elements from the new form with which he was experimenting. Recently, this has been increasingly explored, in essays with titles like "Naturalism or Expressionism: A Meaningful Mixture of Styles in *The*

Dance of Death."[68] But the most striking thing about the work—Part One in particular, which stands on its own as a play and is the one included in this collection—is the circular rather than linear plot. It is close to the circular or "spiraling" plot of the Theatre of the Absurd, a half century before that movement would seize the stage in much of the world. Martin Esslin in his landmark study, *The Theatre of the Absurd*, has acknowledged the peculiar strains of the Absurd in Strindberg.[69] George and Martha in Albee's *Who's Afraid of Virginia Woolf* (1962) are unthinkable without their forebears Edgar and Alice. Both plays portray marriage as mortal combat; both have semi-invited guests appearing, who then become drawn into the couple's secret rules and games; both deal with shifting alliances between the guests and the couple; both deal with power struggles over absent children; and in the end, both plays reveal that these couples despite their savage combat are entirely dependent upon one another—their wars and games are there to give meaning to existence and give form to the void.

What brought this hybrid creation to the page? What was the nature of the subject matter that forced Strindberg to find his way, once again, to an almost entirely new theatrical form?

After the new "vision" of both the world and art that Strindberg acquired in the years after the *Inferno* period, it is true that he turned to more epic, episodic, and dreamlike forms. Yet his talent for mustering the almost Greek intensity of conflict in his naturalistic period would not simply vanish. He was, after all, one of the best known masters of the form. One of his favorite motifs as a painter —in painting his style was always expressionist, though his subjects tended to be nature and landscape as opposed to human—was a lighthouse on an isolated island on a writhing sea. This subject of "maximum focus" in his paintings in the 90s seems to have inspired a similar effort to create a drama of focus and intensity like that of his naturalist plays. Yet Strindberg now read much more meaning into environment and landscape than he did in his early and middle-period dramas. To create the domestic landscape of the Captain (Edgar) and Alice's home, he needed both the middle class parlor or living room—and something else. Their strange "living room" is in almost Beckettian fashion set in a stone tower. They are at sea, their door facing out to sea, with no other society visible than a lone sentry in the distance. They are attached to a fortress, and on top, possibly, of an old dungeon. As we meet them they are sitting in a telling tableau: he is looking tired, she looks expectant. We have arrived during some sort of *time-out* in ongoing rounds of terrible struggle between the two. We do not know that yet. For the moment they are out of ammunition. They play cards. We sense we have arrived during a lacuna in some sort of tension. All that is lacking is the arrival of what we might call the "uninitiated guest" for them to be able to get truly motivated again. The games and the rituals of their absurd existence make sense only when seen against the emptiness of the landscape outside the tower, and the emptiness of the people with whom Edgar and Alice must associate. Without *fresh blood*, for two people it is hard to keep up the series of games and conflicts which give the illusion that something is at stake against nothingness. So the character Kurt, a relative of Alice, must enter. Then the couple can play out the tragifarce of the embattled sexes using him as fodder. When Kurt enters the tower/drawing room, at the same time a quintessentially modern character steps onto the stage for the first time. The "uninitiated guest"—typically a kind of nobody who enters in a state we can only describe as "out of it"—will continue to appear in plays on stages throughout the world, but the trend will not pick up until several decades later. This character type includes: Pinter's Ruth and Teddy, returning to visit Teddy's East End family in *The Homecoming*, and the homeless grubber Davies who enters the flat of two strange brothers in *The Caretaker*; Sam Shepard's Shelly, uninitiated to the strange rites and secrets of her boyfriend Vince's farm family in *Buried Child*; Albee's Honey and Nick in *Who's Afraid of Virginia Woolf*, who find themselves turned into "material" for George and Martha's illusions, games and rituals. All of these unfortunate uninitiated guests will find themselves in a sort of hell that certain people make for themselves when confronted with the void—a world that has lost its meaning.

Edgar is confronting his mortality: or perhaps it is more accurate to say that he is in a state of actively denying it. He needs more distractions than ever. That he is confronting a great Nothingness seems clear from various speeches, particularly his dialogue with Kurt at the end of the play's first scene.

What is happening here is that this apparent drawing-room drama is infused with elements of the expressionism which Strindberg was beginning to bring to a high level of refinement in other works. We are seeing a sort of inner landscape, emerging from the scorched battlefield of Edgar and Alice's lives, working in tension with an external set which has many trappings of a realistic play, and a use of linear time (all the so-called unities of time, space and action for that matter) which the naturalists advocated. But in fact the plot is not linear. It gives us many rounds in a struggle using shifting alliances between the three, which gives it the rhythm of a wrestling or boxing match rather than conventional dramatic action: for the plot is thin, but the rounds of the fight are well defined. Friedrich Dürrenmatt interpreted this element of the play as a *match* literally in his adaptation and staging of the *Dance of Death* as *Play Strindberg* in 1969.[70] It also looks forward to Sartre's depiction of Hell in *No Exit* forty-four years later, in which the trio of characters in Hell (Edgar calls their island "Little Hell" in Strindberg's play) end by concluding: "Let's get on with it." This is an echo of the conclusion of *Dance of Death*.

The many elements of the semiexpressionist *interior landscape* that show up in the play include: the strange sentry in the distance; the sea itself; the interior of the tower and the fortress; the many candles lit by Edgar when he is left alone at night in the second half (Act II in some editions), and throws objects of his accumulated memories out the window to the sea; the collapse of Edgar in a sort of "preliminary" death after dancing to Alice's rendition of the *March of the Boyars*; Alice's suddenly going from dark hair to white hair in the second act; Kurt's sexual advances on Alice, which finally emerge in his gesture of biting her throat in vampire fashion; the absence of the children, who are only present in the play and their parents' lives through the chattering telegraph; the strange and unverified appearance of the old woman almost as a harbinger of death to Edgar. Many of these features, in a play built around naturalistic unities, have caused critics to class Strindberg as a symbolist, who simply follows on the heels of Belgian dramatist Maurice Maeterlinck and Ibsen's late symbolist dramas. But in terms of both structure and message, this play by Strindberg stands apart from the work of the symbolists almost as much as his pilgrimage plays and his *Dream Play*. Whereas Ibsen has a linear plot with a beginning, a middle and an end (what can be more linear and definitive than the avalanche that covers over the couple and their unfulfilled lives in *When We Dead Awaken* [*Når vi døde vågner*])—when one takes Strindberg's *Dance of Death, Part I* by itself, the plot is the repetitive cycle or spiral which will come to be associated with the Theatre of the Absurd after the Second World War. It is precisely because this was seen as a flaw, as wrong-headed dramaturgy, that Strindberg was advised by Emil Schering[71] to create the more conventional sequel *Dance of Death, Part II*: to allow Edgar to finally die instead of going in eternal circles around his mortality, and so that Kurt's son Allan, and Edgar and Alice's daughter Judith, might come together to counter Hell with hope and bring about resolution. With part two, *The Dance of Death* is a symbolist drama, which takes on a linear plot. Without Part Two, the original play stands on its own as a grotesque and ironic portrayal of the trap of the eternal recurrence that daily living and the cycles of life bring with them. It is an unmistakable prototype of the Theatre of the Absurd (which to this day wields great influence over playwrights, though no longer exists as an identifiable movement).

Therefore, one returns to the question of what material, events or ideas spurred Strindberg on to create this hybrid play—and new dramatic form. In an early draft titled *Death in the Dance (Döden i dansen)* Strindberg included notes on a "Fru Tavaststjerna." This actress, Gabrielle Tavaststjerna and her husband Karl August Tavaststjerna, met Strindberg in Weimar in 1892. One could talk with her on any subject before her husband, who was mostly deaf.[72] This earlier draft has a Boat's Captain or Navigator as the protagonist, and the first act takes place in a lighthouse. The second act moves to *Fagervik* (or *Fairhaven*, one of the locales in *A Dream Play*, written in 1901-02).[73]

A later draft was set in the tower of a fortress, with the characters Edgar and Alice playing chess (not cards). In this draft there is a cover page with an outline and character list. The heading on the page is *"Allt går igen"*: that phrase, rich in connotations (everything returns, our acts come back to us, things walk again) appears not only in this play, but elsewhere in Strindberg's late work. Beneath this phrase he writes: "Struggle with death. (Dance Macabre.) / Preparation for death." Some character descriptions have the names of family or acquaintances of Strindberg next to them, but written in Greek letters. The names "Kléen," "Eliasson" and "Hugo" are among them. Kléen was a poet, whom Strindberg had visited daily while he was on his deathbed in Lund in 1898. Anders Eliasson was a physician who has been immortalized as the Doctor character in both *Inferno* and *To Damascus*.[74] Hugo (Philp), Strindberg's brother-in-law, had been quite ill in the year prior to the writing of the play. Strindberg noted in his diary, after a visit to Anna and Hugo's residence in Furusund (1 January 1899), that it had something to do with arteriosclerosis. Strindberg stayed with Hugo overnight, and the two had a "talk about death."[75] In 1900 Strindberg visited the couple again in June, but left in anger for Stockholm shortly after arriving. In October the couple was to celebrate their silver wedding anniversary, but he would not be in attendance. A few weeks later, however, his play about the silver anniversary in "little Hell" was completed.

It can be assumed that, aside from his confrontation with death, Hugo Philp brought something more to bear on the character of Edgar. Strindberg had been for some years resentful and outraged by his sister's husband, whom he saw as one of the exploiter types which he fleshed out into his vampire-figures in a number of his last novels and plays. Philp was ill from the late 1890s until his death in 1906. He was demanding on Strindberg's sister Anna and everyone around him. Anna had given up her career as a conservatory-trained violinist to marry him. Apart from Strindberg's occasional sympathy for Anna, Hugo was guilty of a betrayal Strindberg probably could not forget. He had taken Siri's side during the divorce proceedings eight years prior.[76]

Hugo had descended into bouts of rage and drinking, and what Strindberg perceived as self-centered tyranny. Hugo, as one of the social-radical generation, was a materialist who took a dim view of Strindberg's evolving religious philosophy. In a letter Strindberg described him as "[A] man who has solved all the problems of the universe without having to exert himself."[77] These remarks are strikingly similar to Kurt's comments on Edgar to Alice at the beginning of the second scene. K.I. Hildeman discovered in interviewing Philp's daughter Märta that her unmusical father indeed had a strange passion for Halvorsen's piece *Bojarernas intåg (The March of the Boyars)*, and further came to learn that, in Strindberg's presence, he had danced to the song, with Anna accompanying him, and suddenly collapsed to the floor.[78] Later, ironically—after Hugo's death when Strindberg had twice had his sister living with him and could not tolerate her alleged bohemianism—he broke with her altogether, and began to reflect on Philp more positively. Thus Anna seems to partly inspire the character of the Mother in the *Pelican*, and Hugo was one of his models for the dead and misunderstood Father: that is, not just misunderstood by the children in that play. Strindberg wondered if he himself had misunderstood him.

Lest we be too hasty in this detective work to nail one "suspect" as inspiration for this play, Strindberg's eye for the strange and wondrous would never have allowed him to stop at one model for so earthshaking a character. One out of many other relevant observations by Strindberg: On a visit to Gustaf af Geijerstam's house at Saltsjöbaden in January of 1900 Strindberg recorded "strange goings-on" in his diary. What he saw was a "dance of death" in which Geijerstam's wife, Nennie, with a terminal illness, rose in company to begin dancing. This was to become one of the grotesque scenes of *Black Banners*, in which the wife of Zachris, Jenny—both consciously modeled on Geijerstam and his wife Nennie—does her own *danse macabre*.[79]

Many theatre people who have had the opportunity to work with *Dance of Death* have puzzled over the reputation that Strindberg's family dramas have for being misogynous. Ruthless as Alice is, the balance of darkness and ruthlessness tilts clearly toward the male partner in this inseparable pair. Once again, the play rises above the stereotypes, and the models for characters Strindberg may have used as well. It resonates and is driven by emptiness and the Void, and supplies a surprising amount of humor in the face of death.

Dance of Death is by no means as popular to perform in North America as Strindberg's two world famous naturalist classics, *The Father* and *Miss Julie*. But over time it has come to run a close third. It began its career in Sweden at Strindberg and August Falck's Intimate theatre in Stockholm in 1909. In the course of over eight years, no theatre would take a chance on it. In Sweden from 1902 until 1907 the only new play by Strindberg to be produced was *Carl XII*. The reviews on this play stand as an object lesson to future generations about the reception of a new *way of seeing* when the old still dominates culture and media. *Svenska Dagbladet's* book reviewer, Oscar Levertin, responded unequivocally to the published work. "Permit us to say first off, that a more unpleasant, and what's worse—irritating—play Strindberg has never produced."[80]

> The mere fact that the brutality [in Strindberg's writing] has risen to unprecedented levels, that his simplistic ideas have grown to the point of being insufferable and base, means the crass bickering drowned any trace of thought or feeling in one endless embittered and leaden dissonance. These two spouses . . . [who] throw choicest curses at each other, strike out and spit at one another, seem in the end like a pair possessed by demons, to whose insane rows one cannot bear to listen.[81]

There were other reviews pitched in this key. And it happened again at the premiere in 1909. August Brunius, in *Svenska Dagbladet*, compared it unfavorably with *The Father* (already widely performed and proven). He wrote that the play showed "two awful maniacs with a wondrous virtuosity at the arts of squabbling, slander and abuse":

> At the same time the play is a pathological study of diverse spiritual and physical illnesses: alternately erotic hysteria and sclerosis of the heart. A medical auditorium would undoubtedly profit most from seeing *The Dance of Death*. It can hardly be judged by esthetic or psychological criteria [. . .] The elements

intended to shock, in the end, lie dangerously close to the ridiculous.

This is not by any means to say that Strindberg was simply made a martyr by the press. As always, there were those who were out looking for the new, the previously unexpressed, the valid artistic risk. The reviewer for *Social-Demokraten* wrote that the play "made a powerful impression, that shakes one." Bo Bergman, in *Dagens Nyheter*, saw the play as among "the most impressive works that has been produced in Swedish literature and on the Swedish stage." But even before the production, evaluating the published version, Georg Nordensvan had written in *Dagens Nyheter* that he found an

> impressive ability with character . . . dramatic power and additionally unique ability to structure, consistent in all its capriciousness [. . .] And it should be undeniable that in terms of energy and richness of content, it stands above the latest plays this restlessly laboring author has put forth.

Although there had been no response from Reinhardt on the script, the first production had taken place in Germany as early as 1905. The Altes Stadttheater in Köln premiered it, and then toured it—at a fair financial loss. The Intimate Theatre's small resources and small stage did not allow for the more or less symbolist set that Strindberg called for in the 1909 Swedish production, so the drawing room was more conventional than intended. As one can gather from the reviews, it received a strongly divided response, but was one of the longer running productions the theatre did (approximately fifty performances). Meanwhile, after years of cajoling from Strindberg's side, Reinhardt did his landmark production at Deutsches Theater in Berlin in 1912, and its reputation as a ground-breaking work began to spread—to France and elsewhere.[82] Working against it was the general perception of Strindberg, and the title itself may have raised fears about the supposed Scandinavian penchant for morbidity. Thus, British and American productions until recent years have often been ponderous, laying on the darkness too thick. It was only late in life that Laurence Olivier is said to have realized that the play was in many ways a comedy (He made a film version in 1969). In fact it is only recently that directors have discovered the tremendous sense of irony, delighted outrage and recognition an audience may experience from this play. The company Friteatern in Stockholm toured an openly comic version of the play in 1986-87, in which the colors were brighter, Alice's costumes and memorabilia from her acting career were hung on the walls, and the production began with a bright, upbeat waltz on calliope. And on the final lines, "Let's go on," the music returned and the couple, refreshed by tales about the misfortunes of others, took each other's arms and began a circular waltz. JoAnne Akalaitis in 1996 at Arena Stage made use of a powerfully imagistic set, with Dalì-like pyramidal shining rocks, seen through the transparent wall. The lighting was never somber, and produced a constant "glow" from the sea. The play has been produced in Europe, Russia, Latin America and elsewhere countless times. It is only recently that it has begun to appear on American stages with a regularity accorded other recognized modern classics.

Though *The Dance of Death* cannot be placed in a realist tradition, nor as an expressionist play, and it came into being too early to be classed as Theatre of the Absurd—it has something to do with all these theatre traditions. It contains only small traces of Strindberg's religious thinking, and portrays instead the challenges to human consciousness confronted with a great Emptiness. It is one of the few plays at the dawn of the century that brought existential questions to the fore: a depiction of alienation, of living against the Void, of the absurdity of love and relationships in the midst of the quest for power that seems to be inborn in us all. All this had never so clearly been placed under the lights and before the eyes of a theatre public. In this century, that theatre public has been increasingly prepared to view existence as something neither inherently good nor evil, and something containing both the tragic and comic. The play's—still recent—position as a modern classic indicates that there is a readiness for a theatre that does not create the illusion of resolving human problems, but that can shine a light on the great paradoxes of living.

Opus 3

THE GHOST SONATA

A Chamber Play

(1907)

CHARACTERS

THE OLD MAN, Director Hummel

THE STUDENT, Arkenholz

THE MILKMAID, a vision

CARETAKER'S WIFE

THE DEAD MAN, Consul

THE DARK LADY, daughter of the Dead Man by the Caretaker's Wife

THE COLONEL

THE MUMMY, the Colonel's wife

HIS DAUGHTER, is the Old Man's daughter

THE ARISTOCRAT, called Baron Skanskorg. Engaged to the Caretaker's daughter

JOHANSSON, Hummel's servant

BENGTSSON, the Colonel's servant

THE FIANCÉE, Hummel's fiancée previously. A white-haired old woman

THE COOK

[POOR PEOPLE, beggars]

[1.]

The first and second storeys of the facade of a house, but only the corner of the house is visible — which on the ground floor terminates in a round room, and on the next floor ends in a balcony with a flag staff.

Through the open window of the room, when the blinds are drawn up, a white marble statue of a young woman, surrounded by palms, is starkly lit by sun beams. In the window at the left hyacinths can be seen: blue, white and pink.

On the balcony railing on the upper floor, at the corner, we see a blue silk quilt, and two white pillows. The windows at the left are draped with white linens. It is a clear Sunday morning.

In front of the house, downstage, is a green bench.

To the right, in the foreground, is a public drinking fountain on the "street"; to the left a poster-column.

To the left, at the back, is the front door, through which the stairwell can be seen, with steps of white marble, banisters of mahogany and brass. On either side of the door, on the walk, are sheaths of laurel branches.

The corner with the round room also faces out on a cross-street, which appears to lead off to one side backstage.

To the left of the front door, at street level, is a window in which there is a street reflector.

As the curtain rises, the chimes from several churches are heard in the distance.

The front doors stand open; a woman dressed in black is standing, motionless, on the stairs.

The CARETAKER'S WIFE is sweeping the landing. Later she will sprinkle water on the laurel branches.

Beside the poster column, the OLD MAN *is sitting in a wheelchair reading the paper. He has white hair and whiskers and wears glasses.*
The MILKMAID *enters from the corner, with bottles in a wire basket. She is in a summer dress, with brown shoes, black stockings and a white beret.*

The MILKMAID *takes off the beret and hangs it on the well; wipes the sweat from her face; takes a drink from a ladle; washes her hands; arranges her hair using her reflection in the water.*

The bell from a steamship rings out, and the bass notes from an organ in a nearby church emerge now and then through the silence.

After a couple of minutes of silence, when the girl has finished fixing her hair, the STUDENT *enters from the left, unshaven, looking as though he has gone without sleep. He goes straight to the fountain.*

Pause.

STUDENT May I borrow the ladle?
MILKMAID *(hugs the ladle to her chest.)*
STUDENT Won't you soon be finished?
MILKMAID *(looks at him in terror.)*
OLD MAN *(to himself.)* Who's he talking to? — I don't see anybody!
— Is he crazy?

He continues to watch them in amazement.

STUDENT What are you looking at? Do I look so terrifying? — Of course, I didn't sleep last night, and naturally you're thinking that I've been out carousing . . .
MILKMAID *(as before.)*
STUDENT I'm unshaven, I know that . . . Give me a drink of water, girl, because I've earned it.

Pause.

Well! Then I'll have to explain to you in plain terms, that I have been binding wounds and watching over the injured all night long. I was there, you see, when the house collapsed yesterday evening . . . Now you know.

MILKMAID *(rinses the ladle and gives him a drink.)*

STUDENT Thanks!

MILKMAID *(motionless.)*

STUDENT *(slowly.)* Will you do me a great favor? *(Pause.)* The fact is, I have an inflammation in my eye, as you can see, but my hands have been in contact with the wounded and corpses — so I can't touch my eyes without risk . . . Would you take my clean handkerchief then, moisten it in fresh water, and dab my poor eyes? — Will you be a good Samaritan?

MILKMAID *(hesitates, but does as he has asked.)*

STUDENT Thank you my friend.

He takes out his change purse.

MILKMAID *(makes a gesture of refusal.)*

STUDENT Forgive my thoughtlessness, but I am in a daze . . .

The MILKMAID goes.

*

OLD MAN *(to the Student.)* Pardon me for inquiring, but I heard that you were at the unfortunate event yesterday evening . . . I was just sitting here reading about it in the paper . . .

STUDENT Is it already in there?

OLD MAN Yes, the whole thing, and your picture along with it. But they regret they were unable to get name of the student . . .

STUDENT Really? That's me! Well!

OLD MAN Who was that you were just speaking to?

STUDENT Didn't you see?

Pause.

OLD MAN Would you consider me impertinent if I asked — to have the honor of knowing — your name?

STUDENT What purpose would that serve? I don't like publicity — once you're famous, then the attacks begin — the art of knocking people down to size is developed to such a degree — besides, I'm not asking for any repayment . . .

OLD MAN Wealthy, perhaps?

STUDENT Not at all . . . on the contrary! I am destitute.

OLD MAN Listen— — —it seems to me I've heard that voice— — — I had a friend in my youth who couldn't say "window," but was always saying "win-dau" — I've only met one person with that pronunciation, and that was him. The other is you — Is it possible that you are related to Arkenholz, the wholesaler?

STUDENT He was my father.

OLD MAN Strange are the ways of fate . . . I have seen you as a little child, under rather difficult circumstances . . .

STUDENT Yes, I was brought into a bankrupt estate when I came into the world . . .

OLD MAN Absolutely right!

STUDENT Might I ask your name?

OLD MAN I am Director Hummel.

STUDENT Is that . . . ? Now I recall . . .

OLD MAN You have often heard my name mentioned in your family?

STUDENT Yes!

OLD MAN And mentioned perhaps with a certain disdain?

STUDENT *(remains silent.)*

OLD MAN Yes, I can well imagine! — They said that I was the one who ruined your father? — Everyone who ruins themselves through stupid speculation finds that they have been ruined by whomever they didn't manage to cheat! *(Pause.)* Well, the fact of the matter is that your father deprived me of 17,000 crowns, which comprised all of my savings at that time.

STUDENT It's peculiar how a story can be told in two such contradictory ways.

OLD MAN Surely you don't believe what I've said is false?

STUDENT What am I supposed to think? My father didn't lie!

OLD MAN That's true, of course. A father never lies . . . but I am also a father, accordingly . . .

STUDENT What are you driving at?

OLD MAN I saved your father from misery, and he repaid me with the terrible hatred of those who owe a debt of thanks . . . He taught his family to speak ill of me.

STUDENT Perhaps you made him unthankful by poisoning your help with unnecessary humiliations.

OLD MAN All help is humiliating, sir.

STUDENT What do you want of me?

OLD MAN I'm not demanding my money back. But if you will do me some small favors, I will be well repaid. You see me as a cripple: some say that it's my own fault, others blame it on my parents. As for myself, I'd rather think that it's life itself and it's treachery, for no sooner do you escape one trap than you find yourself in the middle of another. In the meantime, I can't go running up the stairs, can't ring bell cords, therefore I'm saying to you: help me.

STUDENT What can I do?

OLD MAN In the first place: give my chair a push so that I can read the playbills. I'd like to see what's playing tonight . . .

STUDENT *(pushes the wheelchair.)* Don't you have a man to help you?

OLD MAN Yes, but he has gone on an errand . . . coming back soon . . . Are you studying medicine, sir?

STUDENT No, I'm studying languages, but for that matter, I don't know what I'm going to be . . .

OLD MAN Ah ha! — Good at mathematics?

STUDENT Yes, passable.

OLD MAN That's good! — Might you be interested in a position?

STUDENT Well, why not?

OLD MAN Good! *(Reading the posters.)* *Die Walküre* is the matinée . . . Then the Colonel will be there with his daughter, and since he always sits last in the seventh row, then I'll have you sit right beside them . . . Would you go to the telephone booth there, and reserve a ticket for row seven, number eighty-two?

STUDENT Will I be going to the opera at noon?

OLD MAN Yes! And if you do all I bid you to do, then you shall fare
well. I want you to be successful, rich and honored. Your debut
yesterday as the courageous rescuer will make you famous
tomorrow, and then your name will be worth a lot.

STUDENT *(goes to the telephone booth.)* This is an amusing adven-
ture . . .

OLD MAN Are you an adventurer?

STUDENT Yes, that's my misfortune . . .

OLD MAN And we shall change it into a fortune — now call.

He reads the paper.
*The DARK LADY has come down on the walk, and is speaking to the
CARETAKER'S WIFE. The OLD MAN listens, but the audience hears
nothing.*

STUDENT *(returns.)*

OLD MAN Did you manage it?

STUDENT It's done.

OLD MAN You see that house there?

STUDENT I have noticed it, actually . . . I went past here yesterday
when the sun was shining through the windowpanes, and —
imagining all the beauty and luxury in there — I said to my
companion: Whoever owned a flat in there, four floors up, a fine
young wife, two pretty little children, and an income of 20,000
crowns . . .

OLD MAN Did you say that? Did you say that? I too love this
house . . .

STUDENT Do you speculate in houses?

OLD MAN Well . . . yes! But not in the way you mean . . .

STUDENT Do you know the people who live there?

OLD MAN All of them. At my age you know all people, their fathers
and their forefathers, and you are always related to them in some
way or other — I have just turned eighty — but no one knows me,
not really — I'm interested in people's destinies . . .

The blinds in the round room are drawn up. The COLONEL *is seen, in civilian dress. After taking a look at the thermometer, he walks into the room and stops before the marble statue.*

OLD MAN Look, there's the Colonel, whom you'll be sitting beside at noon . . .

STUDENT Is that — the Colonel? I don't understand anything about all this, but it's like something out of a storybook . . .

OLD MAN My whole life is a storybook, sir. But even though the stories are all different, they all hang together on one thread, and the leitmotif returns with regularity.

STUDENT Who is that marble statue of, in there?

OLD MAN That is his wife, naturally.

STUDENT She must have been quite lovely then?

OLD MAN We-ell! Yes!

STUDENT Tell me!

OLD MAN There is no accounting for a human being, my dear child! — And if I tell you that she left, that he beat her, that she came back, remarried him, and that she is sitting in there now like a mummy, worshiping her own statue, you would think I was mad.

STUDENT I don't understand!

OLD MAN I can imagine! — And then we have the hyacinth window. That's where his daughter lives— — —She's out horseback riding, but she'll soon be home . . .

STUDENT Who is that lady in black, who is talking with the caretaker's wife?

OLD MAN Well, you see, it's a bit complicated, but it has to do with the dead man, up there where you see the white sheets . . .

STUDENT Who was he?

OLD MAN A human being, like us, but the most apparent thing about him was his vanity . . . If you were a Sunday-child, you would soon see him come out through the door to look at the flag of the consulate at half mast. He was the Consul, you see, and liked crowns, lions, ruffles in his hat, and colored ribbons —

STUDENT You mentioned Sunday children — I was supposed to have been born on a Sunday . . .

OLD MAN No! Are you . . . I could believe it . . . I saw it in the color of your eyes . . . But then you can see what others cannot, have you noticed that?

STUDENT I don't know what others see, but once in a while . . . well, you don't talk about these things.

OLD MAN I was almost sure of it! But you can talk about it to me . . . because I — understand such things.

STUDENT For example, yesterday . . . I was drawn to that obscure street where the house later collapsed . . . I got there and stopped in front of the building, which I'd never seen before . . . Then I noticed a crack in the wall, heard how the double flooring was creaking. I ran forward and clutched a child that was walking under the wall . . . Within the next second the house came crashing down— — —I was spared, but in my arms where I thought I had the child, there was nothing . . .

OLD MAN That I must say is . . . I thought, in fact . . . Explain one thing to me: Why were you making those gestures just now at the well? And why were you talking to yourself?

STUDENT Didn't you see the milkmaid I was talking to?

OLD MAN *(horrified.)* Milkmaid?

STUDENT Of course. The one that gave me the ladle.

OLD MAN Really? Is that what it was! . . . Ah well, I'm not a seer, but I can do other things . . .

Now a WHITE-HAIRED WOMAN can be seen sitting at the window with the street reflector.

Look at that old woman in the window! You see her? — Good! That was my fiancée once upon a time, sixty years ago. — — —I was twenty. — Don't be afraid, she doesn't recognize me! We see each other every single day, without its affecting me in the least, although we swore to be eternally faithful back then. Eternally!

STUDENT How foolish you were in the old days! We never speak in those terms to girls nowadays!

OLD MAN Forgive us young man, we knew not what we did. — But can you see that this old woman was once young and beautiful?

STUDENT It doesn't show. Yes, she is good looking, but I can't see her eyes!

The CARETAKER'S WIFE *comes out with a basket, and scatters spruce twigs on the ground.*

OLD MAN The caretaker's wife, oh yes! — That dark lady there is her daughter, by her dead man, and that's how her husband got his job as caretaker . . . But the lady in black has a suitor, an aristocrat, who expects to be rich. He is in the process of divorcing his wife, you see, who is giving him a manor house to be rid of him. This noble suitor is the son-in-law of the dead man, and those are his bed linens you see airing there on the balcony . . . It's complicated, I suppose!

STUDENT It is horribly complicated!

OLD MAN Yes it is, inside and out, although it looks simple.

STUDENT But who is the dead man then?

OLD MAN You've just asked me, and I told you. If you could see around the corner, where the service entrance is, you would notice a mob of poor people whom he helped . . . whenever he felt so moved . . .

STUDENT Was he a compassionate person then?

OLD MAN Yes— — —now and again.

STUDENT Not always?

OLD MAN Nah!— — —Such are human beings. Listen, sir, push the chair a bit, so that it is out in the sun. I am freezing dreadfully. When you are never able to move about, your blood congeals — I'll certainly be dying soon, I know that, but before that time I have a few things to attend to — take my hand, you can feel how cold I am —

STUDENT It's beyond belief! *(He recoils.)*

OLD MAN Don't leave me. I am tired, I am alone, but I haven't always been like this, you understand. I have an endlessly long life behind me — endlessly — I have made people unhappy, and people have made me unhappy. The one cancels out the other — but before I die I want to see you happy . . . Our fates are bound together through your father — and some other things . . .

STUDENT But let go of my hand, you're taking my strength, you're freezing me — what do you want?

OLD MAN Patience, and you shall see and understand— — —There comes the young miss . . .

STUDENT The Colonel's daughter?

OLD MAN Yes! Daughter! Look at her! — Have you ever seen such a masterpiece?

STUDENT She is like the marble statue in there . . .

OLD MAN That's her mother, after all!

STUDENT You are right — I've never seen such a woman of woman born. He's a lucky man, whoever takes her to the altar and home!—

OLD MAN You can see it! — Not everyone finds her beauty . . . Well, thus it is written!

*

THE DAUGHTER *(enters from the left, dressed in an English riding outfit, walking slowly, without looking at anyone, to the door, where she stops and says a few words to the* CARETAKER'S WIFE *— and then goes into the house.*

STUDENT *(has placed his hands over his eyes.)*

OLD MAN Are you crying?

STUDENT Where there's no hope, there's only despair.

OLD MAN I can open doors and hearts, if I can just find an arm to do my bidding. Serve me, and you shall rule . . .

STUDENT Is this some kind of pact? Am I supposed to sell my soul?

OLD MAN You need sell nothing! — You see, all of my life I have *taken*. Now I need to be able to give! To give! But no one will receive— — —I am rich, very rich, but have no heirs. Well yes, a blackguard who pesters the life out of me— — —Be a son to me, inherit from me while I'm alive, enjoy existence so I can watch, from a distance at least.

STUDENT What do you want me to do?

OLD MAN First, go and see *Die Walküre*!

STUDENT That matter's taken care of. What else?

OLD MAN This evening, you will be sitting in there — in the round room.

STUDENT How will I get in there?

OLD MAN Through *Die Walküre*!

STUDENT Why exactly have you chosen me as your medium? Did you know me before?

OLD MAN Yes, naturally! I've had my eye on you a long time . . . But look over there, look at how the maid on the balcony is hoisting the flag at half-mast for the Consul . . . and now she's turning the bed linens . . . Do you see that blue quilt? — That was for two people to sleep under, but now it's for one . . .

The DAUGHTER appears now, having changed clothes, and waters the hyacinths in the window.

That's my little girl. Look at her, look! — She's talking to the flowers — isn't she herself like the blue hyacinth? She gives them drink, only clear water, and they transform the water into colors and perfume . . . Here comes the Colonel with the paper! — He's showing her the collapsed house . . . Now he's pointing out your picture! She is not indifferent . . . She's reading about your exploits . . . I believe it's clouding over. Just think, if it starts raining, I'll be sitting in a pretty pickle — if Johansson doesn't come back soon . . .

It clouds over and grows darker. The OLD WOMAN at the street reflector closes her window.

Now my fiancée is closing her window . . . seventy-nine years old . . . The street reflector is the only mirror she uses because she doesn't see herself in it, only the outer world, and from two perspectives, though the world can see her, something she hasn't thought of . . . A handsome old woman at any rate . . .

Now the DEAD MAN *comes through the door in his shroud.*

STUDENT My God! What am I seeing?

OLD MAN What are you seeing?

STUDENT Don't you see, in the doorway, the dead man?

OLD MAN I don't see anything, but it's just as I expected! Tell . . .

STUDENT He's going out to the street . . . *(Pause.)* Now he's turning his head and looking at the flag . . .

OLD MAN What did I tell you? He'll be coming to count the wreaths and read the visitors' cards . . . Woe to them who are missing!

STUDENT Now he's going around the corner . . .

OLD MAN He'll be counting the poor at the service entrance . . . The presence of the poor adds such a nice touch: "He is remembered in the prayers of so many." Yes, but he won't get any prayers from me! He was a great scoundrel, just between you and me. . .

STUDENT But benevolent . . .

OLD MAN A benevolent scoundrel, who was always planning how beautiful his funeral would be . . . When he knew that the end was drawing near, he cheated the state of 50,000 crowns . . . Now his daughter, brought up in someone else's household, is wondering about the inheritance . . . He, the scoundrel, hears everything we're saying, and we can't begrudge him that! — Here comes Johansson!

JOHANSSON enters at left.

OLD MAN Report!

JOHANSSON *(speaks inaudibly.)*

OLD MAN Oh, not home eh? You are an ass! — And the telegraph? — Nothing!— — —Go on!— — —Six o'clock this evening? — That's good! — Special edition? — The whole name! Student Arkenholz, born . . . parents . . . splendid . . . I think it's starting to rain . . . What sort of things did he say?— — —Really! Really! — He won't? — Well he'll have to! — Here comes the aristocrat! — Push me around the corner Johansson, so I can hear what the poor are saying . . . And Arkenholz will wait for me here . . . and he knows why! — Hurry up! Hurry up!

JOHANSSON pushes the chair around the corner.

*

STUDENT *(stays behind and observes the DAUGHTER, who is now raking the dirt in the flower pots.)*

*

THE ARISTOCRAT *(dressed in mourning, addresses the DARK LADY, who is walking on the path.)* Yes, what can be done about it? We must wait!
THE LADY I cannot wait!
THE ARISTOCRAT Is that so? Go to the country then!
THE LADY I don't want to.
THE ARISTOCRAT Come over here, or else they'll hear what we're saying.

They withdraw to the poster column and continue their discussion, inaudibly.

*

JOHANSSON *(enters from the right, to the STUDENT.)* The master bids the gentleman not to forget that other errand.
STUDENT Listen — tell me first: who is the master?
JOHANSSON Yes, well! He is so many things, and has been everything —

STUDENT Is he wise?

JOHANSSON Well, what does that mean? — He's been searching for a Sunday-child all his life, or so he says, but that might not be true . . .

STUDENT What does he want? Is he greedy?

JOHANSSON He wants to rule . . . The whole day long he rides about in his chariot like the god Thor . . . He looks at houses, demolishes them, opens streets, builds on marketplaces. But he breaks into houses too, creeps in through windows, wreaks havoc on people's lives, kills his enemies and never forgives. — Can you imagine, sir, that little cripple was once a Don Juan, although he always lost his women?

STUDENT Where does that fit in?

JOHANSSON Yes, well, he is so cunning that he gets women to go when he grows tired of them— — —In the meantime, he's like a horse thief in the people-market. He steals human beings in all kinds of ways . . . Myself he literally stole out of the hands of justice . . . I had, you see, committed a blunder, hm — which only he knew about. Instead of turning me in, he made me a slave. I slave only for food, which is not the best . . .

STUDENT What does he want to do in that house?

JOHANSSON Well, look, I don't want to say. It is so complicated.

STUDENT I think I'm going to get out of this . . .

JOHANSSON Look, the daughter is dropping her bracelet out the window . . .

THE DAUGHTER has dropped her bracelet through the open window.

The STUDENT goes forward slowly, picks up the bracelet and hands it to THE DAUGHTER, who thanks him in a formal manner. The STUDENT goes back to JOHANSSON.

JOHANSSON Yes indeed! He's thinking of getting out . . . That's not so easy as you think when *he* has got his net over your head . . . And he fears nothing between heaven and earth . . . Well, one thing, or rather one person . . .

STUDENT Wait a minute! Maybe I know!

JOHANSSON How could you know?

STUDENT I can guess! — Is it . . . a little milkmaid he's afraid of?

JOHANSSON He always turns away when he meets a milk truck . . . and then he talks in his sleep . . . He was in fact once in Hamburg and . . .

STUDENT Can one count on this man?

JOHANSSON One can count on him — to say anything!

STUDENT What is he doing there around the corner now?

JOHANSSON He is listening, to the poor . . . He plants a few words here, pulls out a few stones there, a little at a time, until the house collapses . . . figuratively speaking . . . You see, I am an educated fellow and once had a bookstore . . . Are you going to go now?

STUDENT It's hard for me to act ungrateful . . . This man once saved my father, and now he's only asking a small service in return . . .

JOHANSSON What is that?

STUDENT I am going to see *Die Walküre* . . .

JOHANSSON That I don't understand . . . But he's always hitting upon a new idea . . . Look, now he's talking to the police . . . He always sticks to the police, he seeks them out, engages their interest, binds them with false promises and prospects, all the while pumping them for information. — You shall see, that before the night is out he will be received as a guest in the round room!

STUDENT What does he want there? What's his connection with the Colonel?

JOHANSSON Well— — —I suspect but I don't know! You'll see for yourself when you get in there!— — —

STUDENT I'll never get in there . . .

JOHANSSON That depends on you! — Go to *Die Walküre* . . .

STUDENT Is that the way?

JOHANSSON Yes, if that's what he said! — Look! Look at him. In his war chariot! Drawn in triumph by the beggars, who won't get one penny in payment — only a hint that they will get something at his funeral!

The OLD MAN enters standing in the wheelchair, drawn by a beggar, accompanied by others.

OLD MAN Hail to the noble youth, who, by endangering his own life, saved many lives at the disaster yesterday! Hail Arkenholz!

THE BEGGARS *(remove their hats, but without cheering.)*

THE DAUGHTER *(in the window, waves with her handkerchief.)*

THE COLONEL *(stares out of his window.)*

THE OLD LADY *(rises at her window.)*

THE MAID *(on the balcony, hoists the flag to the top.)*

OLD MAN Clap your hands, citizens, it is true it is Sunday, but the ass in the well and the corn in the field will absolve us, and although I am not a Sunday-child, I am the owner of a prophetic gift of healing, for I once brought a drowned person back to life ... Yes, it was in Hamburg on a Sunday morning like this ...

*

THE MILKMAID *(appears, seen only by the STUDENT and the OLD MAN. She reaches her arms above her head like a person drowning and fixes her gaze on the OLD MAN.)*

*

OLD MAN *(sits, and then collapses in horror.)* Johansson! Take me away! Quickly! — Arkenholz, don't forget *Die Walküre*!

STUDENT What is all of this?

JOHANSSON We shall soon see! We shall soon see!

Curtain.

[2.]

Inside the round room: At the back a white porcelain stove with an inset mirror, as well as an ornamental clock and candelabra. To the right, a hallway with a view onto a green room with mahogany furniture. At the left is a statue, in the shadow of some palm trees, and which can be concealed by the curtains. At the back, to the left is the door to the hyacinth room, where the DAUGHTER is seated reading. The COLONEL can be seen from the back, where he is sitting in the green room, writing.

BENGTSSON, the servant, dressed in livery, enters from the hall with JOHANSSON, who is in a dress suit with a white cravat.

BENGTSSON Now Johansson, you will do the serving while I take their coats. Have you ever been part of these functions before?

JOHANSSON During the daytime, as you know, I push around a war-chariot, but in the evenings I serve at parties, and it has always been my dream to come into this house . . . They are strange people, eh?

BENGTSSON Well — yes, a bit unusual, you might say.

JOHANSSON What will it be, a music evening?

BENGTSSON It is the usual ghost supé, as we call it. They drink tea, speak not a word, unless the Colonel talks by himself — and they munch their biscuits, all at once, so it sounds like rats in a storage room.

JOHANSSON Why is it called "ghost supé"?

BENGTSSON They look like ghosts . . . And they've been doing it for twenty years, always the same people, saying the same things, or sitting silently to avoid embarrassing themselves.

JOHANSSON Isn't there a lady of the house as well?

BENGTSSON Oh yes, but she has lost a few marbles. She sits in a closet because her eyes can't tolerate the light . . . She's sitting in there . . .

He indicates a wall-papered door in the wall.

JOHANSSON In there?

BENGTSSON Yes, well, I did say they're a bit unusual . . .

JOHANSSON What does she look like?

BENGTSSON Like a mummy. Would you like to look at her? *(He opens the wall-papered door.)* You see — there she sits!

JOHANSSON Jesus Chr . . .

THE MUMMY *(crowing.)* Why does he open the door? Haven't I said it should stay closed . . .

BENGTSSON Ta, ta, ta, ta. If little chicky is a good girl, she'll get something good! — Pretty polly!

THE MUMMY *(like a parrot.)* Pretty polly! Oh! Is Jakob there? Currrrra!

BENGTSSON She believes that she is a parrot, and that is in fact a possibility . . . *(To the* MUMMY.*)* Polly, whistle a little something for us!

THE MUMMY *(whistles.)*

JOHANSSON I've seen a lot of things, but not the likes of this!

BENGTSSON You see, when a house gets old, it becomes moldy, and when people remain together a long time tormenting each other, then they become mad. This lady of the house — hush Polly! — this mummy has been sitting here for forty years — the same man, the same furniture, the same relatives, the same friends . . . *(He closes the* MUMMY'S *door.)* And the things that have come to pass in this house — I know scarcely anything about it . . . Look at this statue. . . that is the lady when she was young!

JOHANSSON Oh my God! — Is that the Mummy?

BENGTSSON Yes! — It is really enough to make you cry! — But this lady has, through the power of imagination or whatever, acquired some of the traits of that chatterbox bird — so she can't stand cripples and sick people . . . She can't stand her own daughter, because she is sick . . .

JOHANSSON Is the daughter sick?

BENGTSSON You didn't know that?

JOHANSSON No!— — —And the Colonel, who is he?

BENGTSSON You'll soon see!

JOHANSSON *(regarding the statue.)* It is terrible to think . . . How old is the lady now?

BENGTSSON No one knows— — —but it is said that when she was thirty-five she looked nineteen, and that she led the Colonel to believe that she *was* . . . Here in the house . . . Do you know what that black Japanese screen is for, by the chaise longue? — It's called the death screen, and is placed in front of a person who is going to die, just like at the hospital . . .

JOHANSSON It's a dreadful house . . . And the student wanted *in* here, as though it were paradise . . .

BENGTSSON What student? Ah yes, him! The one who is coming here tonight . . . The Colonel and his daughter met him at the opera, and were both quite taken by him . . . Hm! . . . But now it's my turn to ask: Who is his patron? The director in the wheel chair. . . ?

JOHANSSON Yes! Yes! — Is he coming here too?

BENGTSSON He is not invited.

JOHANSSON He'll come uninvited, if necessary— — —

*

OLD MAN *(in the hall, in frock coat, top hat, and on crutches, creeps forward and listens.)*

BENGTSSON He's really an old rogue, eh?

JOHANSSON Full blown.

BENGTSSON He looks like the devil himself!

JOHANSSON He's most likely a wizard too. Because he can pass through locked doors!

*

OLD MAN *(steps forward and grabs JOHANSSON's ear.)* Rascal! —
Watch yourself! *(To BENGTSSON.)* Notify the Colonel of my visit!
BENGTSSON Yes, but company is expected here . . .
OLD MAN I know that! But my visit is somewhat expected, if not
long awaited . . .
BENGTSSON Really! What was the name? Director Hummel!
OLD MAN Absolutely correct! —
BENGTSSON *(goes through the hall to the green room, where the door
closes behind him.)*

*

OLD MAN *(to JOHANSSON.)* Get lost!
JOHANSSON *(hesitates.)*
OLD MAN Get lost!
JOHANSSON *(disappears in the hallway.)*

*

OLD MAN *(looks the room over. He stops before the statue in deep astonishment.)* Amalia!— — —It's her!— — —Her!

*He strolls through the room, fingering things. He arranges his wig in
front of the mirror. He turns back to the statue.*

THE MUMMY *(from inside the closet.)* Prrrr—etty polly!
OLD MAN *(startled.)* What was that? Is there a parrot in the room?
But I don't see any!
THE MUMMY Is Jakob there?
OLD MAN It's haunted!
THE MUMMY Jakob!
OLD MAN I'm starting to get scared— — —They've been hiding such

secrets here in this house!

He contemplates a painting with his back turned to the closet.

That's him! . . . Him!

*

THE MUMMY *(comes out of the closet and pulls his wig.)*
  Currrr—a! Is it a currrrrr?
OLD MAN *(bursts out)* Lord in heaven! — Who's that?
THE MUMMY *(with a human voice.)* Is that Jakob?
OLD MAN My name is Jakob, in fact . . .
THE MUMMY *(with emotion)* And my name is Amalia!
OLD MAN No, no, no . . . Oh Lord Jes . . .
THE MUMMY This is how I look! Yes! — And once looked like that!
  It is edifying to live one's life — I live for the most part in the
  closet, both to avoid seeing and being seen . . . But Jakob, what
  are you after here?
OLD MAN My child. Our child— — —
THE MUMMY She's sitting there.
OLD MAN Where?
THE MUMMY There, in the hyacinth room!
OLD MAN *(observing the DAUGHTER.)* Yes, it's her!

  Pause.

OLD MAN What does her father say, I mean the Colonel? Your husband?
THE MUMMY Once I was angry at him, and then I told him everything . . .
OLD MAN Aaand?
THE MUMMY Instead of believing me, he said: "That's just what all
  wives say when they want to kill their husbands." — It was a

terrible crime, in any case. All of his life has been a forgery, his genealogy as well. I've been reading the peerage register now and again, and then I think: This girl is going around with a false birth certificate like some housemaid, which is punished with time in the spinning house.

OLD MAN A lot of people do that. I would remind you that your date of birth had been changed . . .

THE MUMMY It was my mother, who taught me . . . I couldn't help that!— — —But you were the most to blame for our crime . . .

OLD MAN No, your husband brought on the crime, when he took my fiancée from me. — I was born never to forgive before I punish — I took it as an important duty . . . and still do!

THE MUMMY What are you after in this house? What do you want? How did you get in? — Does it have to do with my daughter? If you interfere with her, you're going to die!

OLD MAN I wish her only well.

THE MUMMY But you must spare her father.

OLD MAN No!

THE MUMMY Then you're going to die: in this room, behind this screen . . .

OLD MAN Come what may . . . I can't drop the bit once I have bitten.

THE MUMMY You want her to marry the student. Why? After all, he is nothing, and owns nothing.

OLD MAN He's going to be rich, through me!

THE MUMMY Have you been invited here this evening?

OLD MAN No, but I intend to have myself invited to the ghost supé here!

THE MUMMY Do you know who is coming?

OLD MAN Not really.

THE MUMMY Baron . . . who is living upstairs here, and whose father-in-law was buried at noon . . .

OLD MAN The one who is getting divorced so he can marry the caretaker's daughter . . . The one who was once your lover!

THE MUMMY And also coming, is your former fiancée, who my husband seduced . . .

OLD MAN A pretty bunch . . .

THE MUMMY God, if only we could die! If *only* we could die!

OLD MAN Why do you associate with each other then?

THE MUMMY Crimes and secrets and guilt bind us together! — We have broken and gone our ways, such an endless number of times, but we're drawn together again . . .

OLD MAN Now I think the Colonel's coming . . .

THE MUMMY Then I'm going to Adèle . . .

Pause.

Jakob, think about what you're doing. Spare him . . .

Pause. She goes.

*

THE COLONEL *(enters, cold, reserved.)* Please sit down!

OLD MAN *(sits slowly.)*

Pause.

THE COLONEL *(fixes his glance on him.)* Are you the gentleman who wrote this letter?

OLD MAN Yes!

THE COLONEL And the gentleman's name is Hummel?

OLD MAN Yes!

Pause.

THE COLONEL Then I know that you have paid off all of my outstanding promissory notes, so it follows that I am now in your hands. What do you intend to do now?

OLD MAN I'd like repayment, in one form or another.

THE COLONEL In what form?

OLD MAN A very simple one — let us not speak of money — only allow me into your house, as a guest!

THE COLONEL If you are content with so little . . .

OLD MAN Thank you!

THE COLONEL And then?

OLD MAN Dismiss Bengtsson!

THE COLONEL Why should I? My faithful servant, who has been with me for a generation — who has earned the fatherland's medal for loyal service — why should I?

OLD MAN All this lovely stuff, that's only the way you imagine him. — He is not what he appears to be.

THE COLONEL Who is, actually?

OLD MAN *(flinching.)* True! But Bengtsson must go!

THE COLONEL Do you intend to make decisions about my household?

OLD MAN Yes! Since I own everything you see here — furniture, curtains, service, linen chest . . . and more.

THE COLONEL What do you mean more?

OLD MAN Everything! Everything you see I own, it's mine!

THE COLONEL Well then, it is yours! But my family crest and my good name are still mine.

OLD MAN No, not even that!

Pause.

OLD MAN You are not nobility!

THE COLONEL For shame!

OLD MAN *(takes out a paper.)* If you will read this excerpt from the Book of Nobility, you will see that the house whose name you bear has been extinct for a hundred years!

THE COLONEL *(reads.)* I have heard rumors to that effect, to be sure, but I take the name from my father . . . *(Reads.)* It is correct. You are right . . . I am not nobility! — Not even that. — There, I'll remove my signet ring. — It's true. It belongs to you— — — Please take it!

OLD MAN *(puts on the ring.)* Now let's go on! — You're not a Colonel either!

THE COLONEL I'm not?

OLD MAN No! You were previously temporarily commissioned as a colonel in the American volunteer army, but after the war in Cuba and the reorganization of the army all previous titles were withdrawn . . .

THE COLONEL Is that true?

OLD MAN *(draws his hand toward his pocket.)* Would you like to read it?

THE COLONEL No, it's not necessary!— — —Who are you, you who have the right to sit there stripping me in this manner?

OLD MAN You'll soon see! But as far as stripping goes— — —do you know who you are?

THE COLONEL Have you no shame?

OLD MAN Take off your hair and have a peek in the mirror — but first remove your teeth and shave off your moustaches, have Bengtsson unfasten your corset, and then we shall see if a certain servant XYZ doesn't recognize himself: the one who used to sponge food in a certain kitchen . . .

THE COLONEL *(reaches for the bell on the table.)*

OLD MAN *(anticipating him.)* Don't touch that bell, don't call Bengtsson, because then I'll have him arrested . . . The guests are coming now — Keep quiet, and we'll go on playing our former roles.

THE COLONEL Who are you? I recognize the look on your face, and the sound of your voice . . .

OLD MAN Don't inquire, just be quiet and obey! —

*

STUDENT *(enters, bows to the COLONEL.)* Colonel!

THE COLONEL Welcome to my house, young man! Your courageous conduct during the great tragedy has brought your name to everyone's lips, and I deem it an honor to have you in my home . . .

STUDENT Colonel, sir, my humble background . . . Your honored name and noble birth . . .

THE COLONEL May I present candidate Arkenholz, Director Hummel— — —Please step inside and greet the ladies, I must conclude a conversation I was having with the Director . . .

STUDENT *(is shown the hyacinth room, where he remains in view engaged in shy conversation with the DAUGHTER.)*

*

THE COLONEL A superb young man — musical, a singer, writes poetry . . . If he were from the nobility and of equal birth, I would have nothing against his . . . well . . .

OLD MAN What?

THE COLONEL My daughter . . .

OLD MAN *Your* daughter! — Apropos of your daughter, why is she always sitting in there?

THE COLONEL She has to sit in the hyacinth room when she isn't out! It's one of her peculiar habits . . . There we have Miss Beata von Holsteinskrona . . . a charming woman . . . supported by the Maidens Foundation, with an income just sufficient for her upkeep . . .

OLD MAN My fiancée!

*

THE FIANCÉE *(enters, white-haired, appears to be mad.)*

THE COLONEL Miss Holsteinskrona, Director Hummel . . .

THE FIANCÉE *(nods and sits.)*

*

THE ARISTOCRAT *(enters; secretive, dressed in mourning, he sits.)*
THE COLONEL Baron Skanskorg . . .
OLD MAN *(aside, without getting up.)* I believe that's the jewel thief
. . . *(To the COLONEL.)* Admit the mummy, and then the assembly
will be complete . . .
THE COLONEL *(through the door to the hyacinth room.)* Polly!
THE MUMMY *(enters.)* Currrr—a!
THE COLONEL Should the young people come in too?
OLD MAN No! Not the young ones! They will be spared . . .

They are all now sitting in a circle, mute.

*

THE COLONEL May we bring in the tea?
OLD MAN What for! Nobody likes tea, and therefore we are not going to sit around like hypocrites.

Pause.

THE COLONEL Shall we converse then?
OLD MAN *(slowly and with pauses.)* Speak about the weather, which
we can see for ourselves, ask how we're doing, which we all know?
I prefer silence, for then you can hear thoughts and see the past.
Silence is unable to hide anything . . . which words can. I read the
other day that the difference between languages actually arose
among primitive peoples for the purpose of hiding one tribe's
secrets from the others. So languages are actually ciphers, and he
who finds the key will understand all the languages of the world.
But that doesn't prevent secrets from being revealed without a key,
and particularly in cases where paternity must be proven. But

proof in a court of law, that's another thing: two false witnesses constitute full proof provided they agree with each other. But in matters such as the one I aim to expedite, one need not bring witnesses. Nature itself has installed in human beings a sense of shame, which seeks to hide that which must be hidden. Still we slide into situations against our will, and the occasion sometimes presents itself when the deepest secrets are revealed, when the mask is torn from the deceiver, when the villain is exposed. . .

Pause. They regard each other in silence.

It's become so quiet!

Long silence.

Here, for example, in this respectable house, in this lovely home, where beauty, culture and prosperity are united . . .

Long silence.

Each one of us sitting here, we know what we are . . . right? . . . That goes without saying . . . and you know me, though you let on that you're ignorant . . . In there at the back sits my daughter, *my daughter*, you know that as well . . . She had lost the desire to live, without knowing why . . . but she was withering in this atmosphere of crime, deceit and every sort of falsehood . . . Therefore I sought a friend for her, in whose presence she could sense the light and warmth which radiate from a noble act . . .

Long silence.

This was my mission in this house: to clean out the weeds, expose the crimes, to settle accounts, so that the young will be able to begin anew in this home, which I have left to them!

Long silence.

Now I grant you all leave to depart, each one in his turn. Anyone who stays I'll have arrested!

Long silence.

You hear how the clock is ticking, like a deathwatch in the wall! You hear what it's saying? "It's time! It's time!— — —"
   When she strikes, in a little while, then your time is up, then you can go, but not before. But she'll start shaking first, before she strikes! — Listen! Now she's giving the warning: "The clock can strike"— — —I too can strike . . .

He strikes the table with his crutch.

Do you hear?

Silence.

*

THE MUMMY *(goes over to the pendulum and stops it. Then, serious and lucid:)* But I can stop time in its tracks — I can transform the past to nothing, undo what has been done. But not with bribes, not with threats — instead through suffering and repentance— — *(She approaches the OLD MAN.)* We are wretched people, we know that. We have committed crimes, we have made mistakes, we just like the rest. We are not what we seem, because we are, basically, better than ourselves, since we disapprove of our offenses. But that you, Jakob Hummel, under a false name, presume to sit in judgment, that shows that you are worse than we wretches! Neither are you what you seem to be! — You're a thief of human beings, for you once stole me with false promises. You have murdered the Consul who was buried here today, by strangling him with bills. You have stolen the student by binding him with a fictitious debt of his father, who never owed you a penny . . .

The OLD MAN has attempted to rise and take the floor, but has fallen back into the chair and sunk down — and he sinks more and more during the following.

THE MUMMY But there is a black period in your life, which I don't really understand, but which I suspect . . . I believe that Bengtsson knows!

She rings the bell on the table.

OLD MAN No, not Bengtsson! Not that!
THE MUMMY Yes indeed! *He* knows!

She rings again.
Now the little MILKMAID appears at the hall door, unseen by everyone except the OLD MAN, who shudders. The MILKMAID disappears when BENGTSSON enters.

THE MUMMY Bengtsson, do you know this gentleman?
BENGTSSON Yes, I know him and he me. Life has its ups and downs, as we all know, and I was once his servant, he at another time was mine. He was consequently a sponger in my kitchen for two whole years — and as he had to leave at three o'clock, dinner was prepared at two o'clock, and the household had to eat warmed-over food after that ox there finished — But he also drank from the bouillon, which then had to be diluted with water — He sat out there like a vampire sucking all the pith out of the house so that we began to look like skeletons — and he attempted to have us put in jail when we accused the cook of stealing.

Later I encountered this man in Hamburg under another name. At that time he was a usurer or bloodsucker. But there he had also been accused of having lured a young girl out onto the ice where she was sucked into the river, inasmuch as she had witnessed a crime which he was afraid would be uncovered . . .

THE MUMMY *(passes her hand over the OLD MAN's brow.)* That is you! Now out with the I.O.U.'s and the will!

JOHANSSON *(appears in the hall door and watches the performance with great interest, since he has now been released from his serfdom.)*

OLD MAN *(brings forth a bundle of papers and tosses them on the table.)*

THE MUMMY *(strokes the OLD MAN on the back.)* Polly! Is Jakob there?

OLD MAN *(like a parrot.)* Jakob's there! — Kakadora! Dora!

THE MUMMY Can the clock strike?

OLD MAN *(clucking.)* The clock can strike! *(Mimics a cuckoo clock.)* Cookoo, coo-koo, coo-koo!— — —

THE MUMMY *(opens the closet door.)* Now the clock has struck! — Get up, go into the closet there where I have been sitting for twenty years grieving for our offenses. — There is a cord hanging in there which can represent the way you strangled the Consul up there, and the way you intended to strangle your benefactor . . . Go!

OLD MAN *(goes into the closet.)*

THE MUMMY *(shuts the door.)* Bengtsson! Place the screen in front! The death screen!

BENGTSSON *(places the screen in front of the door.)*

THE MUMMY It is finished! — God have mercy on his soul!

EVERYONE Amen!

A long silence.

*

Inside the hyacinth room the DAUGHTER can be seen at the harp, on which she is accompanying the STUDENT's recitation.

Prelude and song:

I saw the sun, so it seemed to me
that I beheld the Hidden One;
men take pleasure in their labors,
happy is he who works for good,
for your deeds done out of anger
are no cure for malice;
comfort him you've given sorrow
with kindness, and you've found the cure.
No one fears who's done no evil;
it is good to be innocent.

Curtain.

[3.]

A room, decorated in somewhat bizarre style, with oriental motifs. Hyacinths of all colors everywhere. On the porcelain stove sits a large Buddha with a bulb on its knees, out of which the stalk of a shallot has shot up, which bears a spherical constellation of white star-flowers!

At the back, to the right, the door leading out to the round room. There the COLONEL and the MUMMY are visible, sitting idly and in silence. A part of the death screen is also visible. To the left, the door to the pantry and kitchen.

The STUDENT and the DAUGHTER (Adèle) at the table. She is sitting at the harp, he is standing.

THE DAUGHTER Now sing for my flowers!

STUDENT Is this the flower of your soul?

THE DAUGHTER It's my only flower! Do you like hyacinths?

STUDENT I love them more than all others. Its maidenlike form, which rises straight and slender from its bulb, rests upon water and sinks its clean white roots in the colorless liquid. I love its colors; the pure and innocent snowy-white ones, the honey-yellow ones, the young pink ones, the mature red ones, but above all the blue, day blue, the deep-eyed, the faithful ones— — —I love them all, more than gold and pearls, have loved them since I was a child, have admired them, since they possess all the beautiful qualities I'm lacking . . . Still! . . .

THE DAUGHTER What?

STUDENT My love is not returned, because those lovely flowers hate me . . .

THE DAUGHTER How so?

STUDENT Their scent, which the first winds of spring made strong and pure when they swept over the melting snow, it muddles my thoughts, deafens me, blinds me, forces me out of the room, bombards me with poison darts which make my heart sad and my head hot! Don't you know the story of those flowers?

THE DAUGHTER Tell it!

STUDENT But first what it signifies. The bulb is the earth which rests on water or lies in the soil. And then the stalk shoots straight up, like the axis of the spheres, and at its upper end are the six-pointed star flowers —

THE DAUGHTER Above the earth, the stars! Oh, that is fantastic. Where did you get that, how did you see it?

STUDENT Let me think! — It was in your eyes! — And in the same way *it* is a reflection of the cosmos . . . That's why Buddha is sitting with the bulb of the earth, concentrating his vision so that he will see it grow out and upwards, transforming itself into heaven. This poor earth shall become heaven! That's what Buddha is waiting for!

THE DAUGHTER Now I see — isn't the snowflake also six-pointed, like the hyacinth lily?

STUDENT That's it! — Then the snowflakes are falling stars . . .

THE DAUGHTER And the snowdrop is a snow star . . . grown out of snow.

STUDENT But Sirius, the greatest and most beautiful of stars in the firmament, yellow and red — that's the narcissus with its red and yellow cup, and its six white petals which radiate out . . .

THE DAUGHTER Have you seen the shallot in bloom?

STUDENT Yes, I have in fact! — It brings forth its blossoms in a ball, a sphere which resembles the sphere of heaven, dotted with white stars . . .

THE DAUGHTER Yes, God, so magnificent. Whose thought was that?

STUDENT Yours!

THE DAUGHTER Yours!

STUDENT Ours! We have given birth to something together, we are joined now . . .

THE DAUGHTER Not yet . . .

STUDENT What else do we have to do?

THE DAUGHTER To wait, to face the tests, to have patience.

STUDENT Well, test me! *(Pause.)* Say! Why are your parents sitting in there so silently, without saying a single word?

THE DAUGHTER Because they have nothing to say to each other, because the one doesn't believe what the other says. My father expressed it this way: What good does it do to talk, we can't fool each other anymore.

STUDENT What an awful thing to hear . . .

THE DAUGHTER Here comes the cook . . . Look at her, she's so big and fat . . .

STUDENT What does she want?

THE DAUGHTER She will ask me about dinner. I am managing the house, you see, while my mother is ill . . .

STUDENT Will we have to deal with the cooking?

THE DAUGHTER We've got to eat— — —Look at the cook, I can't look at her . . .

STUDENT Who is this huge woman?

THE DAUGHTER She belongs to the Hummel family of vampires. She is eating us up . . .

STUDENT Why isn't she dismissed?

THE DAUGHTER She won't go! We don't meddle with her. We have gotten her for our sins . . . Haven't you noticed that we are pining away, being consumed . . .

STUDENT Then don't you get any food?

THE DAUGHTER Yes, we get a lot of dishes, but all of the nutrients are gone . . . She boils out the meat, gives us the threads and water while *she* drinks up the bouillon. And when we have steak she cooks the flavor out of it first, eats the sauce, drinks the broth — everything she comes into contact with loses its sap, it's as if she could suck with her eyes. We get the dregs after she has drunk the coffee. She drinks from our wine bottles and tops them with water . . .

STUDENT Drive her away!

THE DAUGHTER We can't!

STUDENT Why?

THE DAUGHTER We don't know! She won't go! No one can manage her — she has taken our strength!

STUDENT Can I drive her out?

THE DAUGHTER   No! Things must be as they are! — Here she comes. Next she will ask what it shall be for dinner. I answer this and that. She raises objections, and in the end she has it her way.

STUDENT   Then let her decide herself!

THE DAUGHTER   She won't.

STUDENT   This is a strange house. It's bewitched.

THE DAUGHTER   Yes! — But she just turned back this way when she caught sight of you!

*

THE COOK *(in the door)*   Naa! That wasn't why!

She grins, baring her teeth.

STUDENT   Get out, you!

THE COOK   When I please. *(Pause.)*   Now it pleases me!

She disappears.

THE DAUGHTER   Don't get exited! — Practice patience. She is one of the tests we are being put through here. But we also have a housemaid! Whom we have to clean up after!

STUDENT   Now I'm sinking! *Cor in æthere!* A song!

THE DAUGHTER   Wait!

STUDENT   A song!

THE DAUGHTER   Patience! — This room is called the testing room — it is lovely to look at, but it consists of nothing but imperfections . . .

STUDENT   Incredible. But that can be overlooked. It is lovely, but a little cold. Why don't you have a fire going?

THE DAUGHTER   Because it gets smokey inside.

STUDENT   Can't you have the chimney cleaned?

THE DAUGHTER   It doesn't help!— — —Do you see that desk there?

STUDENT Extraordinarily fine!

THE DAUGHTER But it wobbles. Every day I insert a wedge of cork under the shorter leg, but the maid takes it away when she sweeps, and I have to cut a new one. Every morning the pen is inky and the point is clogged from use. So I have to clean up after her there every single day the sun goes up.— — — *(Pause.)* What is the thing you hate the most?

STUDENT To do the wash! Ugh!

THE DAUGHTER That's my chore. Ugh!

STUDENT And what else?

THE DAUGHTER To be awakened in the middle of the night because you have to get up and latch the window . . . which the maid forgot.

STUDENT And what else?

THE DAUGHTER To climb up on a ladder and open the register, after the maid has gone and closed it.

STUDENT And what else!

THE DAUGHTER To sweep up after her, to dust after her, and to make the fire in the stove for her — she only puts in the wood! To watch the damper, to dry the glasses, set the table *over again*, tap wine for the bottles, open the windows to air out the house, make my bed *over again*, rinse the water carafe when it's gotten green with algae, buy matches and soap, which are always missing, dry the glasses on the lamps and trim the wicks so that the lamps won't smoke and so that the lamps won't go out, and when we have guests I have to fill them myself . . .

STUDENT A song!

THE DAUGHTER Wait! — First comes the toil, the toil of keeping life's impurities at bay.

STUDENT But you are wealthy, you have two servants!

THE DAUGHTER That doesn't help! Even if you have three! It is difficult to live, and sometimes I get tired . . . And just imagine a nursery in addition.

STUDENT The greatest of all joys . . .

THE DAUGHTER The most expensive— — —Is life worth so much trouble?

STUDENT   I guess that depends on the wages you expect for your labor . . . I would spare no pains to win your hand.

THE DAUGHTER   Don't talk that way! — You can never have me!

STUDENT   Why?

THE DAUGHTER   You mustn't ask about that.

Pause.

STUDENT   You dropped your bracelet out the window . . .

THE DAUGHTER   Because my hand has grown so thin . . .

THE COOK   *(appears with a Japanese soy bottle in her hand.)*

THE DAUGHTER   There's the one who is consuming me, and all of us.

STUDENT   What does she have in her hand?

THE DAUGHTER   It's a bottle of food coloring, the devil's elixer, with scorpion letters on it!   It's the witch, Madame Soya — who changes water into bouillon, which replaces real sauce, which the cabbage is cooked in and which the soup is made from.

STUDENT   Get out!

THE COOK   You sap us and we sap you. We take blood and you get water back — with food coloring. That is food coloring! — I'll go now, but I can stay as long as I want.

She goes.

STUDENT   Why does Bengtsson wear a medal?

THE DAUGHTER   For his meritorious deeds.

STUDENT   Has he no faults?

THE DAUGHTER   Yes, great ones, but you don't get a medal for that.

They smile.

*

STUDENT   You have a lot of secrets in this house . . .

THE DAUGHTER Like all others . . . Let us keep ours!

Pause.

STUDENT Do you like candor?

THE DAUGHTER Yes, in moderation.

STUDENT Sometimes a furious desire comes over me to say everything that I think — but I know the world would come crashing down if there were nothing but complete honesty.

Pause.

STUDENT I was at a funeral the other day . . . in the church — it was very solemn and beautiful!

THE DAUGHTER Was it Director Hummel's?

STUDENT My false benefactor, yes! — At the head of the coffin stood an old friend of the deceased, and he carried the funeral staff. The pastor especially made an impression on me with his dignified manner and his moving words. — I cried, we all cried. — Afterwards we went to a bar . . . There I learned that the man who carried the staff had loved the dead man's son . . .

THE DAUGHTER *(stares at him, to grasp his meaning.)*

STUDENT — And that the deceased had been borrowing money from his son's admirer . . . *(Pause.)* The day after the priest was arrested because he'd embezzled the church funds! — That's just beautiful!

THE DAUGHTER Ugh!

Pause.

STUDENT Do you know what I'm thinking about you now?

THE DAUGHTER Don't tell me, because I'd die! — — —

STUDENT I have to, or I'll die.

THE DAUGHTER In the asylum people say everything they think. . .

STUDENT Absolutely, yes! My father ended his days in a madhouse . . .

THE DAUGHTER Was he sick?

STUDENT No, he was healthy, but he was crazy! Well, it broke out one day, and under the following circumstances . . . He was, like all of us, surrounded by a circle of acquaintances which he, for the sake of brevity, called friends. They were a heap of wretches, you understand, like most people. But he needed to have company, since it wasn't possible for him to sit on his own. Well, people don't say what they think of each other in daily life, and neither did he. He knew how phony they were of course, he sensed they were disloyal at heart . . . but he was a wise man, and well brought up, therefore he was always polite. But one day he held a big party — it was in the evening. He was tired from the day's work, and the strain, partly of keeping silent, and partly of talking this crap with the guests . . .

THE DAUGHTER *(shrinks back at this)*

STUDENT Anyway, he rapped on the table to have quiet, raised his glass to give a speech . . . Then something snapped, and during a long discourse he unmasked the whole gathering, one after another, told them how phony they were. And exhausted, he sat down in the middle of the table and told them all to go to hell!

THE DAUGHTER Ugh!

STUDENT I was nearby, and I'll never forget what happened then! . . . Father and mother started fighting, the guests dashed for the door . . . and father was taken to the madhouse where he died!

Pause.

By keeping still too long we let decay set in on the stagnant waters, and that's how it is in this house as well. There is something rotten here! And I thought it was paradise when I saw you come in here the first time . . . Then one Sunday morning I looked in here. I saw a Colonel who wasn't a Colonel at all, I had a noble benefactor who was a bandit and hung himself, I saw a mummy who wasn't any mummy and a pure girl . . . Speaking of which, where does virginity exist? Where does beauty exist? In nature, and in my mind when it is dressed in its Sunday best!

Where do honor and trust exist? In fairy tales and children's plays! Where is the promise that is kept? . . . In my imagination! — Now your flowers have poisoned me and I have given the poison back to you — I asked you if we could make a home together, we composed things, sang and played, and then the cook walked in. *Sursum Corda!* Try just once to strike fire and purple on that golden harp. . . . Try, I beg you, I ask you on my knees . . . Well then, I'll do it myself.

He takes the harp, but the strings make no sound.

It's deaf and dumb! To think that the loveliest flowers are so poisonous, are the most poisonous, there must be a curse on all of life and creation . . . Why won't you be my bride? Because the source of life in you is sick . . . Now I feel as if the vampire in the kitchen is starting to drain me. I think it's a Lamia that sucks the blood of children. It's always in the kitchen where they nip the growth of children in the bud — if it hasn't happened already in the bedroom . . . There are poisons which take away your sight, and poisons which open your eyes — I was clearly born with the latter in me, because I cannot see ugliness as beauty or call evil good, I cannot! Jesus Christ descended into hell — that was his time of wandering on the earth, in the madhouse, the house of corrections, earth the morgue. And the madmen killed him when he wanted to liberate them, but the bandit was set free — The bandit always gets the sympathy! — Alas for us all! Savior of the world save us, we are going to perish!

The DAUGHTER has sunk down, appears to be dying, rings the bell, and BENGTSSON enters.

THE DAUGHTER Bring the screen! Quickly — I am dying!

BENGTSSON returns with the screen, which he spreads open, and places in front of the DAUGHTER.

STUDENT The liberator is coming! Welcome, pale and gentle as you are! — And you sleep, beautiful, unlucky, innocent, without blame for your suffering, sleep without dreaming, and when you awake again . . . may you be greeted by a sun which doesn't burn, in a home without dust, by friends who have nothing to hide, by a love without flaws.— — —You wise and gentle Buddha, who sits there waiting for a heaven to grow forth from this earth, grant us patience in our trials, and the strength of will so that your hopes will not be disappointed.

A sighing sound comes from the harp's strings. The room is filled with white light.

I saw the sun
so it seemed to me
that I beheld the Hidden One;
men take pleasure in their labors,
happy is he who works for good,
for your deeds done out of anger
are no cure for malice;
comfort him you've given sorrow
with kindness, and you've found the cure.
No one fears who's done no evil;
it is good to be innocent.

A wailing is heard from behind the screen.

You poor little child, child of this world of chaos, debt, suffering and death — world of eternal change, miscalculation and pain! Lord in heaven grant you mercy on your journey . . .

The room disappears; Böcklin's Toten-Insel *appears in the background. Soft music, pleasantly sad, can be heard from the direction of the island.*

Opus 4

THE PELICAN

A Chamber Play

(1907)

CHARACTERS

THE MOTHER, Elise, widow
THE SON, Fredrik, a law student
THE DAUGHTER, Gerda
THE SON-IN-LAW, Axel, married to Gerda
MARGRET, Servant

[1.]

A drawing room; a door at back leads to the dining room; a balcony door to the right in *pan coupé*.

A chiffonnier, a desk, a chaise longue with a reddish-purple shag dust cover, a rocking chair.

The MOTHER *enters dressed in mourning, sits down and idles in an armchair. She listens uneasily now and again.*

Outside someone is playing Chopin's Fantasie Impromptu oeuvre Posthume Op. 66.

MARGRET *the cook enters from the back.*

MOTHER Close the door, please.

MARGRET Are you alone, ma'am?

MOTHER Close the door, please.—Who is playing?

MARGRET Dreadful weather tonight, wind and rain . . .

MOTHER Close the door, please. I cannot stand this smell of carbolic and spruce.

MARGRET I knew that, ma'am, and that's why I said that he ought to be taken to the crypt right away . . .

MOTHER It was the children who wanted to have the funeral at home . . .

MARGRET Ma'am, why are you staying in this place? Why doesn't the family move?

MOTHER The landlord won't let us move, so we cannot budge . . . (*Pause.*) Why have you removed the cover on the red chaise longue?

MARGRET I had to put it in the wash. (*Pause.*) I know you're aware, ma'am, that your husband drew his last breath on that sofa. But if you'd just remove the sofa . . .

MOTHER I can't touch anything before the assessment's been done.
. . . So here I sit, shut in . . . and I can't go into any of the other
rooms . . .

MARGRET What is it?

MOTHER The memories . . . all the unpleasantness, and that hideous
smell . . . Is that my son playing?

MARGRET Yes. He doesn't like it in here. He's restless, and he's
always hungry. He says that he has never experienced a full
stomach . . .

MOTHER He's always been frail, since the day he was born.

MARGRET A bottle-fed baby should have nourishing food once it's
been weaned . . .

MOTHER (*sharply.*) Ooohh? Did he want for anything?

MARGRET Not exactly. But still, you shouldn't have shopped for the
cheapest and chintziest. And to send the children off to school on
a cup of chicory and a crust of bread, that's not right.

MOTHER My children have had no complaints about food . . .

MARGRET Oh? Not to you, ma'am, no, they haven't dared. But
when they grew up they came out to me in the kitchen . . .

MOTHER We have always lived on a tight budget . . .

MARGRET Oh no! I read in the paper that your husband's assets
were assessed at around 20,000 kronor.

MOTHER It all went!

MARGRET Well, okay. But the children are frail. Miss Gerda, I
mean our new bride, she's not filled out yet, even though she's
twenty now . . .

MOTHER What are you talking about?

MARGRET Ah well. — (*Pause.*) Shouldn't I light a fire for you
ma'am? It's cold in here.

MOTHER No thank you, we can't afford to burn up our money . . .

MARGRET But your son is at his studies freezing all day long, so
he's got to go out or keep himself warm at the piano . . .

MOTHER He has always been freezing . . .

MARGRET How'd that come about?

MOTHER Watch yourself, Margret . . . (*Pause.*) Is someone walking
out there?

MARGRET No, there's no one out there.

MOTHER You think I'm afraid of ghosts?

MARGRET Me, I don't know— — —But I'm not staying here too
much longer . . . When I first arrived here I felt I'd been sentenced to look after the children . . . I wanted to leave when I saw
how the servants were treated, but I wasn't permitted, or I could
not . . . Now, since Miss Gerda is married, I feel my mission is at
it's end, and my liberation is at hand, but not just yet . . .

MOTHER I don't understand a word you're saying — the whole world
knows how I sacrificed myself for my children, how I managed my
house and my duties . . . You are the only one who's accusing me,
but what do I care. You can go when you want. I'm not going to
have any more servants when the young people move into this
apartment . . .

MARGRET I hope it works out for you, ma'am . . . Children are not
grateful by nature. And mothers-in-law not likely welcome, as
long as they don't bring money with them . . .

MOTHER Don't you worry . . . I will pay for myself, and help out in
the house too . . . besides, my son-in-law is unlike any other son-
in-law . . .

MARGRET *Is* he?

MOTHER Yes, he is! He doesn't treat me like a mother-in-law, but
like a sister, if not a friend . . .

MARGRET (*makes a face.*)

MOTHER I understand those faces you're making. I like my son-in-
law, I have a right to, and he deserves it . . . My husband didn't
like him, he was envious, not to mention jealous. Oh yes, he
honored me with his jealousy even though I'm no longer so young
. . . Did you say something?

MARGRET I didn't say a thing! — But I thought there was someone
there . . . It was your son, the student, he's coughing! Shouldn't
I light a fire?

MOTHER It's not necessary!

MARGRET Ma'am!—I have frozen, I have starved here in this house,
and that's all very well, but give me a bed, a decent one. I am old
and tired . . .

MOTHER It is too late now, since you are leaving . . .

MARGRET True! I forgot! But for the sake of the honor of your house, burn up my linens, which people have lain and died in, so that you need not be a disgrace to whoever comes after me—if anyone comes.

MOTHER There will be no one!

MARGRET But if someone does come, she will not stay . . . I have seen fifty housemaids go their way . . .

MOTHER Because they were bad folk, and so are all of you . . .

MARGRET Thanks so much!— — —Well! Now your time is coming, ma'am. Everyone gets their turn! Things come round to each in their turn.

MOTHER Will I soon have enough of you?

MARGRET Yes, soon! Very soon! Sooner than you think!

She goes.

*   *

*

The SON *enters with a book, coughing. He stammers slightly.*

MOTHER Close the door, please.

SON What for?

MOTHER Do you answer me like that? — What do you want?

SON May I sit and read here? It's so cold in my room.

MOTHER Oh you, you're always freezing.

SON When you're sitting still you feel it more, when it's cold.

Pause. At first he pretends to read.

SON Have they done the assessment yet?

MOTHER Why do you ask that? Can't we finish grieving first? Don't you miss your father?

SON Yes . . . but — he's doing all right — and I don't begrudge him his peace, the peace he finally found. But that doesn't stop me being concerned about my situation — whether I'm going to make it to my exams without borrowing . . .

MOTHER Your father left us nothing, you know that. Debts maybe . . .

SON But the business must be worth something?

MOTHER There is no business, since there's no inventory, no merchandise, you see.

SON (*at first, thinks this over.*) But the firm, the name, the customers . . .

MOTHER You can't sell customers . . .

Pause.

SON Yes, so they say!

MOTHER Have you been to see a lawyer? (*Pause.*) So that's how you mourn your father's death!

SON No — not at all. — But that's a separate issue! — Where are my sister and brother-in-law?

MOTHER They came home yesterday from their honeymoon, and now they're staying at a boarding house.

SON Then at least they'll be able to eat their fill.

MOTHER You're always talking about food. Have you had any complaints about my food?

SON Certainly not.

MOTHER But tell me one thing. Recently, you remember when I separated from your father a while, then you went off alone with him — didn't he ever talk about the condition of his business?

SON (*engrossed in his book.*) Naah, nothing in particular.

MOTHER Can you explain the fact that he had nothing to leave us, when he earned twenty thousand crowns last year?

SON I know nothing about father's business. But he said that the house was so expensive! And then recently he went and bought this new set of furniture.

MOTHER Oh, did he say that? Did he have debts, do you think?

SON I don't know. He did have, but then they were paid off.

MOTHER Where did all the money go? Did he make up a will? Me
　　he hated, and several times he threatened to leave me penniless.
　　Is it possible that he stashed away his savings?

Pause.

　　Is there someone out there?
SON No, not that I can hear.
MOTHER I'm a little nervous after all that's happened recently, with
　　funerals and finances — In any case, you know that your sister and
　　brother-in-law will be taking this floor, so you'll have to start
　　looking for a room in town.
SON Yes, I know that.
MOTHER You don't like your brother-in-law?
SON No — we've got nothing in common.
MOTHER But he's a good fellow — and so capable. You must like
　　him. It's the least you can do.
SON He doesn't like me — and besides, he treated my father badly.
MOTHER Whose fault was that?
SON Father didn't treat people badly . . .
MOTHER No?
SON Now I think that there *is* someone out there!
MOTHER Light a couple of lamps. But only a couple!

　　The SON *turns on an electric light.*
　　Pause.

MOTHER Won't you take your father's portrait to your room? The
　　one hanging on the wall?
SON Why should I do that?
MOTHER I don't like it. The eyes look malicious.
SON I don't think so.
MOTHER Take it away then. Since you value it, you shall have it.
SON (*takes down the portrait.*) Yes. Then I will!

Pause.

MOTHER I'm expecting Axel and Gerda . . . Do you want to see them?

SON Ah, no! I have no desire . . . and I can go to my room . . . if I can just get a little stove-fire in the room.

MOTHER We can't afford to go burning up money . . .

SON That's what we've been hearing for twenty years, even though we could afford to travel abroad on idiotic vanity trips . . . And we've eaten lunch at restaurants for a hundred crowns, or the value of two cords of birch logs — two cords on one lunch!

MOTHER The way you talk.

SON Yes, there was something wrong here, but that's all over now . . . as soon as there's a settlement . . .

MOTHER What do you mean?

SON I mean the inventory of the estate and the other stuff . . .

MOTHER What other stuff?

SON Debts and things that have not been settled . . .

MOTHER Really!

SON Meanwhile, can I buy myself a few wool clothes?

MOTHER How can you ask that now? You should be thinking about earning something for yourself soon . . .

SON When I've taken my exams!

MOTHER You can take out loans like everyone else.

SON Who's going to lend to me?

MOTHER Your father's friends!

SON He didn't have any friends! An independent man can't have any friends, since friendship consists of binding oneself in mutual admiration . . .

MOTHER Aren't you wise. *That* you have learned from your father.

SON Yes, he was a wise man — who did foolish things at times.

MOTHER No! Listen to that! — Well, are you thinking of getting married then?

SON No thanks! To maintain a party lady for younger gents, to be a legal pimp for some tart, to arm your best friend — that is to say your worst enemy — to lay siege against you . . . No, I'm wary of that stuff.

MOTHER What am I hearing? — Go in to your room! I've had

enough for today! You've been drinking, of course?

SON I've always got to drink a little, partly for this cough, partly so I won't feel hungry.

MOTHER There's something wrong with the food again?

SON There's nothing wrong, but it's so light it tastes like air.

MOTHER (*startled.*) You may go now!

SON Or else the food is so spiced with salt and pepper that eating it makes you hungry! You might say, it's spiced air!

MOTHER I think you are drunk. Get out of here!

SON Well . . . I'll go. I should say something, but for now it can wait! — Yes!

He goes.

* *

*

The MOTHER paces over the floor, goes through the drawers on the table.

*

The SON-IN-LAW enters, hastily.

MOTHER (*greets him heartily.*) Finally! There you are Axel! I've missed you. But where's Gerda?

SON-IN-LAW She's coming later! How are you doing? How are things?

MOTHER Sit down and let me ask first. After all, we haven't seen each other since the wedding. — Why are you coming home so soon? You were supposed to be gone for eight days, and it's been only three.

SON-IN-LAW We-eell, it got so tedious, you know, when we'd talked ourselves to death. Then the loneliness became oppressive, and we were so used to your company that we missed you.

MOTHER Really? Well yes, we three have stuck together through all kinds of stormy weather, and I think that I was good for you.

SON-IN-LAW Gerda is a child who doesn't understand the art of living. She has prejudices which are a little obsessive, fanatic in some cases . . .

MOTHER Well, what did you think of the wedding?

SON-IN-LAW A terrific success! Terrific! And the verses I recited, what did you think of them?

MOTHER Your verses to me, you mean? Well, never has a mother-in-law received verses like those at her daughter's wedding . . . Remember that part about the pelican who gives her blood to her young. You know, I cried, ye-es . . .

SON-IN-LAW At first yes. But then you danced every dance. Gerda was almost jealous of you . . .

MOTHER Oh, that wasn't the first time. She wanted me to come dressed in black, in mourning, as she put it. But I didn't let that bother me. Am I to obey my own children?

SON-IN-LAW Please don't let it worry you. Gerda is crazy sometimes. If I but look at a female . . .

MOTHER What? Aren't you happy together?

SON-IN-LAW Happy? What's that mean?

MOTHER Well? Have you quarreled already?

SON-IN-LAW Already? We did nothing else while we were engaged. And now what's come up is that I have to go off and serve as a lieutenant in the reserves . . . It's curious, but it seems to me she likes me less in my civvies . . .

MOTHER Why don't you dress in uniform then? I must confess that I hardly recognize you as a civilian — you really are another person . . .

SON-IN-LAW I cannot be in uniform other than on active duty or for parades . . .

MOTHER Cannot?

SON-IN-LAW Yes, that's regulations . . .

MOTHER Anyway, it's too bad for Gerda. She was engaged to a lieutenant, but now she's married to a bookkeeper.

SON-IN-LAW What can I do about that? I've got to live! Speaking of living, how is the financial situation?

MOTHER Frankly speaking, I don't know! But I'm beginning to have suspicions about Fredrik.

SON-IN-LAW How so?

MOTHER He was talking so strangely here this afternoon . . .

SON-IN-LAW That mutton-head . . .

MOTHER *Mutton* are crafty in their way, and I'm not sure that there isn't a will or some savings here somewhere . . .

SON-IN-LAW Have you checked?

MOTHER I've looked through all of his drawers . . .

SON-IN-LAW In the boy's?

MOTHER Of course, and I always examine his wastepaper basket, because he's always writing letters which he tears to shreds . . .

SON-IN-LAW That's nothing. But have you checked the old man's chiffonnier?

MOTHER Yes, of course . . .

SON-IN-LAW But thoroughly? Every drawer?

MOTHER Every one!

SON-IN-LAW There are usually secret compartments in all chiffonniers.

MOTHER I didn't think of that!

SON-IN-LAW Well, we'll have to have a look at it then!

MOTHER No, don't touch it. It's been sealed by the executor.

SON-IN-LAW Can't you get past the seals?

MOTHER No, you can't!

SON-IN-LAW Yes you can, if you loosen the boards at the back, all the secret compartments are back there . . .

MOTHER We'll need tools for that . . .

SON-IN-LAW Not really. It can be done without them . . .

MOTHER But Gerda must not know anything about it.

SON-IN-LAW No, of course— — —She'd squeal immediately to her little brother . . .

MOTHER (*closes the doors.*) I'll lock the doors, just in case . . .

SON-IN-LAW (*explores the back of the chiffonnier.*) Well, I'll be . . . someone has been here . . . The backboard is loose . . . I can get my hand in there . . .

MOTHER The boy did it . . . You see, my suspicions . . . Hurry up, someone's coming!

SON-IN-LAW There are some papers in here . . .

MOTHER Will you hurry, there's someone coming . . .

SON-IN-LAW An envelope . . .

MOTHER Gerda's coming! Give me the papers . . . quick!

SON-IN-LAW (*hands her a large letter, which the Mother hides.*) Here.
   Hide it!

*   *
*

The door is pulled. Then someone starts pounding on it.

SON-IN-LAW To think that you would lock it . . . We're in a fix!

MOTHER Quiet!

SON-IN-LAW You are an ass!— — —Open it! — Otherwise I'll open
   it! — Out of the way!

He opens the door.

DAUGHTER (*enters gloomily.*) Why did you lock yourselves in?

MOTHER Don't you say hello first, my little child? I haven't seen
   you since the wedding. Did you have a pleasant trip? Now, tell
   me about it, and don't look so cloudy.

DAUGHTER (*sits in a chair, depressed.*) Why did you lock the door?

MOTHER Because it comes open by itself, and I'm getting tired of
   keeping after people to close it all the time. Shall we think about
   how to furnish your apartment now. You will be living here?

DAUGHTER We've got to— — —it's all the same to me — what do
   you say Axel?

SON-IN-LAW Yes, it will be fine here, and it won't be so bad for
   Mother— — —since we get on well together . . .

DAUGHTER Where is Mama going to live then?

MOTHER Here, my child. I will just put in a bed.

SON-IN-LAW Are you going to put a bed in the drawing room, dear?

DAUGHTER (*thrown by the word "dear."*) Did you mean me?

SON-IN-LAW I mean Mother . . . but things will work out . . . we've got to help one another, and with what Mother pays in we'll be able to live . . .

DAUGHTER (*brightens.*) And so I'll have some help with the house-keeping . . .

MOTHER Of course, my child . . . But I don't want to do the dishes!

DAUGHTER How could you think such a thing! Anyway, this will be fine, as long as I have my husband to myself. They can't even look at him . . . Like they were doing at the boarding house, and that's why we cut our trip short . . . But anyone who tries to take him from me — I'll kill her! So there! —

MOTHER Now we'll go out and start moving furniture . . .

SON-IN-LAW (*fixes the Mother with his glance.*) Good! But Gerda can start here . . .

DAUGHTER How come? I prefer not to be alone in here . . . once we have moved in, I'll be able to relax here . . .

SON-IN-LAW Since you are afraid of the dark, then we'll all three go together . . .

All three of them go.

*　　*

*

The stage is empty. There is a wind outside howling in the window and in the woodstove. The back doors begin to open and close, papers from the desk fly around the room, a palm on a pedestal shakes furiously, a photo falls from the wall. Now the SON's voice is heard: "Mamma!" Immediately thereafter: "Shut the window!" Pause. The rocking chair moves.

MOTHER (*enters, wild, with a paper in her hand which she is reading.*) What is it! The rocking chair's moving!

SON-IN-LAW (*in, behind her.*) What was that? What's that say? May I read it? Is it the will?

MOTHER Close the door! We'll all be blown away. I had to open a window because of the smell. That's not the will — it's a letter to the boy, where he's slandering me and — you!

SON-IN-LAW Let me read it!

MOTHER No, it will only poison your thoughts. I'm tearing it up — what luck that it didn't fall into his hands . . .

She tears the paper to pieces and throws it into the wood-burning stove.

Just think. He rises up and speaks from the grave — he is not dead! I can never live here — He writes that I murdered him. . . I did not! He died of a heart attack, the doctor verified that . . . but he says other things as well, which are all of them lies! That I ruined him! . . . Listen, Axel, see to it that we get out of this apartment. I can't take this! Promise me! — Look at the rocking chair!

SON-IN-LAW It's the draft.

MOTHER Let's leave this place. Promise me!

SON-IN-LAW I can't do that . . . I was counting on an inheritance, since you alluded to the fact there was one, otherwise I wouldn't have gotten married. Now we'll have to accept things as they are, and you can consider me your sucker son-in-law — and a ruined one at that. We've got to pull together to live! We have to start saving money, and you're going to help.

MOTHER You mean that I'm going to be employed as a maid in my own home? I won't do it!

SON-IN-LAW When necessity calls . . .

MOTHER You're a crook.

SON-IN-LAW Watch your manners, old lady.

MOTHER Your maid!

SON-IN-LAW Now you'll know how your maids have felt, starving and freezing — something you won't have to do!

MOTHER I have my annuity.

SON-IN-LAW That won't get you even a attic. But here it will cover
the rent, if we stay right where we are . . . and, if you don't stay
right where you are, then I'm going!

MOTHER From Gerda? You have never loved her —

SON-IN-LAW You know more about this than I do . . . You rooted
her out of my mind, pushed her out of everything, except for the
bedroom, that she got to keep . . . And should a child arrive, you
will take that from her too . . . She knows nothing yet, understands
nothing, but she's beginning to wake from her sleepwalker's sleep.
The day she opens her eyes—watch out!

MOTHER Axel! We have got to stick together . . . we mustn't split
up . . . I cannot live alone. I'll go along with everything — but not
the chaise longue . . .

SON-IN-LAW Oh yes! I will not wreck this apartment by having a
bedroom here — get that straight!

MOTHER But let me have another . . .

SON-IN-LAW No, we can't afford it, and this one is lovely.

MOTHER Ugh! It's a bloody slaughter block!

SON-IN-LAW Say what you like . . . But if you won't do it, all that's
left for you is an attic and solitude, the chapel and the poorhouse.

MOTHER I give up!

SON-IN-LAW Now you're talking sense . . .

Pause.

MOTHER Still, imagine, he writes to his son that his death was a
murder.

SON-IN-LAW There are many ways to commit murder . . . and your
way had the advantage that it doesn't fall under the criminal code.

MOTHER Call it *our* method! Because you went along and did your
part, when you drove him into a frenzy and desperation . . .

SON-IN-LAW He was in the way and wouldn't budge. So I had to give
him a shove . . .

MOTHER The only thing I reproach you for is that you lured me out
of my home . . . And I can't forget that evening, the first one at
your home, when we were sitting enjoying our meal, and from

down in the gardener's plot we heard these horrible cries, which we thought came from the prison yard or the madhouse . . . do you recall? It was him, walking about in the gardens in darkness and rain, howling out of loneliness for his wife and children.

SON-IN-LAW Why are you bringing all that up now? And how do you know that it was him?

MOTHER It was in his letter!

SON-IN-LAW Well, what's that to us? He was no angel . . .

MOTHER No, he wasn't. But he possessed human feelings from time to time . . . yes, a bit more than you.

SON-IN-LAW Your sympathies are starting to go back to him . . .

MOTHER Don't be angry now! We have to keep the peace here.

SON-IN-LAW We have to. We are condemned to . . .

Hoarse yelling from within.

MOTHER What's that? You hear that? It's him . . .

SON-IN-LAW (*coarsely.*) Which *him*?

MOTHER (*listens.*)

SON-IN-LAW Who is that? — The boy! He's been drinking again.

MOTHER Is that Fredrik? It was so much like *him* — I thought— — — I can't take this! What is going on with him?

SON-IN-LAW Go and see. The bum is drunk, most likely.

MOTHER How can you say such a thing! He is my son, after all!

SON-IN-LAW Yours, after all! — (*Takes out his watch.*)

MOTHER Why are you looking at your watch? Won't you be staying this evening?

SON-IN-LAW No thanks. I don't drink tea water and never eat rancid anchovies . . . or porridge . . . Besides, I have to go to a meeting . . .

MOTHER What kind of meeting?

SON-IN-LAW Business, that's no concern of yours! Do you want to attend as my mother-in-law?

MOTHER Are you going to leave your wife alone your first night home?

SON-IN-LAW That's no concern of yours either!— — —

MOTHER Now I know what's in store for me — and my children! Here comes the unmasking —

SON-IN-LAW Here it comes!

Curtain.

[2.]

Same set.

Someone is playing, off: "Berceuse" from Jocelyn.

The DAUGHTER is sitting at the desk.

A long silence.

SON (*enters.*) Are you alone?

DAUGHTER Yes. Mamma is in the kitchen.

SON Where is Axel then?

DAUGHTER He's at a meeting . . . Sit down and let's talk, Fredrik. Keep me company!

SON (*sits.*) Well, I don't think we've ever talked before. We've always stayed out of each other's way, not having anything in common.

DAUGHTER You've always taken Father's side, and I've taken Mother's.

SON Maybe that's changing now. — Did you really know your father?

DAUGHTER A strange question! But I actually only saw him through Mother's eyes.

SON But you saw that he was fond of you.

DAUGHTER Why did he want to prevent and break up my engagement?

SON Because he didn't consider your fiancé to be the kind of support you need.

DAUGHTER He was punished for that too, when Mamma left him.

SON Was it your husband who persuaded her to leave?

DAUGHTER It was him and me! Father had to feel what it's like to be separated, since he wanted to separate me from the man I was engaged to.

SON Meanwhile, this shortened his life . . . And believe me, he only wanted the best for you.

DAUGHTER You stayed with him. What did he say? How did he take it?

SON His pain I couldn't begin to describe . . .

DAUGHTER Then what did he say about Mamma?

SON Nothing . . . Anyway, after all I have seen I will never get married.

Pause.

SON Are you happy, Gerda?

DAUGHTER Well, yes! When you've gotten what you wanted, then you are happy.

SON Why is your husband leaving you alone your first night back?

DAUGHTER He has business, a meeting.

SON At the café?

DAUGHTER What are you saying? Do you *know* that?

SON I thought you knew.

DAUGHTER (*cries into her hands.*) Oh God, my God!

SON I'm sorry if I hurt you.

DAUGHTER Yes, it hurts! hurts! Oh, I want to die!

SON Why didn't you stay longer on your honeymoon?

DAUGHTER He was anxious about business . . . he wanted to see Mamma. He can't be away from her . . .

They look each other in the eyes.

SON Really? (*Pause.*) Did you have a pleasant trip in any case?

DAUGHTER Well, yes!

SON Poor Gerda.

DAUGHTER What are you saying?

SON Well, you know of course, Mother is curious about things, and she can use a telephone like nobody else.

DAUGHTER What's that mean? Was she spying?

SON She always does . . . she's likely listening behind some door to this very conversation . . .

DAUGHTER You always think the worst about our mother.

SON And you always think the best! How can that be? You know what she is like . . .

DAUGHTER No! And I don't want to know . . .

SON That's another thing, you don't want to know. You have some reason not to . . .

DAUGHTER Hush! I am walking in my sleep, I know that. But I don't want to be wakened! I wouldn't be able to go on living.

SON Don't you think we're all sleepwalking? — I'm studying Law, as you know, case records. So, I'm reading about great criminals, who cannot explain how things came about the way they did . . . and thought that they were doing the right thing, right up till the moment that were caught and woke up! If that isn't a kind of dream, it certainly is a kind of sleep!

DAUGHTER Let me sleep! I know that I will wake up, but I hope I have a long ways to go before I do. Ugh! All these things, that I don't know, but suspect! Do you remember when we were children . . . People call you bad if you say what is true . . . "You are so bad," they always said to me when I maintained that something wrong was *wrong* . . . so I learned to keep quiet . . . then I was liked for my good manners. So I learned to say what I didn't mean, and then I was ready to step out into life.

SON (*listless.*) Of course, one should overlook the next person's mistakes and weaknesses, that is true . . . but then you're one step from what they call bowing and scraping . . . It's hard to know the best way . . . Sometimes it's a duty to speak out . . .

DAUGHTER Be quiet.

SON I'll be quiet.

Pause.

DAUGHTER No, it's better to talk, but not about *that*! I hear your thoughts in the silence! . . . When people come together, then they talk, talk ceaselessly, just to hide their thoughts . . . to forget, to deaden themselves . . . Of course they want to hear news about other people, but their own lives they hide.

SON Poor Gerda.

DAUGHTER Do you know what hurts the worst? (*Pause.*) To see, in your greatest happiness, nothingness.

SON Now you're talking!

DAUGHTER I'm freezing. Light us a fire.

SON Are you freezing too?

DAUGHTER I'm always freezing and hungry.

SON You too? It's odd about this house. — But if I go out now to get some wood, she'll make it living hell here for a week.

DAUGHTER Maybe it's been put in the woodstove. Mamma used to lay in firewood once in a while to fool us— — —

SON (*goes to the woodstove and opens the door.*) There really are a few sticks of wood here! (*Pause.*) But what's *that*? — A letter! Torn in pieces, we can light it with that . . .

DAUGHTER Fredrik, don't light it. She will nag us about it forever. Come and sit down again and we can talk . . .

SON (*goes and sits at the table, spreading the letter out before him.*)

Pause.

DAUGHTER Do you know why Father hated my husband the way he did?

SON Well, your Axel came and took his daughter and wife from him, so that he ended up sitting on his own. And then the old man noticed that his son-in-law was getting better meals than he did. You'd lock yourselves in the parlor, playing music and reading, but always the things that our father couldn't abide. He was elbowed out, eaten out of his home, and that's why he ended up at the bar.

DAUGHTER We weren't thinking of what we were doing . . . poor Father! — It's good to have parents with an irreproachable name and reputation, and we can be thankful . . . Do you remember our parents' silver anniversary? The verses and speeches people made for them?

SON I remember, but I thought it was a sorry spectacle, celebrating a marriage as if it were happy, when it was a dog's life . . .

DAUGHTER Fredrik!

SON I can't help it. But you know how their life was . . . Don't you remember when Mamma wanted to go out the window and we had to hold onto her?

DAUGHTER Please, hush.

SON There are reasons, which we don't know . . . and during their separation, when I was watching over the old man, he seemed to want to talk, several times, but the words didn't come to his lips . . . I dream about him sometimes . . .

DAUGHTER So do I! — Then, when I see him he's thirty again . . . he looks at me kindly, meaningfully, but I don't understand what he wants . . . Sometimes Mamma is there too. He is not angry at her, because she was always dear to him, despite everything, even recently. You remember the lovely way he spoke of her at the silver anniversary, thanking her, *in spite of everything* . . .

SON In spite of everything! That's saying a lot, but not enough.

DAUGHTER But it was lovely. She really did deserve it . . . She has managed her household.

SON Yes, that is the big question.

DAUGHTER What are you saying?

SON See, you all stick together! No sooner is housekeeping mentioned, then you're on the same side . . . it is like freemasons, or a Camorra . . . I have even asked old Margret, who is my friend, things concerning the household finances. I have asked her why everyone must always be hungry in this house . . . this person who could talk your head of! She goes silent and gets mad . . . Can you explain that?

DAUGHTER (*short.*) No!

SON I can hear from your voice that you're a mason too.

DAUGHTER I don't know what you mean!

SON Sometimes I wonder whether father fell victim to that Camorra which he must have uncovered.

DAUGHTER Sometimes you talk like an idiot . . .

SON I remember father using the word Camorra from time to time, as a joke. But in the end he got quiet . . .

DAUGHTER It's awful how cold it is here. Cold as a grave . . .

SON Then I'm going to light a fire, whatever it costs!

*He picks up the torn letter, at first thoughtlessly. Then it catches his
eye and he starts to read.*

SON What's this here? (*Pause.*) To my son . . . It's Father's writing!
(*Pause.*) It's to me then!

He reads. He falls into a chair and continues reading in silence.

DAUGHTER What are you reading? What is it?
SON It's awful.

Pause.

SON   It's too terrible!
DAUGHTER Tell me, what is it!

Pause.

SON It's too much . . . (*To the DAUGHTER.*) It's a letter from my
dead father, to me! (*He reads on.*) Now I'm waking from my
sleep.

*He throws himself on the chaise longue, and howls as if from pain,
but stuffs the papers in his pocket.*

DAUGHTER (*on her knees beside him.*) What is it Fredrik? Tell me
what it is! — Fredrik, are you sick? Tell me, tell me!
SON (*sits up.*) I don't want to live anymore.
DAUGHTER Tell me what it's about!
SON It's just too incredible! . . . (*He pulls himself together, standing
up.*)
DAUGHTER It might be untrue.
SON (*irritated.*) Oh no. He can't be lying from the grave.
DAUGHTER He might have been suffering from a sick man's fan-
tasies . . .
SON Camorra! Are you back to that again? Then I *am* going to tell

you what it's about!— — —Now listen!

DAUGHTER I think I know everything already. But I still don't believe it.

SON You don't want to believe it. — Anyway, here it is. Our mother
who gave us life was a master thief!

DAUGHTER No . . .

SON She stole from the housekeeping funds, she created phony bills,
she bought the worst quality for the highest price, she ate in the
kitchen in the mornings and gave us our meals warmed over and
watered down, she skimmed the cream from the milk, that's why
we're depressed, her children, always sick and hungry. She stole
from the money for firewood, so we had to freeze. When our
father discovered this, he gave her a warning. She promised things
would improve, but kept on, and made discoveries: soya and
cayenne pepper!

DAUGHTER I don't believe a word.

SON Camorra! — But here's the worst of it! That sleazy guy who
is now your husband, Gerda — he has never loved you, but your
mother!

DAUGHTER Uhh!

SON When father found this out, and when your husband borrowed
money from your mother, our mother, then the wretch covered his
tracks by proposing to you. This is the broad outline. You can
work out the details for yourself.

DAUGHTER (*is crying in a handkerchief. Then:*) I already knew
this. But still, I didn't know it . . . it never came to awareness in
my mind. Because it was too much!

SON What can be done now, to save you from this humiliation?

DAUGHTER Leave!

SON Where to?

DAUGHTER Don't know!

SON Wait then, and see how things turn out.

DAUGHTER A person's defenseless against her mother. I mean, she
is holy . . .

SON The hell with that!

DAUGHTER Don't say that.

SON She's as cunning as an animal, but her self-love often blinds
    her . . .

DAUGHTER Let's run away from here.

SON Where? No, stay, till the bastard drives her out of the house!
    — Sssh! The bastard's coming home! — Ssshh! Gerda, now the
    two of us will be freemasons. I'll give you the word. The
    password: "He struck you on your wedding night!"

DAUGHTER Remind me of that often! Otherwise I forget. I want
    so much to forget.

SON Our lives have been wrecked . . . nothing to respect, to look up
    to . . . it's impossible to forget . . . Let's live to restore our lives,
    and the memory of our father.

DAUGHTER And to get justice!

SON Call it vengeance.

*   *
*

The SON-IN-LAW comes in.

DAUGHTER (*acting.*) Hello there! — Did you enjoy your meeting?
    Did something good come of it?

SON-IN-LAW It was called off.

DAUGHTER They called you out, did you say?

SON-IN-LAW Called off, I said.

DAUGHTER Well, are you going to do some chores around the house
    tonight?

SON-IN-LAW You are in such a good frame of mind tonight. But
    Fredrik is cheerful company.

DAUGHTER We've been playing freemasons!

SON-IN-LAW Watch yourself.

DAUGHTER Then we'll play Camorra instead! Or *vendetta*!

SON-IN-LAW (*ill at ease.*) You are talking so strangely. What are you
    up to? Secrets?

DAUGHTER You don't talk about your secrets. Or do you? Maybe you don't have any secrets?

SON-IN-LAW What's happened? Has somebody been here?

SON Gerda and I have become mediums. We've been visited by a
departed spirit.

SON-IN-LAW Let's cut the joking now, or things will take a bad turn.
Although it suits you, Gerda, when you're a little bit happy, you
are usually gloomy . . . (*He attempts to give her a pat on the cheek,
but she pulls away.*) Are you afraid of me?

DAUGHTER (*drops her role-playing.*) Not at all! There are feelings
which seem like fear, but are something else. There are gestures
which say more than looks, and words which hide what movements
and expressions don't reveal.

SON-IN-LAW (*amazed, fingers the books on a shelf.*)

The SON *gets up from the rocking chair, which continues rocking
until the* MOTHER *enters.*

SON Here comes Mother with her mush.

SON-IN-LAW Is it . . .

*   *
*

The MOTHER *enters, sees the rocking chair moving; shudders but
calms herself.*

MOTHER Will you come and have some porridge!

SON-IN-LAW No thanks. If it's oatmeal, then give it to the hounds,
if you have any. If it's rye, spread it on your boil . . .

MOTHER We are poor and have to save . . .

SON-IN-LAW On twenty thousand a year you're not poor.

SON Yes, if you lend out money to those who don't pay you back.

SON-IN-LAW What's that? Is the boy crazy?

SON Maybe he *was*, once.

MOTHER Are you coming?

DAUGHTER Come on, let's go. Courage gentlemen. You shall get a sandwich and a steak from me . . .

MOTHER From you?

DAUGHTER Yes, from me in my house . . .

MOTHER Have you heard the like!

DAUGHTER (*with a gesture to the door.*) Please, gentlemen. This way!

SON-IN-LAW (*to the MOTHER.*) What is all this?

MOTHER Something's up.

SON-IN-LAW I think so too!—

DAUGHTER Please, this way gentlemen.

They all move toward the door.

MOTHER (*to the SON-IN-LAW.*) Did you see the rocking chair moving? *His* rocking chair?

SON-IN-LAW No, I didn't. But I saw something else!

Curtain.

[3.]

The scene is the same.

The waltz "Il me disait" by Ferraris is being played.

The DAUGHTER is seated with a book. The MOTHER enters.

MOTHER Do you recognize it?
DAUGHTER The waltz? Yes.
MOTHER Your wedding waltz, to which I danced until morning!
DAUGHTER "I" danced? — Where's Axel?
MOTHER What do I care?
DAUGHTER Well well! Have you quarreled already?

Pause. They exchange looks.

MOTHER What are you reading, dear?
DAUGHTER Your recipe book. But how come it doesn't say anything
   about how long something should be cooked?
MOTHER (*embarrassed.*) It varies so much, you see. People have such
   different taste. The one does it this way, the other does it that
   way . . .
DAUGHTER I don't understand that. Food has got to be served as
   soon as it's done, otherwise it's got to be warmed up and therefore
   spoiled. Yesterday, for example, you fried a grouse for three
   hours. During the first hour this whole floor was filled with the
   aroma of fresh game cooking. Then it got quiet in the kitchen.
   And when the food was served the aroma was gone and it tasted
   like air. Can you explain that?
MOTHER (*flustered.*) I don't understand.
DAUGHTER Then explain why there was no sauce on it. Where did
   it go? Who ate it all?

MOTHER I don't understand any of this!

DAUGHTER But now I've been asking myself about these things, and
I have figured out a great deal . . .

MOTHER (*cutting in.*) I know that, and you're not going to be
teaching me anything new. But I can teach you about the art of
managing a house . . .

DAUGHTER You mean with soya and cayenne pepper. I already
know about that. And how to choose dishes for guests that no
one will eat so that you have leftovers the next day . . . or by
inviting people when the pantry is filled with scraps . . . I know
how all that is done now, and that's why from this day forward
control of this household is in my hands.

MOTHER (*furious.*) Am I to be your maid?

DAUGHTER I'll be yours and you mine. We'll help each other. —
Here comes Axel.

*   *
*

The SON-IN-LAW *comes in, with a thick cane in his hand.*

SON-IN-LAW We-eell? What do you think about the chaise longue?

MOTHER Ooohhh, good heavens . . .

SON-IN-LAW (*threateningly.*) Isn't it all right? Is there anything wrong
with it?

MOTHER Now I begin to understand.

SON-IN-LAW Really!— — —Meanwhile, since we cannot get enough
to eat in this house, Gerda and I intend to eat by ourselves.

MOTHER And what about me?

SON-IN-LAW You're getting fat as a barrel, so you don't need much.
It would be better for your health if you thinned down a little, as
we have done . . . Meeaan-while — would you step out for a
moment Gerda — meanwhile you can get a fire going in the
woodstove.

Gerda goes.

MOTHER (*trembles with rage.*) There is wood in there . . .

SON-IN-LAW Oh no, there are a few sticks. But now you're going to go get some wood, enough to fill the stove!

MOTHER (*hesitates.*) So we're going to burn up our money?

SON-IN-LAW No, but it takes wood to make a fire to make us warm! Fast!

MOTHER (*hesitates.*)

SON-IN-LAW One, two — three!

He slams his cane on the table.

MOTHER I think all the wood is gone . . .

SON-IN-LAW Either you're lying, or you have stolen the money . . . because we bought a quarter cord of wood day before yesterday!

MOTHER Now I see who you are . . .

SON-IN-LAW (*sits in the rocking chair.*) You would have seen that long ago, if your age and experience had not made a dupe of my youth and inexperience . . . Quick! Go! For wood, or else . . .

He raises his cane.

MOTHER (*goes out quickly, comes back immediately with wood.*)

SON-IN-LAW Now light a decent fire, and don't just fake it! — One, two three!

MOTHER How you resemble the old man now, sitting there in his rocking chair!

SON-IN-LAW Light it!

MOTHER (*cowed, but in a rage.*) I will, I will!

SON-IN-LAW Now you will watch the fire, while we go out to the dining room and eat . . .

MOTHER What do I eat then?

SON-IN-LAW The porridge Gerda put out for you in the kitchen.

MOTHER With the blue skim milk . . .

SON-IN-LAW Since you ate up all the cream, it's only right! and just!

MOTHER (*dully.*) Then I'll go my way.

SON-IN-LAW You can't, because I'm locking you in.

MOTHER (*whispers.*) Then I'll jump out the window.

SON-IN-LAW You should. You ought to have done that long ago,
then the lives of four people would have been spared. Light it
now! — Blow on it! — Like that!   Sit right here until we get
back.

He goes.

*   *

*

Pause.

*The MOTHER stops first at the rocking chair; then leans against the
door; then she takes some of the wood out of the stove and hides it
under the chaise longue.*

The SON enters, somewhat drunk.

MOTHER (*pulling herself together.*) Is it you?

SON (*sits in the rocking chair.*) Yes.

MOTHER How are you feeling?

SON Bad. Soon it'll be over for me.

MOTHER That's just your imagination! — Don't rock like that! —
Look at me, someone who has reached certain . . . a ripe age. . .
and still I've worked and toiled and seen to my duties toward my
children and my house. I've done that, haven't I?

SON Ah! — And the pelican, who never gave her heart's blood. The
zoology books say that's a lie!

MOTHER If you've had any complaints, speak up.

SON Listen mother. If I were sober I wouldn't answer that honestly
because I wouldn't have the strength. But now I'll tell you that I

have read father's letter, which you stole and threw in the wood-stove . . .

MOTHER What are you saying? What sort of letter?

SON Always lies! I remember when you first taught me how to lie. I'd barely learned to speak yet. Do you remember?

MOTHER No! I don't remember anything about it. Stop rocking!

SON And when you lied to me the first time? — I remember also as a child, I'd hidden under the piano, and then one of our aunts came to visit you. You sat there lying to her for three hours and I had to listen to it all!

MOTHER That's a lie!

SON But do you know why I've turned out so worthless. I was never breast-fed, I had a nanny with a glass bottle. And when I got older, I got to go with her to her sister's place, who was a prostitute. And there I got to see those secret scenes which otherwise only dog owners provide for children on the open street during fall and spring! When I told you about it — I was four years old — what I had seen in the house of sin, you said it was a lie. And you hit me for being a liar, even though I'd told you the truth. This nanny, encouraged by your assent to all this, initiated me at the age of five to all the secrets. I was five years old . . . (*In tears.*) And then I started to go hungry and cold, like father and all of us. Now for the first time I know that you stole from the household funds and the money for fuel . . . Look at me, pelican, look at Gerda, thin and flat-chested. — How you murdered my father, you know that very well — since it was you who brought him to despair, which is not a crime the law can punish. How you murdered my sister, you know better than anybody. But now she knows it too!

MOTHER Stop rocking! — What does she know?

SON Things you know, but I cannot make myself say them. (*Crying.*) It is horrible that I've said all this, but I've got to. I know that when I get sober I'll shoot myself. So I'm going to keep on drinking. I don't dare become sober . . .

MOTHER Why don't you lie some more.

SON Once father said in anger that you were nature's biggest fraud

... that as a child you didn't learn to talk like other children, but learned to lie instead ... That you always shook off your duties to be able to go to parties. And I remember that when Gerda was sick and at the brink of death, you went to the opera that evening — I remember your words: "Life is hard enough without our having to make it harder!"— — —And that summer, three months, you were in Paris with father and did so much merry-making that the household went into debt, while my sister and I lived here in the city, closed in with two maids in this flat. In the master bedroom a fireman was living with the housemaid — and that intimate pair put the marriage bed to good use —

MOTHER Why haven't you talked about this before?

SON You've forgotten that I talked about it, and that I got a beating for tattling, or lying, to use your alternate word for it. Because no sooner did you hear a true word than you called it a lie!

The MOTHER paces the room like a captured wild animal.

MOTHER I have never heard the like from a son to his mother!

SON It is a bit unusual. And it's completely against nature, I know that. But for once it must be said. It was like you were walking in your sleep and could not be awakened. That's why you couldn't change. Father said: that if you were "put on the rack" you "wouldn't admit to a fault or confess" that you had lied ...

MOTHER Father! You think he had no faults?

SON He had great faults, but not in his relations with his wife and children! — But there are other secrets in your marriage which I sensed, suspected, but never wanted to admit to myself ... Father took those secrets with him to the grave, some of them!

MOTHER Have you talked enough now?

SON Now I'm going out to drink ... I can never take the exam. I don't believe in the justice system. The laws seem to be written by thieves and murderers in order to absolve the criminals. One man with the truth is not competent to witness, but two false witnesses constitute full proof! At eleven-thirty my case is just, but after twelve o'clock I've lost in court. A slip of the pen, a mistaken note in the margins can land me — innocent — in jail. If I am merciful to a crook, then he tries to sue me for defamation of character. My contempt for life, humanity, society and *me* is so infinite that I can't be bothered with the effort of living . . .

He goes to the door.

MOTHER Don't go!

SON Are you scared of the dark?

MOTHER I am nervous.

SON That's logical.

MOTHER And that chair there is driving me crazy! It was always like two butcher knives when he sat in it . . . hacking at my heart.

SON You don't have such a thing.

MOTHER Don't go! I can't stay here. Axel is a bastard.

SON I thought so too, until recently. Now I think he is the victim of your criminal tendencies . . . Yes, the young man who got seduced.

MOTHER You must seek out bad company.

SON Bad company. Yes. I've never been in good company!

MOTHER Don't go!

SON What can I do here? I would just torture you to death with my talking . . .

MOTHER Don't go!

SON Are you beginning to wake up?

MOTHER Yes. I'm waking now — like out of a long, long sleep. It is terrifying! Why couldn't somebody wake me before?

SON Since no one could, then of course it was impossible. And since it was impossible, you can't be held responsible, I guess.

MOTHER Say those words again!

SON I guess you couldn't be any other way.

MOTHER (*kisses his hand, servile.*) Tell me more!

SON I can't say any more. — Yes, I'll ask you: don't stay here and make what's bad worse.

MOTHER You're right. I will go — away.

SON Poor mamma.

MOTHER Do you feel some pity for me?

SON (*in tears.*) Yes, of course I do! How often haven't I said: She's so sick, we should be sorry for her.
MOTHER Thank you for that. — Go, go on Fredrik.
SON Can't we do something about this?
MOTHER No, nothing can be done.
SON Yes, that's it. Nothing can be done.

He goes.

* *
*

Pause.

The MOTHER *alone, with her arms crossed over her breast a long moment. Then she goes to the window, which she opens and looks down into the depths. She draws back into the room, and positions herself to leap out; but then she changes her mind when someone knocks three times at the door at back.*

MOTHER Who is it? What is it? (*She closes the window.*) Come in!

The door at back is opened.

Is there someone there?

The SON is heard howling inside the apartments.

It's him, down in the gardens! Isn't he dead? What am I going to do? Where will I go?

She hides behind the chiffonnier.
Now the wind begins to blow as before, so that papers go flying around the room.

Close the window, Fredrik!

A flower vase is blown over.

Close the window! I'm freezing to death, and the fire's going out!

She turns on all the electric lights; closes the door, which opens again. The rocking chair is moved by the wind. She paces round and round the room until she throws herself prostrate on the chaise longue and hides her face in the pillows.

*   *

*

"Il me disait" is being played, off.

The MOTHER is lying as before on the chaise longue with her head hidden.

The DAUGHTER comes in with the porridge on a tray, which she puts down. Then she turns off the electric lights, all but one.

MOTHER (*wakes, rises.*) Don't turn them off.
DAUGHTER Yes, we must economize.
MOTHER Are you back so soon?
DAUGHTER Yes, he didn't think it was any fun without you there!
MOTHER Well, thanks a lot!
DAUGHTER Here is some supper.
MOTHER I am not hungry.
DAUGHTER Yes you are hungry. But you don't eat porridge.
MOTHER I do, sometimes.
DAUGHTER No, never! But it's not because of that, but because of your spiteful smile every time you tortured us with oatmeal. You enjoyed our suffering . . . and you cooked the same thing for the

dogs out back.

MOTHER I can't eat things with blue milk. Chilled skim milk makes me freeze.

DAUGHTER Since you always skimmed away the cream for your eleven o'clock coffee! — Help yourself!

She serves the porridge on a small table.

Eat now. Let me see you eat!

MOTHER I can't!

The DAUGHTER leans down and takes a log from under the chaise-longue.

DAUGHTER If you don't eat, then I'm going to show Axel that you stole wood.

MOTHER Axel, who was missing my company . . . He won't do anything to me! Do you remember the wedding when he was dancing with me . . . to *Il me disait!* There it is!

She hums the second reprise, which is now being played.

DAUGHTER It would be more discrete of you not to remind me of that outrage . . .

MOTHER And *I* had verses read to *me*, and the most beautiful flowers!

DAUGHTER Quiet!

MOTHER Shall I read the verses for you? I know them by heart. . .
"In Ginnestan— — —"
Ginnestan is a Persian word for the garden of delights in Paradise, where the fairest peris live on perfume . . . Peris are jinns or fairies, created in such a way that the longer they live, the younger they become . . .

DAUGHTER Oh, good Lord. Do you think you're a peri?

MOTHER Well, that's what it says here. And uncle Victor has proposed to me. What would you say if I were to marry again?

DAUGHTER Poor mamma! You're still walking in your sleep, as we've all been doing. But aren't you ever going to wake from this? Don't you see how people smile behind your back? Don't you understand when Axel is insulting you?

MOTHER Does he? I've always thought he's been more courteous to me than he is to you . . .

DAUGHTER Even when he lifted his cane at you?

MOTHER At me? It was at you, dear child.

DAUGHTER Mother dear, have you lost your mind?

MOTHER He did miss my company this evening. We always have so much to talk about — he is the only one who understands me, and you are only a child . . .

DAUGHTER (*takes her mother by the shoulders and shakes her.*) Wake up, for God's sake!

MOTHER You aren't fully grown yet, but I am your mother and have nourished you with my blood . . .

DAUGHTER No, you gave me a baby bottle and put a rubber nipple in my mouth, and later on I had to go to the cupboard and steal, but there was only hard rye in there, which I ate with mustard, and when my throat started burning I cooled it down by drinking from the vinegar bottle. The tablecloth and the bread box, that was our whole pantry!

MOTHER Oh, you were *already* stealing as a child! That's just lovely. And you're not ashamed to talk about it? To think, I've sacrificed myself for such children?

DAUGHTER (*in tears.*) I could forgive everything. But not that you took my life from me — Yes, he was my life, because with him I began to *live* . . .

MOTHER I had no control over the fact he preferred me. Perhaps he found me, how should I say it? . . . more pleasant? . . . Yes, he had better taste than your father, who didn't know how to appreciate me before he got rivals— — —

There are three knocks at the door.

MOTHER Who is that knocking?

DAUGHTER Don't you speak a bad word about Father! I don't think I'll live long enough to repent my offenses against him. But you're going to pay for that, you who turned me against him! Do you remember when I was a little, little child — you taught me to say nasty, cutting words to him which I didn't understand? He had sense enough not to punish me for the arrows that hit him, because he knew who had drawn the bow! Do you remember when you taught me to lie to him, that I needed new books at school? And when you and I tricked him out of his money we divided it between us! — How will I ever forget all of this past? Isn't there any drink which wipes out memory without snuffing out your life? If I had the strength to get out of it all — the whole thing . . . But, I'm like Fredrik. We are powerless, submissive victims. Your victims . . . You hard woman — you feel no remorse for your own crimes!

MOTHER Do you know about *my* childhood? Do you have any idea what a bad home I came from? What wrongs I was taught there? It's like it's passed on as an inheritance, right down to the present. But from whom? From the first parents, as it says in the children's books, and that would make sense . . . Don't blame me then, and I will not blame my parents, who could have blamed their own, and so on! Anyhow, it's the same in all families. Even though outsiders never get to see it . . .

DAUGHTER If that's the case, then I don't want to live. But if I'm forced to, then I want to walk deaf and blind through this misery. But with the hope of something better to come . . .

MOTHER You exaggerate everything, dear. If you have a child there will be other things to think about . . .

DAUGHTER I'm not going to have any children . . .

MOTHER How do you know?

DAUGHTER The doctor has made that clear.

MOTHER He is mistaken . . .

DAUGHTER There you're lying again . . . I am sterile, my growth was stunted. Me just like Fredrik. And that's why I don't want to go on living . . .

MOTHER The way you talk . . .

DAUGHTER If I could do the hateful things I'd like to, you would not be standing here anymore! Why should it be so hard to act on hate. When I lift a hand against you, I strike myself!— — —

The music stops suddenly. The SON is heard howling outside.

MOTHER He's been drinking again!

DAUGHTER Poor Fredrik, yes . . . What else can he do?

*   *
*

The SON enters, half-inebriated, stammering.

SON There's . . . smoke, I'd say . . . in the — kitchen!

MOTHER What are you saying?

SON I think . . . I . . . I think that it's . . . burning!

MOTHER Burning? What are you saying?

SON Yes, I . . . think . . . that it's burning!

The MOTHER runs toward the back and opens the doors, but is met by the red glow of a fire.

MOTHER Fire! — How will we get out! — I don't want to burn! — I don't want to!

She circles, rushes about.

DAUGHTER *(embraces her brother.)* Fredrik! Run! The fire's coming in! Run!

SON I can't.

DAUGHTER Run! You've got to!

SON Where? . . . No, I don't want to . . .

MOTHER It's better if I go out the window . . .

She opens the balcony doors and throws herself out.

DAUGHTER Oh dear God. Help us!

SON It was the only thing left.

DAUGHTER You did this!

SON Well, what should I have done? — There was nothing else to be done. — Was there anything else?

DAUGHTER No. It all must burn. Otherwise we'd never get out of this. Hold me in your arms, Fredrik. Hold me tightly, brother. I am happier than I have ever been. It's getting brighter. Poor Mama, she was so sick, so sick . . .

SON Sister, poor Mama, do you feel how warm it is, so lovely, now I'm not cold anymore, you hear how it's crackling out there, all the old things, all the things, foul, evil and ugly . . .

DAUGHTER Keep holding me, little brother, we won't burn. We'll be smothered by the smoke, you see how good it smells, it's the palm trees burning, and Papa's laurel wreath, now the linen chest is burning, it smells of lavender, and now, the roses! Little brother! don't be afraid, it will soon be over, dearest, dearest, don't fall, poor Mama! she was so sick! Hold onto me, harder, *squeeze*, like Papa used to say! It's like Christmas eve, when we got to eat in the kitchen, to dip bread in the cooking pots, the one day we could eat our fill, like Papa always said, smell the scent in the air, it's the cupboard, with the tea bags and coffee, and the spices, the cinnamon and cloves . . .

SON (*in ecstasy.*) Is it summer? Yes, the clover is blooming, summer vacation's starting, you remember when we went down to the white steamships and clapped their hulls, when they were freshly painted and waiting for us, then Papa was happy, then he really felt alive, he said, and we were finished with our notebooks! This is how life should always be! he said, it was *he* who was the pelican, because he drained himself for us, his trousers were always worn at the knees and he had a threadbare coat collar while we went around like little princes . . . Gerda, hurry, the steamboat bell is ringing, Mama's sitting in the observation deck, no, she's not with us, poor Mama! she's not here, did we leave her on shore? where is she? I don't see her, it's no fun if Mama's not there — there she comes! (*Pause.*)— — —Now our summer can begin!

The rear doors open and the red, bright glaring light comes through.

The SON and DAUGHTER sink to the floor.

Curtain.

End!

CARL XII

A Play in Five Tableaux

(1901)

CHARACTERS

CARL XII
ULRIKA ELEONORA, his sister
GÖRTZ
ARVID HORN, a count
KARL GYLLENBORG, a count
FEIF, secretary
HULTMAN, table-setter
KATARINA LESZCZYNSKA, former queen of Poland
EMERENTIA POLHEM, daughter of the famous scientist
EMANUEL SWEDENBORG, scientist and philosopher
THE DWARF LUXEMBOURG

SECONDARY CHARACTERS

THE MAN
THE WOMAN
A MALCONTENT
COUNCILLOR OF THE REALM
SPEAKERS OF THE FOUR ESTATES
A SAILOR
COAST GUARD
[THE ADJUTANT]
[DÜRING]
[ROSEN]
[THE PROFESSOR]
[THE SKIPPER]
[A LACKEY]
[COUNTESS PIPER]
[A GROUP OF PETITIONING WOMEN]
AND OTHERS[1]

---

[1] Characters in brackets are left off of Strindberg's cast list.

SCENES

TABLEAU 1: On the coast of Scania

TABLEAU 2: In the King's audience room in Lund

TABLEAU 3: On the square outside Görtz's residence in Lund

TABLEAU 4: In the yard outside Görtz's residence

TABLEAU 5: Before Fredrikstens fortress in Norway

TABLEAU I

It is a windy morning in December 1715 on the coast of Scania. A cottage, dilapidated and abandoned during the plague of 1710 stands with its foundations buried in shifting sands. The windows are knocked out, the roof shingles torn away, the door off its hinges. Visible through the ruins of the front wall are the fireplace and chimney covered with soot. Outside of the cottage is a leafless, wind-blown apple tree with only a single apple remaining, which is being shaken by the wind. Alongside it there is a rubbish heap with withered burdocks. To the right of the cottage lie the burned remains of a church and several dwellings. Beyond lies the dark sea. On the horizon appears a light gray streak of dawn.

A MAN clad in rags walks through the ruins, searching for something.
A COAST GUARD enters.

COAST GUARD Halt! *Wer da?*
MAN *(hides behind a column in the church ruins)*
COAST GUARD Halt! *Wer da!* *(He approaches the MAN.)*
MAN Who am I? — Once I was a soldier. Once there was a town here!
COAST GUARD What are you looking for?
MAN I'm looking for a house which once existed, but no longer does.
COAST GUARD Speak up. The wind's carrying off your words.
MAN Wasn't there a town here that was called Stavstorp?
COAST GUARD Oh yes! You see the remains: here stood the church, here stood the school.
MAN Where was the soldier's cottage?
COAST GUARD There!
MAN There! Why isn't it there anymore?
COAST GUARD Because first the plague took all the inhabitants, and then the enemy burned all the houses.

MAN When did the plague come?

COAST GUARD Right after Poltava!

MAN Where'd the plague come from?

COAST GUARD From Russia, that's where Poltava is — from Russia, which swallowed up our king and our army. You were with the army?

MAN Yes, and at Poltava and in Russia and in Siberia.

COAST GUARD What were you doing there? Should've stayed at home.

MAN You're telling me! *(Examines the cottage.)* That's absolutely right! Here was my cottage, here was my home, here sat my wife and my two children. My pudding was cooked in this oven, my children played at this window, my wife sat at this doorstep waiting, patching clothes— — —That's fifteen years ago— — — Fifteen!— — —I planted this apple tree before I left. I never got to see the fruit . . . Now I can see it, but it's rotten! *(He shakes the tree, but the apple doesn't fall.)* Enough of that. *(He rummages in the heap of refuse.)* Look, here's my shattered kitchenware, stoneware plates, tin spoons, the salt cellar. . . . and the sole of a shoe . . . It's my wife's — she had a pretty little foot, and walked so soft and quiet — here! Well, what's the use of wailing!— — — This is most likely the way the whole kingdom looks!— — —A ruin, a garbage heap — and one rotten apple at the top . . .

COAST GUARD Which should be shaken off!

MAN *(enflamed.)* By whom?

COAST GUARD By a man with a heart in his chest!

MAN You see here the soldiers' plaque, which was over the door of my cottage. Number seventy-three, southern Scania. That was me — — —What are you looking for out at sea?

COAST GUARD Don't you know? Don't you understand?

MAN No.

COAST GUARD You haven't heard that Stralsund has fallen?

MAN We-lll! And the crook?

COAST GUARD Has fled!

MAN Exactly like at Poltava! The crook always flees, excepting when he wins! One time he fled from a woman!

COAST GUARD One time? He's always fled from women.

MAN Why is it that the crook has always fled from women?

COAST GUARD Because the crook has no self-confidence about handling women-folk!

MAN Most likely!— — —What do you see out on the water?

COAST GUARD I see a Danish frigate chasing a brigantine!

MAN Brigantine? Doesn't *brigand* mean "crook"?

COAST GUARD Yes indeed!

MAN Then it's the crook on board the brigantine.

COAST GUARD Exactly!

MAN Aren't there any reefs, sandbars, underwater clefts or turbulent currents here?

COAST GUARD Yes. But he who's doomed to hang cannot be drowned.

MAN Is there any hemp left in this kingdom of Svea?

COAST GUARD In Karlskrona there's rope, but there's no one who dares take it in hand!

MAN No?

COAST GUARD Do you know anyone?

MAN Yes, I do!— — —Is he going to be landing here?

COAST GUARD That's the plan!— — —What did you do in Siberia?

MAN First I went to school, then I became a teacher.

COAST GUARD That's why you know what "brigand" means! Anyway, can you spot those gentlemen there, trotting along the beach?

MAN I see them!

COAST GUARD Then you are looking at the Councillor of the Realm and the Speakers of the Four Estates!

MAN Do you think if a signal fire were lit here, right here, both brigand and brigantine would turn course away from the world of the living, thereby saving the kingdom?

COAST GUARD Remarkable that you and I, meeting each other for the first time, should be inspired by the same thought.

MAN Perhaps there's only one thought in the whole country? Shall I light a fire?

COAST GUARD Light it! Even though I don't think it will help. Till now neither spear nor blade, fire nor water, has had any effect on him. And nothing *will* have an effect, until his time is out!

MAN *(lights a fire in the cottage's fireplace.)* When the crook sees this
  fire, he'll say to himself: Look, they're celebrating with a fire. —
  Yes it could be a celebration, but not just yet!

COAST GUARD Why are you constantly calling him "the crook"?

MAN You know as well as I and all the rest of the people in this
  country — all — no, half, because a half of them are dead . . . But
  tell me, what is the government doing here on this beach?

COAST GUARD Well, they're afraid of losing their heads, since they
  called together parliament in his absence and demanded his,
  whatever you call it, suspension . . .

MAN Suspension? You can suspend a drunk priest, a bungling official, a cowardly officer . . . that's a good word!

COAST GUARD Look!— — —The fire is having an effect out on the
  water! The brigantine is turning leeward. — The Danish frigate is
  falling off and sailing away for fear of running aground . . . A boat
  has set out from the beach— — —He is saved!

MAN Then it's time we saved ourselves as well!— — —

COAST GUARD First, give me your hand, countryman.

MAN Here!

COAST GUARD Which way are you headed?

MAN Who can say?— — —Goodbye. The government is coming!

COAST GUARD The government — on the main road. The King —
  on the back roads! — O this land! This land!

They go, each his own way.

*

A shot is heard in the distance. The wind and rain grow in intensity.

*

*The COUNCILLOR OF THE REALM enters together with the SPEAKERS
OF THE FOUR ESTATES. They are clad in wet capes, and are pale as
corpses due to their night-long vigil, rain, cold and anxiety.*

COUNCILLOR The King is coming!

NOBLEMAN God have mercy upon us!

THE PRIEST What have we done?

THE BURGHER Our duty!

THE FARMER More than our duty — we've made sacrifices!

COUNCILLOR *(takes out a paper, which he protects from the rain.)* This is what I've written: The country, abandoned by its king for fifteen years, bids him welcome home, and prays for peace . . .

THE NOBLEMAN That he will never stand for.

THE PRIEST Pity the land whose king is a lunatic.

THE BURGHER Pity us, who should be judged by a lunatic!

THE FARMER Pity the land whose king is a crook!

Applause is heard from off.
The COUNCILLOR and the SPEAKERS draw together in dread.

COUNCILLOR What did the farmer say?

THE FARMER Crook, I said!

COUNCILLOR Quiet! The wind could carry your words to that same ear which heard in Turkey what was being whispered in Sweden!

THE FARMER That same ear, which could make itself deaf to the prayers of an entire people, their justified protests, cries of agony! Lord God, hear us in your heaven. Lord, punish him. Lord, have mercy upon us!

ALL Amen!

*

ADJUTANT The King! — Away from there, you people!

COUNCILLOR The government is not "you people"!

ADJUTANT The government? — Is that the government? *(Makes a gesture with his arms: "away"!)*

COUNCILLOR *(forward.)* Does the Adjutant recognize me?

ADJUTANT Councillor?— — —What is your errand?

COUNCILLOR To gain an audience with the King, and present the kingdom's . . .

ADJUTANT We've heard all that, long . . .

THE FARMER Hear it one more time then!

ADJUTANT None of your insolence, farmer!— — —Look sharp, the
King is coming!

NOBLEMAN *(to the others)* No one on your knees!

FARMER No kneeling!

BURGHER Agreed!

*

DÜRING *(enters from the left at breakneck speed, catches sight of the
fire, gets wood from the cottage and throws it on.)*

ROSEN *(enters from right.)* Stand aside, farmers!— — —

HULTMAN *(enters from right with a box under his arm.)*

NOBLEMAN That's the King's entourage!

THE PRIEST *Courreur de table!*

THE FARMER Plate-lickers!

THE DWARF LUXEMBOURG *(enters with a violin under his arm.)*

BURGHER The court fool. — What a crew!

THE FARMER With a government like that you can go far! The giant
seeks out the dwarf . . .

*

Two BODYGUARDS *with rapiers drawn hold back both* COUNCIL-
LOR *and* SPEAKERS, *who withdraw to the left, and fall on their knees
with hands outstretched toward the right.*

The KING *enters from the right, pale, frozen, wet, in his cloak. He
walks hastily past the* COUNCILLOR *and the* SPEAKERS, *who are
hidden by the* BODYGUARDS, HULTMAN *and* LUXEMBOURG. *He
enters the cottage, throws off the cloak, and positions himself calmly,
immobile, in front of the fire.*

The ADJUTANT *approaches the* KING, *who quietly gives him an order; whereupon the* ADJUTANT *goes out to the* COUNCILLOR *and*

SPEAKERS, from whom he accepts letters, which he immediately delivers to the KING.

Respectful stillness and silence reign while the KING opens the letters. He glances through them and tosses them in the fire. Then he gestures for the ADJUTANT. He appears to be consulting with him about what route they will be traveling. Then he tightens his belt, and pulls his hat down over his face. ROSEN puts his cloak on him, with the collar turned up.

The ADJUTANT goes out. He commands: Attention! — and makes a motion toward the foreground to the right. The BODYGUARDS move off in that direction, in front of the church ruins. The KING follows with rapid steps. ROSEN follows, but waves to HULTMAN and LUXEM-BOURG to stay. DÜRING follows the KING.

*

NOBLEMAN *(to the BURGHER.)* Why did we kneel?

BURGHER I don't know! What else could we do!

THE FARMER Was that the King? So there is something different be tween him and other people. It's just as if someone were going before him to clear his path . . . I can't understand — *(brushing off his knees)* — but it was as if somebody knocked your legs out from under you— — —I mean, it wasn't me who kneeled . . .

NOBLEMAN No doubt!

COUNCILLOR He is the ruler and the Lord's anointed servant, do you understand that now? — No! — But you see, that's the dif- ference between us and you!

*

THE DWARF *(forward with an open snuff box.)* Since the weather's turning fair, we'll have a pinch of snuff to celebrate.

He invites the FARMER first.

THE FARMER *(takes some with pleasure.)* Thanks for the offer!
THE DWARF That stuff's not for dogs to sniff at!

He offers some to the BURGHER.

BURGHER Praise and thank you!
THE DWARF Will that do? *(Offers it to the PRIEST.)* Now to your
   questions.
PRIEST *(feigns a sniff.)* Is the dwarf working in a court capacity?
THE DWARF No, I am only working as court dwarf! He despises me
   as much as anyone else, but I keep him amused. It's not everyone
   who can! *(Offers snuff to the NOBLEMAN.)* Be my guest!
NOBLEMAN No, thank you!
THE DWARF Now that's a fine chap — I like that! We should have
   more like him! — If I were now to offer some to the Councillor of
   the Realm, he would have to, according to nature's hierarchy and
   ours, toss the whole boxful in my eyes, and I don't want that. . .

                              *

HULTMAN Do they intend for us to live here in burned-out ruins, or
   what?
THE DWARF Hultman. Don't ask, but rather live. Live life one
   moment at a time. No one knows what tomorrow bears in its
   womb, and there are no pleasures after death.
HULTMAN Cynicus! Epicurus! I'm only asking where I'll next be
   setting the King's table. And I'm asking neither about tomorrow's
   womb nor death's pleasures . . . My lord and King, the greatest of
   all men and rulers, is the most perfect of human beings born, and
   his smallest wish is my command, his pleasure is my gospel . . .
   Right now I'm asking where my King commands that I shall set his
   silverware, which I have dragged around with me in the cities of
   Saxony, in the villages of Poland, round the steppes of Russia and
   in the gardens of Turkey . . .
THE DWARF Hultman! The sun will soon be rising. Cut the gab. . .
HULTMAN This silver, which I rescued from the siege of Stralsund,

from the Danish frigate, from . . .

THE DWARF Put on the brakes, Hultman! Make him put on the brakes, damn it all, or he'll never come to the point!

HULTMAN Look, the Adjutant's back again!

*

ADJUTANT The King bids and commands that the Councillor of the Realm and the Speakers of the Estates promptly return to their posts in the capital to there await his majesty's further decision— — —

COUNCILLOR Now this?

ADJUTANT I beg pardon? Was there some remark? Has the King legal right to run the kingdom as he sees fit?

COUNCILLOR He does. — But . . .

ADJUTANT Did you break your oath when you voted to depose him? — The silence answers yes! — Go then, and thank God in heaven that he has not taken off your heads. Allez!

*

HULTMAN *(to the DWARF.)* He's one hell of a speaker. — Oh yes! These are the traitors who wanted to depose our gracious lord because he'd had some setbacks. Well, such is the world, and such are men.

ADJUTANT *(to the COUNCILLOR and SPEAKERS.)* You gentlemen ought to remove yourselves quickly, for the execution of other traitors will be taking place here!

THE DWARF *(to HULTMAN.)* It's the skipper of the brig *Snapp-Opp* who's going to be shot because he did not make it to the meeting place.

ADJUTANT Yes, that's right! And the crew will be publicly flogged as well.

HULTMAN And then they complain that there is no law and justice in this country!

The COUNCILLOR *and* SPEAKERS *(draw away toward the wings, pressing each other's hands.)*

*

SKIPPER *(led in, bound, by two soldiers.)* Let go of me, I say, in the name of Jesus Christ. It is not my fault if the ice floe blocked the maneuver— — —Let go. I haven't done anything! Let go!

THE DWARF *(who is tuning his violin.)* Don't shout, man.

SKIPPER They want to kill me!

THE DWARF Well, that's hardly anything to shout about.

SKIPPER I haven't done anything. I don't control the wind and weather. I can't break up ice floes. Let me go!

ADJUTANT Off with him, quick!

SKIPPER *(being led out.)* Let go! I haven't done anything!

*

HULTMAN Hasn't the Adjutant heard whether our gracious King has expressed his wishes regarding his quarters, his table, and that sort of thing?

ADJUTANT Yes. Hultman, you have horses in the next village, which will convey you to the city.

HULTMAN Of course! I need only have the order!

THE DWARF And what about me?

ADJUTANT You? Who cares about you?

THE DWARF Am I being sacked? Has he gotten some new dwarf? Is that the intention, to cast me out? Don't I deserve better? Was I not the first dwarf of the kingdom: Luxembourg, the one and only . . .

ADJUTANT *(as he goes.)* Hultman your horses are in the next village!

THE DWARF Yes, Hultman, the great liar, the indispensable . . . Such is life! Trust ye not in princes . . .

He plays a melancholy saraband by Sebastian Bach.

HULTMAN *(as he goes.)* For shame!

THE DWARF "The one shall be taken, and the other left." Go table-setter, and tell your lord that you saw Luxembourg cast up on a beach where no roses grow . . .

HULTMAN has gone off. The DWARF is alone. He looks around; rises in rage.

Wait you! I may be little and can only play the fiddle! But I shall play— — —and then you shall dance by my life and by my knife! You shall dance!

Curtain.

TABLEAU II

The KING's audience room in Lund. To the right a large fire-place: close by it a hat and coat stand. To the left a big table with paper and writing materials on it: a huge armchair with a crown and ermine mantel. Two very low and soft easy chairs in the middle of the floor, facing the KING's. Alongside the KING's chair there is a footstool. Farthest down to the left a camp bed covered with blue silk.

GYLLENBORG and HORN stand at the hearth warming themselves.

GYLLENBORG Do you know why we were called here?

HORN No. But everyday it's someone new.

GYLLENBORG Do you think there's anyone who knows the King's plans?

HORN Does he have some plans?

GYLLENBORG What a question!

There is a creaking sound in the boards of the wooden house. They give a start and look around.

HORN What was that?

GYLLENBORG The cold, the temperature's sinking.

Pause.

GYLLENBORG Have you ever experienced anything as ghastly as this?

HORN Never.

GYLLENBORG Have you seen him since he came home?

HORN I saw him yesterday.

GYLLENBORG We-ll?

HORN A dead man, whose shell walks and haunts the living.

Now the DWARF's *saraband is heard in the distance.*

GYLLENBORG What kind of infernal music is that I've been hearing
all morning?
HORN It sounds like a locust . . .
GYLLENBORG I think it sounds like the fall wind between the panes
of the double windows. Or a child crying. — Do you know that
sixty thousand infants died when the plague last broke out among
children?
HORN Lucky them.

*

The PROFESSOR *enters, stealing in from the back. He looks around
uneasily; walks on tiptoes over to the hearth and examines the register.*

GYLLENBORG Who would that be?
HORN Are you going to shut the register before the fire has burned
down?
PROFESSOR *(half-aloud, afraid.)* There was a problem with the reg-
ister that I was going to examine.
HORN Is he the stove repairman?
PROFESSOR They said it was smoking, and we are very afraid of fire
since our town burned a few years back.
HORN Is this the fire inspection?
PROFESSOR Oh-eh! Therefore . . . I'll just shift the coals around
with the gentlemen's permission . . .
GYLLENBORG Is he in his right mind?
PROFESSOR Because, you see, it is my house, oh-eh, I'm allowed to
stay up in the loft . . . If the gentlemen would keep an eye on the
fire, that would make me happy. *(He exits at right.)*
HORN People look like ghosts here in this city.
GYLLENBORG What can the King want with us?
HORN The inscrutable one.

They walk toward the rear and stop before the coat stand.

GYLLENBORG Look at this coat!

HORN It's faded under the belt, and you can see where he's drawn his sword— — —

GYLLENBORG There's a button missing!

HORN Sssshh!

GYLLENBORG Just think, inside this door is the great man, the feared man, who is on the minds of all the monarchs of Europe. — — —Is he tall?

HORN Hard to say. Because he defies being sized up in the usual way— — —I have seen him as huge as a Theseus and as little as a page. And his face?

GYLLENBORG What about it?

HORN Well, I have seen twenty different ones. He is not a human being, because he is legion!

GYLLENBORG You're saying strange things, but . . . many have said the like.

The door on the left opens. They draw together.

*

FEIF *enters.*
They regard each other with searching glances.

FEIF His majesty the King will be here directly! *(Silence.)* I am serving as secretary today! *(Silence.)* My name is Feif! *(Silence.)* May I tell you gentlemen one thing!— — —*(Silence.)* One does not inform the King about anything, but responds only to his questions, more or less exhaustively, all according to whether his majesty shows greater or lesser interest in the response tendered. *(Silence.)* And one does not employ the occasion to report anything about the condition of the kingdom or its wishes, since he is well acquainted with those matters. *(Silence.)* As far as ceremonial is concerned, one sits when commanded by word or gesture.

(Silence.) Finally, I'd like to inform you that the King, who has come down with a case of tonsillitis, can only speak aloud with difficulty, and therefore begs the gentlemen's pardon that he speaks softly.

He bows and exits the same way he came.

*

GYLLENBORG That was *Feif!* . . . Once he was a hatter's apprentice.
HORN We've been made schoolboys, Gyllenborg!
GYLLENBORG That's true!

They go back to the fire.

HORN I'm so cold my teeth are rattling.
GYLLENBORG And it's so dark here.
HORN I wish I were a half an hour older.
GYLLENBORG It's as if you could feel his spirit filling the room in here. I've never been afraid before . . .

The KING has entered without a sound from the left, reading a piece of paper. He is dressed in blue and yellow garb, without his rapier. He now looks up from the piece of paper and regards the men from the back. He is serious, collected, dignified and secretive, with an undecided look on his face, which is sickly ash-gray. When he rustles the paper the two lords turn and kneel.

The KING signals for them to stand. He then sits in the armchair with FEIF — who has just entered — at his side.

The KING and FEIF look through some papers. Thereafter, the KING gestures for the lords to sit. They sit down in the low easy chairs and sink deep down, to the point that they appear uncomfortable.

THE KING *(speaks with FEIF, so softly that only a mumble is audible.)*

FEIF *(turns to the lords.)* His majesty calls upon the Count Gyllenborg . . .

THE KING *(makes a gesture of "stop" to FEIF and mumbles again.)*

FEIF Will Count Horn tell his majesty all that he knows of the much
discussed . . .

The KING mumbles again to FEIF.

FEIF . . . the much-discussed Baron Görtz.

HORN *(rises, looks at GYLLENBORG in astonishment.)*

THE KING *(gestures for HORN to sit.)*

HORN *(sits down unwillingly, and appears bothered by the low, uncomfortable chair.)* His majesty's request is a command, certainly. . .

THE KING *(looks before him at the tabletop. Then he takes up a
pen and begins to draw geometric figures.)*

HORN . . . but . . .

FEIF His majesty desires a short, so to speak, character sketch of the
person in question.

HORN Such a task requires a closer personal acquaintance with the
subject, and I must confess that Baron Görtz is not among my
closer . . .

THE KING *(looks up and rivets his eyes on HORN, who is overcome by
fear.)*

HORN Yes, well. According to all I've heard, Baron Görtz is . . .

*He tries with a few glances to discern the KING's opinion of GÖRTZ,
also trying to compare it with the expression on FEIF's face.*

HORN . . . that this man is . . . a most unusual personality, and his
desire to be unusual can only be matched by his boundless lust for
power.

THE KING *(draws without looking up.)*

HORN It's been alleged that he looks upon himself as the center of
the world, that he searches the papers every morning to see
whether Europe's destiny has undergone any changes while he's
been sleeping, and the learnéd Swedenborg . . .

THE KING *(is attentive.)*

HORN ... assures us that if Görtz died today, tomorrow he would raise the kingdom of the dead against the heavenly powers.

THE KING *(stops moving his pen, though without looking up.)*

HORN This enormous greed for glory he hides — attempts to hide — beneath a simple exterior and a paternalistic manner toward subordinates ...

GYLLENBORG *(is displaying nervousness.)*

THE KING *(reddens.)*

HORN ... subordinates, whom he actually detests, as he detests all human beings ...

THE KING *(bends his head down to his chest.)*

HORN These most obvious character traits of Baron Görtz, coupled with the most exemplary insensitivity to the suffering of others, would appear to be irreconcilable with a religious temperament, but Baron Görtz is not without religion. You might say that he is God-fearing, without fearing God.

FEIF *(till now impenetrable, fixes his eyes on HORN with horror.)*

THE KING *(puts his hands to his throat as if he were suffocating.)*

HORN *(proceeds undaunted, absolutely unaware of the involuntary hints.)* The learnéd and devout Swedenborg regards Baron Görtz's use of religion as a kind of magic, through which he procures himself support and power, even in purely criminal doings— — —For example, for extorting funds, for revenge on his enemies ... since one of his traits is that he can never forgive.

THE KING *(fixes HORN with his glance, as if he wanted to read his innermost thoughts and discover whether there are any ulterior motives. His mouth is open, but his upper lip twitches.)*

HORN In a word, a great weakness masked so as to give the appearance of incredible strength. Knee-jerk willfulness, but not enough to break his own stubbornness ...

THE KING *(makes a noise with his spurs.)*

HORN *(as if waking from a dream, and realizing the infernal situation he is in, becomes mute with fear.)*

They all regard one another in mutual embarrassment, without any-

one being able to break the silence.

*

There is a pounding at the door: three knocks.

THE KING *(mumbles to FEIF, who rises and goes out through the door from which the knocking came.)*

*

THE KING *(in a loud whisper, hardly audible voice.)* Does Gyllenborg know the man who was just sitting here at my side?

GYLLENBORG Secretary Feif. I've only heard Baron Tessin express an opinion of him.

THE KING And . . .

GYLLENBORG With permission, and as your majesty commands— —
—Feif is diligent, good-hearted, honest, pure in appearance, habits and heart as well as a loyal Swede.

THE KING What has Horn heard about Feif?

HORN *(hesitates.)*

THE KING Speak!

HORN *(hesitates.)*

THE KING *(knowingly.)* I didn't think Horn was frightened.

HORN In the field chancery Feif is regarded as less capable, but more self-serving than Piper, and rude as well, vengeful, faithless and hated by everyone who is acquainted with him!

THE KING Can Gyllenborg tell me what I am to believe about Feif?

GYLLENBORG Impossible to say, your majesty!

THE KING Can Horn tell me then what I am to believe about — *(significantly)* — Baron Görtz?

HORN *(parrying.)* The same as your majesty believes about secretary Feif!

THE KING *(smiles.)* Gentlemen, you may go!

GYLLENBORG & HORN *(rise and withdraw backwards.)*

THE KING *(goes back to drawing.)*

*

ADJUTANT Baron Görtz!

THE KING May wait!

GYLLENBORG & HORN *(look at each other in confusion, and exit.)*

FEIF *(re-enters.)*

THE KING Let old Görtz wait!— — —Tell me, Feif, who is Horn nowadays?

FEIF Count Horn is a man of honor.

THE KING And Gyllenborg?

FEIF A knight, in the finest sense of the word.

THE KING Feif is a wise man, for it is wise to always speak well of one's neighbor. Meanwhile — has Feif ordered the reinforcements?

FEIF Yes, your majesty.

THE KING Then I'll have Görtz jailed, but I'd like to speak with him first and look him in the whites of his eyes.— — —Here on this paper it says that he is the greatest rogue that's ever lived, the lowest charlatan, and worse. That he conspired with Russia to depose me is motive enough to secure myself against this person. — — —Feif may go!

FEIF *(hesitates.)*

THE KING Why do you hesitate, Feif?

FEIF Forgive me, majesty, but is it advisable to remain alone in the room with an enemy as formidable as the Baron?

THE KING I am not alone, Feif. I am never alone . . . Go now!

FEIF exits at left.

*

THE KING *(passes his hand over his eyes as if he were collecting memories and thoughts. Then he takes hold of the bell; stops in midgesture and stares at the door to the right. Then he rings.)*

ADJUTANT *(enters.)*

THE KING Baron Görtz may enter!

ADJUTANT *(goes.)*

*

GÖRTZ *(enters, cautiously, unsure, looking about inquiringly. He is refined, a man of the world; he has a beautiful face, but is blind in his left eye, so that now as he enters from the right his face, in profile, appears to be dead. He goes down on one knee.)*

Pause.

THE KING Is that Baron Görtz?

GÖRTZ Yes, it is!

THE KING *(signals: stands up.)* What are you looking for?

GÖRTZ *(with emphasis.)* My hero, my king . . .

THE KING *(angry, his voice trembling, without being raised.)* Has the Baron studied his Machiavelli so poorly that he thinks a king is taken by flattery?

GÖRTZ Machiavelli? I never read that!

THE KING No? Then the Baron does not know how a prince ascertains whether a rogue is speaking the truth or not?

GÖRTZ *(attempting to find a way to strike the right note.)* Can one learn something like that?

THE KING The Baron has been in the company of princes, formerly?

GÖRTZ *(elegantly.)* Everything has its season, your majesty, and I had mine as well. Now that is past . . .

He notices he has missed the mark. He turns quickly.

THE KING The Baron appears to have attained, with the years, a certain self-knowledge.

GÖRTZ Have I?

THE KING So the Baron knows his own little weaknesses?

GÖRTZ Small and great, I'm not ignorant of any of them — rather, they've been there to read about in all the newspapers of Europe for almost ten years now.

THE KING And the Baron acknowledges them all?

GÖRTZ All.

THE KING Now that's an unusual man!

GÖRTZ Oh no.

THE KING The Baron has had, for example, a weakness for writing letters?

GÖRTZ Yes, that was my forté.

THE KING *(laughs with antipathy.)* Preferably to princes, kings, and even emperors . . .

GÖRTZ To the extent that the Czar is an emperor.

THE KING Well, now we've made progress!— — —Has the Baron, for example, written this letter to the Czar?

He places a letter before him.

GÖRTZ *(takes out a lorgnette, inspects the letter, front and back.)* With your permission, I have only one eye and see a bit poorly. Dare I ask what it's about?

THE KING It is about . . . Baron Görtz's plans to depose the King of Sweden, to wed his nephew to the Czar's daughter, and at the same time have his nephew named heir to the Swedish throne.

GÖRTZ Really? But that's really magnificent! A Swedish prince later heir to the Russian throne! That's really brilliant! All difficulties cleared away with one blow! Poltava revenged, August driven out of Poland, the Baltic dominion secured, and Sweden once again a great power as it was at the death of Gustav Adolf. That's really colossal!

THE KING What did you say Baron?— — —The Czar's daughter and Karl Fredrik?

GÖRTZ Absolutely!

THE KING And . . . A . . . A . . . ugust in Poland!

GÖRTZ August in Poland out on his head. And the short end after!

THE KING *(pondering this.)* Does the Baron know the Czar's opinion on this matter?

GÖRTZ *(warming up.)* It is the Czar's greatest wish and boldest dream to create blood ties with the Swedish royal house, and at the same time render old, rotten Poland superfluous. Poland, once a Euro-pean outpost against an uncivilized Russia, is no longer needed, since Russia has become European, and is itself keeping guard against Asia. It is no longer a question of August or Stanislaus — trifles — but rather of Poland or Russia and consequently — Sweden!

THE KING *(draws again.)*

Pause.

THE KING *(as if to himself.)* If I had one man . . .

GÖRTZ To send to the Czar, yes!— — —If I hadn't made such a beastly mess of things, if I wasn't in such poor repute, I would offer my services, because there is no one who knows the courts and secrets of Europe like I do.

THE KING *(draws, and sharpens his pen.)* Is the Baron really in such — poor repute?

GÖRTZ Yes, to the extent that no foreign ambassador can be seen in my company.

THE KING That is surely an exaggeration.

GÖRTZ By my faith — that's not an exaggeration!

THE KING What have you done, then?

GÖRTZ You test fate a little here, you cheat a little there . . .

THE KING How can they . . . how can they . . .

GÖRTZ Your majesty knows how people and the world are . . .

THE KING *(looks up, severe.)* What do I know?

Pause.

If my impoverished country could only set up an army . . . then I'd be tempted to begin reflecting . . .

GÖRTZ Impoverished country? Sweden impoverished? One of the richest lands in Europe? Doesn't the Royal Bank have masses of dead capital stowed away? Are there no crown goods to speculate with! Yes, but one has to put up with a bureaucracy that doesn't have the first idea about high finance.

THE KING What are you driving at?

GÖRTZ There are millions stagnating in the cellars of the Royal Bank getting rusty. The depositors only require their interest. Well then, give them four percent interest and invest the capital in the market at six percent, and then you'll gain two percent immediately. Capital in this country sits in its stall all day long like an ox. Then the balance of trade comes along and says: get out ox and get to work!

THE KING *(laughs softly.)* The Baron is amusing.— — —But he has one thing to his credit — he doesn't see any difficulties.

GÖRTZ Difficulties? I love difficulties, but the lazy man sees difficulties everywhere! And this blessed land is the land of difficulties, because the nation is lazy. If I were someone other than who I am — hm! — I'd have sixty thousand men on their feet within sixty days . . .

THE KING Sixty?

GÖRTZ Sixty thousand.

THE KING And what would Görtz do with them?

GÖRTZ I would take Norway, naturally, as compensation for Finland. When I can't go east, then I go west till I hit the ocean!

THE KING *(amazed.)* Have you been reading my thoughts?

GÖRTZ No. But . . . your majesty . . . I have, at a distance, followed your dizzying path. I have, at a distance, lived your life, shared your fate— — —Sire, I am your man, the man you're looking for!

THE KING *(rises to his full height, angry, and rings the bell.)* Görtz! Don't forget who I am and who you are!

GÖRTZ *(makes a move to talk, but is interrupted.)*

THE KING You have forgotten the basis for this conversation — that you are a traitor, who worked to depose me! Do you deny that!

GÖRTZ Yes!

THE KING Did you write this letter?

GÖRTZ Yes! But it's only a snare that diplomats customarily use.

THE KING Write one thing and mean another?

GÖRTZ Yes!

THE KING I need not believe that, and therefore I am securing myself against your person!

GÖRTZ Then I can do no more.
THE KING *(rings.)*

*

The ADJUTANT enters with letters.

THE KING What do you have there?
ADJUTANT Dispatches of the utmost import.
THE KING Give them here.
ADJUTANT *(leaves the letters and goes.)*

*

THE KING *(sits reading the letters, which appear to trouble him.)*
GÖRTZ *(remains immobile, attempting to read the King's expression.)*
THE KING *(regards GÖRTZ now and again with a furtive glance.)*
GÖRTZ Your majesty!
THE KING Silence!

Pause.

THE KING *(rises and exits through the door at left.)*
GÖRTZ *(looks about uneasily.)*

*

ADJUTANT *(enters with two soldiers.)* Are you Baron Görtz?
GÖRTZ Yes sir.
ADJUTANT I arrest you in the name of the King!
GÖRTZ Me? To what purpose?
ADJUTANT For interrogation.
GÖRTZ What does that mean? Interrogation. Interrogation under
    torture perhaps? I protest!
ADJUTANT Under torture or not, it's no concern of mine.
GÖRTZ *(trembles in his whole body.)* Torture then! I won't go! That

cannot happen, I challenge the validity of these measures. I am not a Swedish subject! I have not done anything!

ADJUTANT I have no way of knowing that. — Soldiers! Do your duty!

The SOLDIERS put manacles on GÖRTZ's arms.

GÖRTZ *(beside himself, but confident.)* You shall regret this. That's for sure, that's for sure . . .

He is led out.

Pause.

*

THE KING *(enters again with FEIF; he walks, exhausted, to the camp bed and lies down.)* Feif!

FEIF Your majesty.

THE KING I think I'm sick— — —Give me the bell.

FEIF gets him the bell.

THE KING Now I have six enemies.

FEIF Six?

THE KING Russia, Poland, Saxony, Prussia, Hannover, Denmark! *(Pause.)* And the Czar is arriving in Copenhagen. You can see his ship out in the sound from the window there! *(Pause.)* Where will I find a defense?

FEIF In a secure peace.

THE KING You are so stupid! *One* can't fight a war, it takes at least two to do that! *One* can't conclude a peace, it takes two to do that — at least! *(Pause.)* Get me an army!

FEIF Impossible!

THE KING Difficulties, the country of difficulties — and the people!

FEIF The country is impoverished — and the people!

THE KING And that is my fault! — Did I cause the plague, did I cause the crop failures, did I cause the fires — did I declare war? — — —No, I have only defended myself, my country, my royal inheritance!— — —

(Pause.)

THE KING Where did Görtz head off to?
FEIF He's probably been taken to the jail.

The KING rings.

*

The ADJUTANT enters.

THE KING Baron Görtz is only to be placed in detention in his own rooms — only that! And is to be treated decently.

The ADJUTANT goes.

*

THE KING Now, Feif! Tell me one thing. Why should the deposits in the bank be sitting in the cellars instead of being out on the market working up some interest?
FEIF Because the deposits are the property of individuals.
THE KING In the Roman state there were no individuals, only members of the state. And when the state was in danger, property ceased to be private and became the state's.
FEIF Those are dangerous teachings.
THE KING Everything is dangerous for cowards.— — —*(Pause.)* If there were just one man in this kingdom! *(Pause.)* What does Feif think of Emanuel Swedenborg?
FEIF Swedenborg is a terrifically learnéd man, pious of temperament, morally pure.

THE KING Is he in the city?

FEIF He is in the city with Counselor Polhem, to whose daughter he is engaged.

THE KING Ah, is he engaged?— — —It is said, you know, that he is a bit strange.

FEIF He is said to exercise a great, almost inexplicable influence on those around him.

Pause.

THE KING Would Feif go and find Swedenborg, and request him to expect me in one hour — at his house!

FEIF It shall be done, your majesty.— — —But . . . can I leave you alone, your highness?

THE KING I am never alone, I've told you . . .

FEIF But the King's lodgings are supposed to be opened to the public at this hour, to set their minds at rest about disturbing rumors.

THE KING What does that matter? They'll be able to see me as well, if they want!— — —Now I'm going to rest a bit— — —Goodbye Feif!

FEIF Your majesty doesn't desire a doctor?

THE KING No, my friend. For my illness there is only one doctor.

FEIF *exits at left.*

THE KING *lies on his back and shuts his eyes.*

Pause.

THE KING *opens his eyes and rings.*

*

The ADJUTANT enters.

THE KING Go and find Baron Görtz, and tell him that he is free, but that he may not leave the city.

ADJUTANT Your majesty, in that case the doors will remain unguarded . . .

THE KING That doesn't matter!

ADJUTANT *(exits.)*

*

THE KING *(closes his eyes again.)*

The saraband is being played on a violin out in the street.

The KING opens his eyes, but remains motionless.

*

The PROFESSOR enters from the back on tiptoes, without noticing the KING. He goes to the hearth and stirs the fire with the iron fork, and tries the register as well. Then he exits on tiptoe at back.

The KING has turned his head to see who it is, but says nothing, only watches the PROFESSOR's activities. Then he draws up his arms and supports the back of his head on his hands.

*

The MAN (= the soldier who returned home from Siberia in the first tableau) enters from the right, ill-clad, with a cap on his head and a thick knotted cudgel in his hand. He walks slowly up to the KING's bed, stops at its foot, crosses his arms over his chest and gazes at the KING with a look of insolence. The MAN appears to have been drinking and to have lost his senses.

THE KING *(lies motionless looking at the MAN.)*

THE MAN Crook!

THE KING *(as before.)*

THE MAN Crook — I said!— — —

THE KING *(motionless.)*

THE MAN Do you have a tongue in your head?— — —*(Pause.)* This then, is the King of Sweden, who's been lying in bed for seven years while the country is dying— — —It's a King who leaves his capital and his government, who dares not return to his home and his own up in Stockholm, since he is ashamed of his fiasco! He'd sworn, to be sure, that he'd return home across North Bridge under a triumphal arch, and have a conquered kingdom on every finger!— — —He is ashamed!— — —

THE KING *(motionless.)*

THE MAN Do you know where I've come from?— — —From the mines of Siberia, from the steppes of Russia! There I met your friends Piper, Rehnsköld, Lewenhaupt, whom you left in the lurch while you lay low in Turkey like an ass. But I've come also, by way of Denmark, where I saw your best man, your truest servant, Stenbocken, working in irons, because you refused to pay ransom.

THE KING *(has moved slightly.)*

THE MAN Crook! Do you know who I am?— — —

THE KING *(motionless but fixes his glance on the MAN.)*

THE MAN Do you remember Krasnokutsch?— — —Do you remember Taube's Dragoons? Do you remember the cavalryman who saved your life, and as thanks for which he was dismissed and thrust in with the foot soldiers — because he, with fervor and zeal to serve, prevented the king from saving himself — as it was put.

THE KING *(rises on his elbows and stares at the MAN.)*

THE MAN Yes — I was number fifty-eight, *Starve*, of Taube's Dragoons. And that I saved your life I now repent, for if you'd perished Poltava would never have happened, and we'd be enjoying six years of peace now!

THE KING *(lies down again.)*

THE MAN Yes, it was nice to get to speak right out for once. And now, we might just as well be friends . . .

THE KING *(rings.)*

THE MAN Ye-es. No one comes, because there is nobody out there!

Well yes, there is a lady— — —a little Polish queen without a throne . . .

THE KING *(rings.)*

THE MAN And a once mighty king protected her and her Lord. And this once mighty king was a splendid man who didn't pinch pennies . . . Look there, by Jove, now there *is* someone coming!— — — Then I'm going. — It's all yours! You are welcome to it!

He goes.

The KING *has risen and attempted to yell, but is unable to get a word out. He rings again.*

*

HULTMAN *enters from the back.*

THE KING *(rubs his eyes.)* I believe that I have been sleeping. — Was there somebody here?

HULTMAN I didn't see anybody.

THE KING Hultman! Give me the cavalry's register for the year 1709, Taube's Dragoons.

HULTMAN *(goes to a shelf and searches.)*

THE KING A blue folio with a yellow spine.

HULTMAN *(comes to him with the desired portfolio.)*

THE KING Look up number fifty-eight under Taube.

HULTMAN *(searches through the register.)* Number fifty-eight?— — — Number fifty-eight has been vacant since seventeen hundred seven!

THE KING *Was denn?* — Look for the dragoon named Starve!

HULTMAN *(again looking.)* Starve?— — —A strange name— — — There is none!

THE KING *(rubbing his eyes.)* Then I've been dreaming. — It was dreadful!— — —Have you been out in the town?

HULTMAN Yes, your majesty!

THE KING Tell me something diverting.

HULTMAN In the town there's nothing that's *diverting.* In the town there's much that's *disturbing.*

THE KING What are the people saying?

HULTMAN Well — what they are saying I wouldn't want to repeat. Not even I.

THE KING They are angry at me because I am not dead.

HULTMAN Lord protect us!

THE KING And this resurrection of mine has crossed many plans.

HULTMAN Yes, that's one thing for certain.

THE KING I'm thinking that Hultman, too, has lost courage.

HULTMAN *(with agitation.)* Your majesty. In truth — yes!

THE KING Do you think my story's reached its end?

HULTMAN *(remains silent.)*

THE KING *(rises and crosses the floor.)* You think so then.— — —

Pause.

THE KING Is there any money in the casket?

HULTMAN None.

THE KING How is the enlistment going?

HULTMAN Badly.

Pause.

THE KING *(leans on the mantel, hiding his face in one hand.)* Difficulties. The land of difficulties!

Pause.

THE KING Hultman . . . Go out into the city. Seek out Baron Görtz. And bring him here at once!

HULTMAN Baron Görtz?

THE KING Baron Görtz! At once!

HULTMAN *exits.*

Curtain.

TABLEAU III

A city square with planted trees, and a well in the middle. In the background, the ruins of burned buildings. Farthest up to the left in the background, GÖRTZ's house, with green shutters that are all closed. There is a Swedish flag with the national coat of arms over the door. This house comprises a corner of the background, where a lane opens up. Downstage at the far left stands a smithy. To the right, in the foreground, a tavern with tables and benches outside.

The MAN *(from the first tableau) and the* DWARF *are sitting at the table smoking clay pipes and drinking beer. They are concealed by several other guests as well as a kind of arbor.*

DWARF And still you didn't let him have it?

THE MAN Naa! But I read him the riot act till he turned white — you'd better believe it.

DWARF Why didn't you let him have it? That's what I would've done!

THE MAN It wouldn't do any good to let him have it. — Besides, I felt sorry for him.

DWARF Sorry for him?

THE MAN He looked sick and unhappy — and they say he's not having a fun time of it. Everyone is after him for money.

DWARF Yes, but there will be money now, since old Görtz has gotten his hands on the economy.

THE MAN Yes, old Görtz! — You see that the shutters are closed at his house up there?

DWARF I can see that — and what's going on in there no one knows.

THE MAN They say that he makes gold like Paykull!

DWARF Oh? No!

THE MAN Whatever they're doing, it's crap. Just think, that villain is all-powerful Minister of the whole kingdom of Sweden, and the crook is in there with him all day long! — He's in there right now, my dear friend!

DWARF Imagine, this Baron, of whom the whole world knows that he's a cheat, an adventurist, tossed out of every state in Europe, and that he's conspired to depose our King! And there is not a single loyal Swede who can say that to the King!

THE MAN Who would dare to?

DWARF There was one, Dean Boëthius, but he went to prison first, and from there to the madhouse! There *is* one, and that's — Emanuel Swedenborg.

THE MAN Yes, him, yes. There's a man for you. And so learnéd then. He's a learnéd one.

DWARF You know that I loved this King, worshiped him — I once kissed his boots. — But now: If I had a cask of powder I'd set it under that house there! Not simply because he dumped me on the road . . .

*

A man, a MALCONTENT, approaches the table.

THE MAN Sit down! and tell!

MALCONTENT The skipper of the brig *Snapp-Opp*, because ice delayed his arrival at Stralsund — and the even more innocent crew — have been publicly flogged!

THE MAN What else!

MALCONTENT His daughter is in town to seek an audience with the crook!

THE MAN What else!

MALCONTENT The students have been driven out of their residences and have been pressed into service!

THE MAN Good!

MALCONTENT The maids and the farmhands from the villages are roaming the roads, since the crown has taken half their wages in war taxes.

THE MAN Wonderful!

MALCONTENT The houses of the bourgeoisie are being assessed, and all their silverware is being seized in exchange for receipts!

THE MAN Magnificent!

MALCONTENT The Councillor of the Realm and the Speakers of the Four Estates are still seeking audiences with the king, who is not receiving . . .

THE MAN That is the limit!

MALCONTENT — — —since he has locked himself in with that adventurist who is busy making counterfeit money!

THE MAN What will you give me if I set fire to that house there?

MALCONTENT That's not necessary, since others are bound to do it.

THE MAN Is there more?

MALCONTENT The Princess Ulrika Eleonora has come to meet with her brother . . .

THE MAN The succession to the throne to boot! The crook's successor!

DWARF *(begins tuning his violin.)* You mustn't call him a crook. — Well I just think it's sad to see a great man slowly degenerate— — —It's sad!

He plays a few bars of the saraband.

THE MAN Why is he always playing that lament?

DWARF Because I used to play it for my King, when he was so sad he was sick to death.

THE MAN Would you listen to that!

DWARF And it was a king who composed this lament! Sebastian Bach, King of the Land of Sorrow and the Realm of Pain— — —

He plays the saraband.

*

THE MAN *(to the MALCONTENT.)* Look out, people are coming!

MALCONTENT I promise you I will!

THE MAN You tell me what you see, because I've been in the

realm of the dead, and no longer recognize the living.

*

WOMEN DRESSED IN MOURNING from the upper classes enter from the right. They approach the doors of GÖRTZ's house. They stop and confer quietly.

MALCONTENT The widows of the captured lords — I call them widows, since the king refuses to ransom their captive husbands, buried alive in Russia and elsewhere. — The widows Piper, Rehnsköld, Lewenhaupt, Stenbock— — —among others.
THE MAN Why doesn't he have the prisoners released?
MALCONTENT Some people say: he will not — others: he cannot! — Look at them now! — I'll bet you that he doesn't receive the women! He never was much good at handling women.— — —The one who is ringing is Countess Piper. But the Stenbocks are the saddest case. Måns Bock, who saved Scania. An honorable man. But the King says he deserves his fate since he did not follow orders!
COUNTESS PIPER *(rings the bell timidly.)*
THE MAN No answer from that silent house.

THE WOMEN withdraw fearfully down to the square in a group and confer.

MALCONTENT New additions!— — —The widows Bjelke, Boëthius, Patkull, Paykull!

FOUR MORE WOMEN dressed in mourning approach the door. One of them rings. A little window on the door is opened and is then shut. THE WOMEN withdraw and cry in their handkerchiefs.

MALCONTENT Look now! Here come the discarded favorites. Just look at them! Yesterday regal, today rebels. — Rosen, Düring, Sparre and Gyllenborg, Wellingk, Cederhielm, De la Gardie,

Mörner, d'Albedyhll, Schwerin, Wrede— — —Horn, Arvid Horn the great— — —

The line of lords approaches the door.

HORN *(rings the bell three times, each time more violently.)*
THE MAN Now he — he is not afraid!
MALCONTENT Because he has a nation behind him! And a future before him!
HORN *(yanks off the bell cord, winds it together and tosses it to the ground.)*

The window on the door opens.

FEIF *(sticking his head out.)* Who do you want?
HORN The King!
FEIF Not receiving! *(He slams the window shut.)*

*

Murmuring among everyone on the square.

MALCONTENT Now! The Councillor of the Realm and the Speakers of the Four Estates!

*

The COUNCILLOR and the SPEAKERS enter. They approach the door, but are stopped by HORN.

COUNCILLOR So it has come to that!
HORN The consequences of absolutism.
COUNCILLOR *(to the SPEAKERS.)* Absolutism—which these little masters were demanding in order to crush the big masters. There

you have it!

MALCONTENT The thieves are fighting: "The farmer gets his cow back!" . . . Quiet! Horse hooves on the toll road . . . Couriers!

*

A POOR WOMAN with a petition in her hand walks to the door. She looks for the bell cord, and when she can't find it, knocks. When no one answers, she pulls on the shutter of the window, which comes open. She quite simply sticks the petition through the opening and sits on the stairs to wait with her hands folded.

MAN She knew how to take the matter straight on!

*

COUNTESS PIPER *(approaches the WOMAN.)* What is the woman requesting?

WOMAN *(simply, humbly.)* I'm requesting mercy for my father.

COUNTESS PIPER Who is the woman's father?

WOMAN He was the skipper of the ship that was supposed to meet the King outside of Stralsund. But then there was ice obstructing his way — and even though he had no control over that, he was sentenced to death.

COUNTESS PIPER *(clasps her hands together and moans.)*

EVERYONE *(who overheard the conversation expresses indignation.)*

*

SAILOR *(approaches the WOMAN.)* What are you doing sitting there?

WOMAN Ye-ess — I'm going to sit here!

SAILOR No you're not. Because your father was a criminal!

WOMAN Could you say such a thing of your own father?

SAILOR He was not my father. And as he was a criminal, I'm going to say he was one!

WOMAN But he was my father . . .

SAILOR But not mine! *(He takes her by the arm.)* Come on!— — —
COUNTESS PIPER What does the gentleman want with that woman?
SAILOR It's nobody's business because that's my wife. *(Murmuring.)*
And her father, the skipper, was a traitor, who hoisted a false flag
on the Danish frigate and wasn't stopped by any ice!
WOMAN Imagine, the nerve to call my father a traitor!

Murmuring.

SAILOR When he was one! And I know that, as a member of the
crew onboard— — —We were whipped, though we were innocent
. . . But I'm not complaining, 'cause that's no kind of man who
can't take a few lashes for his King! That's right — that's no kind
of man!— — —*(Murmuring.)* And sometimes you get it when you
shouldn't, and sometimes you slip by when you should get it!
(Murmuring.) And there are many here who should be whipped
. . . That's right!
WOMAN Just think! A man so foul he calls my father a traitor. My
father!

*

MAN *(who has listened and observed.)* That's one hell of an ungov-
ernable woman!

He leans forward to observe.

MALCONTENT What's he staring at?
MAN Naah, it's not possible— — —
MALCONTENT What is it? What is it?
MAN I thought— — —well, what difference does it make anyway.
MALCONTENT What?
MAN *(sits down.)* I thought that was my deceased wife.
MALCONTENT Haha!— — —A courier! A courier! News!

*

Movement on the square. Everyone looks off to the right.

*

The COURIER *hurries across the stage causing a great commotion, and disappears on the path at the corner of GÖRTZ's house, heading for the back door.*

*

HORN *(to the* COUNCILLOR.*)* Important news!
COUNCILLOR Any hunches?
HORN I have some hunches!

They whisper. Everyone whispers.

*

THE WOMAN *(walks to the corner.)* Well I never! I think you can get in at the back!
MALCONTENT That's really one hell of a woman.
MAN And so like Karolina!

*

HORN *(to* GYLLENBORG.*)* What's happened? There are bells ringing in there, and doors slamming.
GYLLENBORG Haven't got a clue.
HORN Is it peace or war?
GYLLENBORG War of course. Always war!

*

A LACKEY *in red livery comes out through the door.*

MALCONTENT Would you look at that devil!

MAN What kind of parrot is that?
MALCONTENT Görtz's lackey!

The LACKEY walks down the stairs, turns his back to the square, and tramps on the toes of those standing near him without any apologies. Thereupon, he lowers the flag to half mast.

HORN What has happened?
LACKEY *(his back to HORN.)* I haven't learned.
HORN Learn some manners at least!

*

THE WOMAN *(has come back and attempts to slip in through the door.)*
LACKEY *(squeezing her between the door and the jamb.)* Get out of here, you!
WOMAN I want to see the King!
LACKEY Out of here, hag!
WOMAN *(slips inside.)*
MAN Bless my soul — I believe that is Karolina!
MALCONTENT But she's dead.
MAN Who the hell knows?

*

HERALD *(preceded by kettledrummers, who strike up a fanfare.)* In view of his majesty, most holy King of France, Louis the Fourteenth's passing from temporal existence, all parties concerned are commanded to display fourteen days of deep mourning.

*

HORN *(to GYLLENBORG.)* That's it! . . . Absolutism is dead!
GYLLENBORG And Sweden's only friend!
COUNCILLOR Now something new is at hand in Europe.
NOBLEMAN New evil.

PRIEST And new good.
BURGHER AND FARMER Amen!

*

HERALD The people will vacate the square, as mourning salvos will be fired for his most holy majesty, King of France. In addition the chimes from the church towers of the city proclaiming his death shall commence immediately!

The kettledrums play.

The groups dissolve and draw out to the sides, talking and murmuring.

MALCONTENT Absolutism is finished!
MAN Not yet. But soon. And then?
MALCONTENT That's no concern of ours.

*

DWARF Then it'll be Tuesday's soup — the same as Sunday's, but with a bit more water, without butter!

*

FEIF *(comes out through the door, leading the WOMAN.)* Go now, my good woman. Your father has been sentenced by the court as a traitor . . .
WOMAN Do the judges also call my father a traitor?
FEIF *(angrily.)* Since he was a criminal, well?
WOMAN Just think! Judges like that!
FEIF *(yells.)* But your father himself confessed that he was a criminal! He has confessed!
WOMAN That is a lie!

FEIF goes in, slamming the door behind him.
The WOMAN knocks weakly on the door.

*

Now the memorial chimes are heard from the city's churches; kettle and snare drums play.

SAILOR *(enters again, yelling at his wife.)* Karolina!

MAN No — now I'm starting to get scared!— — —

MALCONTENT Is it her?

MAN *(horrified.)* I don't know!— — —

DWARF Royalism's dead!— — —God save the king! anyway, even though he dumped me!

MALCONTENT Anyway! — To think, I can't really be angry at that man either.

DWARF *(as he goes.)* Is *that* so necessary?

MAN Yes, it's absolutely necessary.

Curtain.

TABLEAU IV

A large park. At the right a pair of tall, latticed iron gates leading out to a lane. The gates are partly concealed by trees and bushes. Not far above is a tent-covered veranda of the KING's house; outside of it are the KING's desk and chair. In front is his camp bed.

In the center of the stage is a balustrade of short Tuscan columns, and three blue-and-white faience pots. On the middle of the balustrade stands an old, white statue of Venus.

Visible at the left, GÖRTZ's house with its green shutters and veranda with benches.

At back, a lane against a garden wall, on which there are doors made of planks, furnished on top with "Spanish horsemen" spikes.

HULTMAN *(straightens up the table.)*

PROFESSOR *(puttering with flowerpots.)*

HULTMAN Aren't you a physician, professor?

PROFESSOR Yes, I am indeed.

HULTMAN The fact is, the King is feeling ill, mostly since Baron Görtz's departure.

PROFESSOR Ha - ha - has Baron Görtz departed?

HULTMAN Yes, he's down in Copenhagen dealing with money matters, among other things. But he is expected home at any time.

PROFESSOR Wha - wha - what is his majesty's problem?

HULTMAN Insomnia, uneasiness and irritability.

PROFESSOR Yes, yes, yes. And the Princess sits in town waiting for an audience — his own sister!

HULTMAN Oh? Sister? There are many sorts of sisters. I've got one that's a shrew and a hag . . .

PROFESSOR His own sister! — And she's just married too! Listen Hultman, is it true that the King intends to get married?

HULTMAN No, I haven't heard that . . . We've no time for getting married— — —But the fact that the skirts are starting to swarm,

I find disturbing.

PROFESSOR Respect for women, Hultman! Respect!

HULTMAN Respect for children, respect for servants, respect for me, everyone is hollering for respect, but everyone is suspicious with respect to other people.

PROFESSOR Hultman, you are a misogynist.

HULTMAN You're right there — although that's only half the truth as always— — —Look, here comes Dr. Swedenborg with his skirt.

PROFESSOR The daughter of the great Polhem—Emerentia.

HULTMAN A conceited, proud flirt, who's sworn to get the King at her feet. Because she's used to getting students and ensigns — to dance!

PROFESSOR Oh no. Oh no! But does her boyfriend suspect his fiancée's ambitious plans?

HULTMAN Swedenborg? No. He's deaf and blind like anyone intoxicated by love . . . Look, there they are!

The PROFESSOR and HULTMAN move off into the tent at right.

*

SWEDENBORG and EMERENTIA enter from the lane at right.

SWEDENBORG My love, I have to leave you for a time. My King and my country require my services.

EMERENTIA But you'd promised me that tomorrow would be the day we would exchange rings . . .

SWEDENBORG I'd promised on the condition that no higher duties called me. Now I've got to depart this evening . . .

EMERENTIA Then you don't love me.

SWEDENBORG Alas! What shall I say? What shall I do to show you my love?

EMERENTIA Stay till the day after tomorrow.

SWEDENBORG The King will not allow it.

EMERENTIA Your King, who hates women!

SWEDENBORG No, his thoughts are only on other things.

EMERENTIA May I beg his permission for you to stay?

SWEDENBORG No, my friend. The troops are ready to march, and they are awaiting me.

EMERENTIA Let them wait!

SWEDENBORG Let my people and country wait — at the whim of a little girl?

EMERENTIA Little girl. Watch out!

SWEDENBORG You have made threats so often that I'm almost longing for the blow to fall. What should I be watching out *for*? That you will leave me? —

EMERENTIA It is you who are leaving me!

SWEDENBORG Hm. I've got to go, but to return again for good. But you would go, never to return. There is a difference.

EMERENTIA Is the King in there?

SWEDENBORG Yes, but you're going to promise me not to try to approach him.

EMERENTIA And why should I?

SWEDENBORG He is not receiving.

EMERENTIA That's *my* problem.

SWEDENBORG And mine! Because he'll think that I sent you, and then I'll be disgraced.

EMERENTIA That's not the reason. You have another which you're not telling.

SWEDENBORG Promise that you will not try to see the King.

EMERENTIA You're afraid.

SWEDENBORG (*remains silent.*)

EMERENTIA Of a dream you have had.

SWEDENBORG (*remains silent.*)

EMERENTIA I am not afraid of dreams!

SWEDENBORG So strange. You say you love me — often I believe it. But just the same, every word you speak is like a poison needle. Is that love?— — —

EMERENTIA You call me a poison needle! . . . You have never loved me! — Goodbye!

She walks off to the right on the lane.

SWEDENBORG (*stricken.*) This is love! Earthly love!—O heavens!

He walks off to the left on the lane.

*

The KING emerges from the tent. He looks sick and anxious.
FEIF follows.

THE KING Feif!—Will Görtz be able to get back soon?
FEIF Yes, your majesty.
THE KING That strange man. When he's around, I find him
  engaging, upright, loyalty itself. When away, he takes on the most
  bizarre shapes in my mind—becomes ghostlike, frightening, ghastly.
  (*Pause.*) Do you think his budget estimates are correct?
FEIF Your majesty is the mathematician, not I.
THE KING You can't substantiate his calculations with known
  formulas . . .
FEIF What is the opinion of Polhem and Swedenborg?
THE KING They have nothing to say. (*Pause.*) The whole city has
  nothing to say. The whole country has nothing to say. A deadly
  silence is beginning to close in around us! (*Pause.*) And then I
  am sick. (*Pause.*) The streets are empty. No one comes to visit.
  No one protests!—Nobody says anything! (*Pause.*) Say something!
FEIF I have nothing to say, your majesty.
THE KING Nothing?— — —Won't it soon be lunchtime?
FEIF Your majesty, it is already afternoon.
THE KING My gosh, yes. I remember now . . . (*Pause.*) Why don't
  I ever see Müllern, Sparre, Gyllenborg anymore?
FEIF They don't dare to disturb you.
THE KING Why does everyone leave me alone? Even Hultman goes
  off to sulk.— — —And if I send for anyone — he's sick. (*Pause.*)
  And this silence. This silence!— — —Once I had Luxembourg to
  play for me, but he vanished after Stralsund— — —Get me a
  spider to play with! (*Pause.*) Do you think the country can
  tolerate ten million worth of new token coins?

FEIF Baron Görtz thought two million would be the maximum.

THE KING Oh yes.— — —Why won't the Princess come, since I've invited her? My sister, I mean.

FEIF Her royal highness set the condition that her consort, the Viscount of Hesse, should be allowed to accompany her.

THE KING The one who is waiting out my life. To get the throne. — — —There are more and more people waiting out my life. (*Pause.*) Feif! Go up to her residence and bid the Princess come, regarding a matter of import to her. Without the Viscount!

FEIF exits on the lane to the left.

THE KING (*alone, in despair.*) Oh my God! Let this cup pass from me!

*

EMERENTIA appears on the lane at right. She carries a bouquet of roses; fixes herself to appear attractive, and advances toward the KING. But when she catches sight of him, she turns away, and is gripped by sympathy and respect.

The KING, who has had his face in his hands, looks up now, and when he perceives EMERENTIA, he appears not to know whether it is a dream or a revelation. He then speaks, looking embarrassed.

THE KING With flowers for me! Why do you give me roses?

EMERENTIA My hero has seen enough of laurels . . .

THE KING And thorns. Perhaps it's time for cypresses!

EMERENTIA Not yet. First, myrtle.

THE KING (*prattling.*) You little child, what are you saying?

EMERENTIA What am I saying?—Thus sings the most beautiful woman in Europe, on whom, even so, the hero once turned his back:

"Carl! Your steadfastness o'ercomes any resistance,

For you, your exploits mere games of persistence;
With a thousand cunning plans they've vainly striven,
You are, just as you were, not to be beaten.

But, young hero, when your laurels wrap you,
When honor still is keeping to your side,
It seems that only joy is hidden from you,
And no pleasures may follow on your ride.

Tell how your eyes, and figure shaped by gods,
Have still not found a sweeter recompense?
Forgive my boldness. I placed secret odds
That e'en the hero has a lover's sense.

She, the beauty capable of winning
The greatest mortal's faith, sinks at his feet,
For her then would our altars all be burning.
But open your embrace, the goddess is received."

THE KING (*has regarded her with glowing looks.*) Thank you my child. For having awakened the memory of a happy, bygone time — The compliments, for what they're worth, we'll let be— — — Now tell me, what's your name?

EMERENTIA A little girl's name? What does that matter to a great king?

THE KING A little girl can give a sad king back his confidence and his lust for life.

EMERENTIA Why is the great king sad?

THE KING You sweet little thing.— — —Can you play chess?

EMERENTIA Yes, your majesty! I can!

THE KING Then you shall come and play with me.

EMERENTIA But if I put the king in checkmate, then he'll be angry.

THE KING No child. He'll never be angry. But you won't be able to do that.

EMERENTIA Sure I can! — I've put the great mathematician Polhem in checkmate.

THE KING My Polhem! You? — Do you know him?

EMERENTIA As well as my own father.

THE KING Then you know Swedenborg too? The dreamer?

EMERENTIA A little.

THE KING (*looks at her searchingly.*) Do you like him?

EMERENTIA He is boring.

THE KING (*gives a look of astonishment.*) Whom do you like then?

EMERENTIA (*turns down her eyes.*)

THE KING Shall I guess?

EMERENTIA (*holds her hands before her eyes.*)

THE KING Let me see your pretty eyes . . .

EMERENTIA (*flattered.*)

THE KING I know nothing so sweet as the eyes of a child.

EMERENTIA (*grimaces, crestfallen.*)

THE KING Yes, because you are a child in relation to me— — —

EMERENTIA (*takes hold of the KING's hand, which he pulls away.*)
    Then like me a little.

THE KING You may be my friend . . . Do you know music?

EMERENTIA I play harpsichord!

THE KING You've learned that from Swedenborg.

EMERENTIA That awful man.

THE KING (*with a strange expression.*) Shame!

EMERENTIA (*gives him a questioning look.*)

THE KING Shame, I said!— — —Are you a little bit fond of me?

EMERENTIA (*hides her face in her hands.*)

THE KING Does that mean *very fond*?

EMERENTIA (*takes the KING's hand and kisses it.*)

THE KING Is that the child or the woman?

EMERENTIA (*falls to her knees at the KING's feet.*) It's the woman!

                    *

THE KING (*rises in anger.*) Emerentia Polhem! Get up!

EMERENTIA (*looks up.*)

THE KING Now *you* are lying at the King's feet. — Stand up and go.
    You do not deserve the man who loves you, and therefore you

shall never take Emanuel Swedenborg as your husband.

He turns his back to her.

EMERENTIA Your majesty! Grace!
THE KING *Dis*-grace!— — —

EMERENTIA steals out on the lane to the right.

*

FEIF enters from the lane at left.

THE KING Speak up!
FEIF (*glances after* EMERENTIA.) Her royal highness will be here directly!
THE KING Without the Viscount?
FEIF That was not specified!
THE KING Feif!— — —You've been married?
FEIF Yes, your majesty.
THE KING We-ell?
FEIF It's . . .
THE KING (*smiles.*) We-ell?
FEIF (*with a shrug of his shoulders.*) It's . . .
THE KING That's what you all say. But I never get any answers.
FEIF We neither!
THE KING Maybe there is no — answer— — —
FEIF Maybe so!

*

Kettledrums and the clatter of arms.

THE KING That's the Princess. Feif, you may go! . . .

He walks toward the lane at right.

FEIF goes into the tent.

*

THE ADJUTANT (*enters on the lane at right.*) Her royal highness!

Pause.

*

ULRIKA ELEONORA enters from the right.
THE KING goes to receive her, offers his hand and leads her to the table.

THE KING Welcome, sister of my heart!
ULRIKA ELEONORA Many thanks, my dear brother!

They sit.

THE KING It's a little untidy here, but we live on battle-footing.

The conversation proceeds with pauses and mutual embarrassment.

ULRIKA ELEONORA War-footing. Let us soon be on peace-footing.
THE KING Has the Viscount come along?
ULRIKA ELEONORA No, my consort is hunting.
THE KING Ohh? Are you happily married, sister?
ULRIKA ELEONORA Is Baron Görtz away?
THE KING It has been a long time since my sister and I have met
  face to face.
ULRIKA ELEONORA (*picks up EMERENTIA's roses.*)   Roses, I
  believe.
THE KING What's the news from the city?
ULRIKA ELEONORA Is it true that you are going to march against
  Norway?
THE KING Does that interest the Viscount?

Pause.

ULRIKA ELEONORA (*gives the* KING *a sharp look in response.*)
THE KING A lot has changed during these last years.
ULRIKA ELEONORA (*remains silent, playing with her fan.*)
THE KING That's an especially fine fan!
ULRIKA ELEONORA Has my brother heard mention of the latest broadside printed in Holland?
THE KING Spare me that.
ULRIKA ELEONORA It's the filthiest thing I've ever read.
THE KING Would you please spare me that!
ULRIKA ELEONORA King David went out on his roof, and there he saw Uriah's wife Bathsheba—and so he sent Uriah to war.
THE KING *Was denn?*
ULRIKA ELEONORA These are pretty roses here. They smell so good!
THE KING You're welcome to them.
ULRIKA ELEONORA Me? Used flowers? No, thank you very much.
THE KING (*tosses the roses away.*) Speak in plain language, sister. But don't come here with gossip, because I'm not going to respond to that.
ULRIKA ELEONORA I'd thought — that is to say — I'd hoped that my dear brother had enough confidence in his sister, that he would not hide his plans where it concerned others — the sacred interests of those closest to him.
THE KING You mean the succession to the throne?
ULRIKA ELEONORA Though one be ruler, one should not be brutal.
THE KING No beating around the bush! Or I go my way!
ULRIKA ELEONORA You, you always go! When it's a matter of — —
THE KING Sister!— — —They say you are unhappily married.
ULRIKA ELEONORA Me? Not at all. I am very happy. Very happy!
THE KING They say that your consort is a pig. And we do not want to have any pigs on the Swedish throne.
ULRIKA ELEONORA But idiots? As if your belovéd Karl Fredrik isn't an idiot. But you like idiots. For example this Baron Görtz!
THE KING Keep to the subject.

ULRIKA ELEONORA Karl Fredrik of Holstein, whom you want on the throne, is a good-for-nothing, ruled by his valet Ropstock. So upon your death a valet will rule Sweden!

THE KING Woman!

ULRIKA ELEONORA Yes, that's how you are. You are very great, but you are stupid. Yes you are. But why you are great, I don't know. For the last eighteen years you've been doing nothing but stupid things, and I don't know the name of a single battle other than Poltava, where you fled. Only defeat, and without honor!— — — That's what you get for "woman," you woman-hater!

THE KING Take care.

ULRIKA ELEONORA About what?

THE KING That my sympathies don't transfer to your spouse, who's clearly had one hot hell — like all married men, for that matter!

ULRIKA ELEONORA Look how he blooms now! Oh! Your sympathies go to that wretched Viscount. *That* I could just believe — that dishonorable man, who treats his wife— — —Yes — what — I — haven't — had to suffer . . .

THE KING Just now you were so happy.

ULRIKA ELEONORA Just now?— — —Haha! Just now! He says. . .

THE KING Remember that I am not married to you!

ULRIKA ELEONORA Meaning what?

THE KING That you treat me as your brother and monarch, and don't give me curtain lectures like your consort.

ULRIKA ELEONORA You married? — Yes, why aren't you married? Because you are scared of women. The hero is scared.

THE KING When I listen to you, then I really do get scared. And in the course of these brief moments I've been seized by the greatest sympathy for the Viscount. I almost love him!

ULRIKA ELEONORA (*cries in her handkerchief.*) Yes, yes, yes . . .

THE KING Don't cry, whatever you do — swear instead! Tears are the most hideous thing I know.

ULRIKA ELEONORA Since you love the Viscount, name him successor.

THE KING Let me die first. There's enough time to choose successors.— — —Sister, I may soon reach the end of my road — this may be the last time we shall meet.

ULRIKA ELEONORA (*serious, mild.*) My belovéd brother, my heart. The way you talk!

THE KING Yes, to you, my mother's child, I want to confess that the situation of the kingdom is hopelessly desperate.

ULRIKA ELEONORA That's been rumored for some time now. But it was thought that Görtz . . .

THE KING I thought so too, but . . . He has miscalculated, or he doesn't understand finances . . . I know all the man's vices, but relied on his superior wisdom and abilities . . . But even these showed themselves to be . . . hollow . . .

ULRIKA ELEONORA Dear heart, are things so desperate?

THE KING There's absolutely nothing to be done!— — —I wish I were dead.

ULRIKA ELEONORA Can I do anything for my brother . . . Have you any wishes . . .

THE KING No, my friend. — And who shall inherit the throne, leave that in God's hands . . . Forgive me, I am sick . . . and must lie down.

He lies down on the bed.

ULRIKA ELEONORA (*on her knees by the bed.*) What's wrong, my brother? What is it, my heart?

THE KING "The moments of life ebb out. Smiling will I die!" — You recall what that is?— — —It's Ragnar Lodbrok in the snake pit. (*Pause.*) They considered me inscrutable because I wasn't a talker. And I didn't talk because I wasn't a drinker. Alone in preserving my wits among the intoxicated, I was regarded as a madman . . . (*Pause.*) Ulla! Put your hand on my brow. Now you are like my mother. The only woman I have loved, because she was my mother, and consequently— — —was not a woman to me. (*Pause.*) There is not one action that I cannot defend. But I don't care to defend myself— — —(*Pause.*) The apprentice calls the journeyman a tyrant, and the journeyman calls the master a despot. Every man's superior is seen as a despot.

They would gladly be in that position themselves given the chance!
If they could! (*Pause.*) Yes, you women. I have stood outside the
window and looked into homes, so I saw more than others — for
those who are inside can hardly see what they've got. — The
sweetest things and the most bitter! — Love, only a hair's breadth
from hate. (*Pause.*) Now I'm going to sleep. Sleep's the best thing
. . . next best.

He sleeps.
The saraband is being played in the distance.

*

ULRIKA ELEONORA rises, walks toward the back and waves in a
chamberlain.
The CHAMBERLAIN enters.

ULRIKA ELEONORA Taube, I have placed unlimited trust in you, for
reasons known by you alone! — Am I right?
CHAMBERLAIN (*bows.*)
ULRIKA ELEONORA Seek out the Viscount immediately. Tell him
that the situation favors us, and to prepare himself to embark to
Norway!

The CHAMBERLAIN bows and goes.

*

ULRIKA ELEONORA follows him out a few steps, and returns with
KATARINA LESZCZYNSKA, wife of the deposed Stanislaus Leszczynsky.

ULRIKA ELEONORA Katarina Leszczynska! — The audience that was
never granted you, I grant you now.
KATARINA So I get to see this man, who has played so much with
my fate and my people's . . .
ULRIKA ELEONORA Hush! He's asleep. But you shall wait . . .

KATARINA (*creeps forward and regards the* KING.) Is this he?

ULRIKA ELEONORA My poor brother is sick . . . He may not have long to live.

KATARINA Is this he? Fallen so low? — Just as low as we.

*

THE KING (*moves, and breathes deeply.*)

ULRIKA ELEONORA (*walking upstage to the right.*) He's waking. — Let me wait for you at the residence.

She goes.

*

KATARINA positions herself with her arms crossed as if she awaited the KING's *awakening in order to read him the law.*

The KING *awakens, rising in a calm and dignified manner, and stands.*

THE KING Katarina Leszczynska! I dreamt about you, perhaps because I was expecting you— — —Please, sit down.

KATARINA Sire, you were not expecting me.

THE KING Do you mean to say that I am lying? — Do you have a statement to address to me?

KATARINA I would like to ask you, sire, where my husband and children are!

THE KING Please adjust your tone of voice when you address a monarch.

KATARINA Please employ another tone when you're addressing a woman.

THE KING A woman? Pah!— — —That's one form of sovereignty I've never honored. — Meanwhile, to assist you with your audience — things I love to keep short — I shall state your errand so that it won't get muddled up with chatter. — Please sit down.

KATARINA (*furious.*) This I have got to hear!

THE KING You shall hear, and the King shall speak! — — Well then: Where a man and children may be keeping themselves, that's no concern of mine— — —But when I once appointed Stanislaus, your husband, King of Poland, and I thought him born to rule, I was mistaken — because he lacked the courage to make use of the power that the nation had given him. He was born to obey, and so he had to go.— — —He did so with pleasure, by the way. Yes, he ran! Since then I have ordered the payment of subsidies to him and his family, nearly a hundred thousand rix-dollars annually with no strings attached. The fact that these funds have not been produced with regularity is no fault of mine. No one else's either — for there *were* no funds. And nothing comes of nothing, etcetera. But now there *is something.* So, go to the finance office and collect.

KATARINA King Stanislaus . . .

THE KING Stanislaus could not rule. Just as little as king August — who let himself be ruled by women . . . The audience is over.

He rings.

*

THE ADJUTANT enters.

THE KING Have Doctor Swedenborg come in!

KATARINA Now there's a man!

THE KING (*to the ADJUTANT.*) Escort the lady out!

KATARINA exits.

The KING holds his head as if he had a headache.

*

SWEDENBORG enters, looking distressed.

THE KING Emanuel!— — —Are you prepared to go to Norway with
the Corps of Engineers?

SWEDENBORG Your majesty!

THE KING In the evening? This evening? — I know that you were
supposed to exchange rings tomorrow . . .

SWEDENBORG It's a matter of my future happiness . . .

THE KING Future happiness? — A woman! There's always a woman
coming along to take away my best man.— — —Emanuel. Your
country requires you, your King entreats you — go with us!

SWEDENBORG The allegiance of my heart is holy . . .

THE KING Have you no heart for king and country first?

SWEDENBORG Your majesty!

THE KING (*with his knee on an armchair.*) It is Emerentia. Listen:
Who is Emerentia?

SWEDENBORG That — is an angel.

THE KING This is to me the most inexplicable of the diseases of the
mind. Love! Is she an angel?

SWEDENBORG Yes.

THE KING Emanuel. Even if it costs me your friendship, hear it you
shall!— — —Emerentia was here just now.

SWEDENBORG Here? Despite my pleas?

THE KING She is not the woman you will marry— — —I'd been prepared for the fact, through gossip I'd heard, that she'd sworn to
have me at her feet. Well, her attempt was rather simple — and
I could overlook all that — but she stooped to speaking ill of you.
She held you up to ridicule!

SWEDENBORG (*weeps.*)

THE KING Look at that! Now he's crying!— — —You know lads,
I've now had enough of your affairs with skirts— — —Does it hurt
that much? — (*He claps him on the shoulder.*) — Emanuel, pull
yourself together and be a man!— — —You, a *Nasir*, born to lofty
achievements and great dreams, what's this wine and women to
you? Are you going to lay your head on some lap and let the hair
which gives you strength be cut?

SWEDENBORG I have promised her to be faithful . . .

THE KING But she has broken her promise when she was unfaithful

. . . Unfaithful like that lord of the ladies King August was . . . Up!
Emanuel! Honor and duty call you.

*

FEIF (*enters from the tent.*) Pardon me your majesty.
THE KING What is it?
FEIF Baron Görtz has returned!
THE KING Bring him here.— — —Emanuel, go in there and wait.

SWEDENBORG starts to enter the tent.

THE KING (*to SWEDENBORG.*) If they don't get them, they cry. And
if they get them, they cry then too. — A strange game, that. Mad
man's game or sad man's game!— — —No wait!— — —Stay here
and listen!— — —What's coming now is for you, Emanuel. —
Emanuel deciphered means: God with us!

SWEDENBORG stops.

*

GÖRTZ enters quickly from the left.

*At the latticework gate people are gathering, among whom can be
seen the MAN (from the 1st Tableau), the MALCONTENT, the WOMAN
(from the 3rd Tableau). They are silent, but have a sinister look
about them.*

THE KING Speak. But quickly!
GÖRTZ All is lost!
THE KING In what regard?
GÖRTZ Ruin, bankruptcy! The country in flames— — —They al-
most killed me.
THE KING Is it the emergency coin?
GÖRTZ The emergency tokens and their consequences! But who was

it that released twenty million instead of two!

THE KING Twenty? Lord Jesus! I thought it was only ten. I have seven on my conscience since I last calculated. But who released the other ten?

GÖRTZ Who? No one knows, but now the green copper river's overflowing its banks, poisoning the whole country with verdigris!

THE KING Great God. We've become counterfeiters against our will.

GÖRTZ They're already threatening me with the scaffold!

THE KING Not as long as I live.

GÖRTZ But what's worse: the country's most popular man at the moment is the Viscount of Hesse!

THE KING The Viscount? My brother-in-law? How's he done that?

GÖRTZ Hate always results in love — love for another. And he has been promising them— — —freedom.

THE KING What a word.

The squalid figures of men and boys begin to hover about the wall at back. They emerge silently, imperceptibly, and sit on it, one, two, three, but are still not noticed by the others on stage.

GÖRTZ (*uneasily.*) There's something going on in the vicinity here which makes one uneasy, something I don't understand . . . and it smells like the clothing of the poor . . .

THE KING Do you see anything? I don't see anything. But I hear this terrible silence!— — —Wait a minute. Let me think!

Pause.

THE KING (*sits down, desperate.*) He's promising freedom?

GÖRTZ Your majesty. Don't turn me over to them! I am not guilty!

THE KING We bear a little guilt, but the intentions were honest — fairly honest *this* time. — What are you scared of?

GÖRTZ (*looks around without looking at anything in particular.*)

Pause.

The KING collects himself and rings.

*

The ADJUTANT enters.

THE KING My sword! My coat! And my hat!
ADJUTANT (*goes to get the requested items.*)

*

THE KING (*rising.*) Görtz! Now go to the residence and look for the
  Viscount of Hesse, whom I have appointed Generalissimo over the
  army.
GÖRTZ When was that?
THE KING Now. Just now.— — —Thereafter I take to the field —
  this very afternoon.
GÖRTZ And me?
THE KING You follow.
GÖRTZ Against Norway?
THE KING Against— — —the enemy— — —whoever will. . . toward
  victory . . . or else defeat's a given! (*To Swedenborg.*) Now, you've
  decided to follow us?
SWEDENBORG Now I'll follow, your majesty.
THE KING (*points at the statue of Venus.*) And not *that* goddess!— —
  — Görtz, lead us out, your way!— — —

*

The ADJUTANT enters with sword, hat and coat.
The KING puts them on; appears to look for words which he cannot
find. He pulls on his gloves.

THE KING I should have said something to Hultman . . . But it's all
  the same— — —So, we go then!

He exits through GÖRTZ's *house, followed by* GÖRTZ *and* SWEDEN-BORG.

Now the latticework gate opens, and sinister figures slip in, silently, ghostlike, curious, and they finger everything. The figures on the wall come down to join them.

Curtain.

TABLEAU V

At Fredrikstens fortress in Norway. Farthest up at the back a part of the fortress is visible. The roof resembles a great, black sarcophagus. Beneath the terrace-shaped terrain, trenches with breastworks. To the left in the foreground, at the extreme front, a simple table with two camp stools. Beside it, the king's camp bed covered with blue and gold silk beneath a tent canopy. To the right of the bed, a campfire. Alongside the bed are lit torches.

At the left in the background, another campfire with stools.

At the right in the background, a third campfire with stools.

At the right in the foreground, Secretary FEIF's table — lit by a large lantern.

It is evening. There is moonlight with racing clouds and a chilly wind.

GÖRTZ is sitting on a cannon not far from the KING.

THE KING lies clad in his greatcoat on the bed staring into the fire.

HULTMAN is attending to the kettle over the fire — with the assistance of kitchen boys.

FEIF and SWEDENBORG are sitting at FEIF's table.

In the background high- and low-ranking officers stroll about.

Supply carriers and camp-followers can be seen at the campfires.

Farthest down at right, in circular branch-basket masking, in a group, sit the MAN, the MALCONTENT and the DWARF.

SWEDENBORG (*to FEIF.*) Doesn't it seem as if everyone were waiting for something?

FEIF Yes, they're clearly planning an assault on the fortress toward morning.

SWEDENBORG That's not what I meant . . . Feif, have you seen what the roof of the fortress looks like?

FEIF This country is clearly impenetrable.

SWEDENBORG Someone is protecting it well too.

FEIF Even if we take the fortress, what's the use of that? You can't bombard mountains. And besides, half the people live at the sea!— — —

SWEDENBORG The King also seems to be waging war to keep himself occupied, while he's waiting for something . . .

FEIF And Görtz seems to expect to fly through the air. Look at how he's sitting — on the cannon. Many's the man who'd like to be the one to light the primer. — And in headquarters the Viscount and the Duke are waiting for the throne. Arvid Horn is waiting for the Viscount and freedom. Gyllenborg is waiting for the Duke and absolutism— — —What is the King waiting for?

SWEDENBORG You tell me— — —Look how he lies there staring into the fire. A great, rich life is passing . . .

FEIF Has passed — a great man!

SWEDENBORG Great man? Not a "great" man. Can you measure a man with such small words? — Are you weary, Feif?

FEIF We are all weary.

SWEDENBORG Yes, perhaps.

FEIF It's the first Sunday of Advent today. It will soon be Christmas.

SWEDENBORG And the new year! — Poor Görtz.

FEIF He's sitting there with his one eye cocked as if he were aiming a rifle— — —It *is* strange that the King, these last years, surrounded himself with one-eyed people.

SWEDENBORG Ah! No!

FEIF Yes! Frölich, Müllern, Grothusen and Görtz all see with only one eye.

SWEDENBORG That would be ridiculous, if there wasn't a hidden meaning in it.

FEIF Bah! Coincidence!

SWEDENBORG No, Feif . . . But you'd never comprehend that . . .

FEIF Dreams, Swedenborg, I never comprehend.

SWEDENBORG Hush! Great men are coming this way!— — —

FEIF (*looks around.*) Horn and Gyllenborg.

*

HORN and GYLLENBORG enter at right in the foreground.

HORN (*sees the KING.*) Is he sleeping?

GYLLENBORG No. His eyes are open, and he's looking into the fire.

HORN Gyllenborg! We are not friends. But for the sake of the fatherland we've got to stick together.

GYLLENBORG A truce, Horn. Gladly!

HORN After all, it's no great secret that our King is physically and spiritually played out — in a word, what they call — finished. And the odd thing is that nobody notices his presence anymore, or even bothers with him. I don't know if there's been talk or rumors in the camp, but it seems as though there's a silent consensus that something's got to happen here — that we've come this far, but go no farther. They're waiting for an omen, a flash of lightning from the sky, an earthquake. Yes, there are those who have been dreaming of — a shot!— — —And this has become so obvious that, without reasonable justification, at headquarters horses are already saddled and couriers ready to mount and set off.

GYLLENBORG To where?

HORN To Stockholm, of course.

He sees that he has misjudged the situation, and gives GYLLENBORG a penetrating look.

HORN Gyllenborg. Do not betray my trust!

GYLLENBORG By no means. Cross my heart! — Go on.

HORN (*carried away by his own eloquence.*) This man, who lies there now, awaiting his funeral procession — for he is dead — he was once chosen by Providence, and success followed him as long as he took the paths of justice. — But then, when eighteen years ago he wanted to forge his own paths and steer the fates of peoples and countries — then Providence took him by the ear and played blind-man's bluff with him.— — —

And now he stands — or lies — divided against himself. He has squandered eighteen years to uphold one oath: that Peter in Russia and August in Poland would be eradicated from the earth! Around these two poles his life revolved. And now: now he is negotiating family ties with the Russian one day, and friendship with Poland the next — all the while he is meddling with Norway. With Norway!— — —

And what looks like a colossal enterprise consists of this paradox: He wanted to raise a strong Poland against Russia, but then he broke up Poland and played into the hands of the Russian! Wanted one thing and accomplished the other! That's how Providence plays with those who would play with Providence.

GYLLENBORG Horn, can't you, as you are so eloquent, try to get this across to the King?

HORN (*fixes* GYLLENBORG's *glance and goes on.*) No. I don't want to speak to him. He has insulted me and I dislike associating with him.

GYLLENBORG To what do you attribute all of these misfortunes of the King and the country?

HORN Absolutism, of course.

GYLLENBORG Absolutism is not so bad, if only it falls into the right hands, eh?

HORN I don't understand . . .

GYLLENBORG (*slyly*) No? —

HORN I don't understand at all.

GYLLENBORG Try. You've got such a good intellect Horn, after all.

HORN There was someone who said to me: "No one wants to be enemies with Gyllenborg, but he's bloody friends with the devil!"

GYLLENBORG Horn — are you swearing?

HORN Yes. In the company of Gyllenborg!

GYLLENBORG In good company, a man can show his colors.

HORN I am not playing poker.

GYLLENBORG Will we be meeting in Stockholm, then?

HORN I promise you that!— — —As soon as . . . this spectacle here plays itself out.— — —What a King!

GYLLENBORG Hush!

HORN He's ashamed of old Görtz — doesn't want to talk to him. But doesn't dare let him go.

Now the stage is occasionally lit by fireballs shot from the fortress.

GYLLENBORG The shooting's going to start again soon.
HORN It's just as well.— — —He's moving now!

HORN and GYLLENBORG withdraw toward the back.

*

The KING rises from his bed. He dismisses HULTMAN with a gesture. He walks forward on the stage and gazes at the fortress. Then he approaches FEIF's table, where he sits down.

THE KING (*weary, indifferent.*) The mail!
FEIF (*gives him letters.*)
THE KING (*opens letters and looks through them; he stops at one.*) That is wretched!— — —That wild woman, whose father was executed as a confessed traitor because he'd given up his ship, has succeeded in convincing the French ambassador— — —Doesn't it sometimes seem as if lies had a patron saint? (*Pause.*) And here! Katarina Leszczynska claims I used violence against her. (*Pause.*) And the princess— — —nothing but women the whole way!— — — And it was they who hated *me* because I would not recognize their supremacy . . . It's all too much! (*Pause.*) Here we have a life-saver! This will interest Emanuel. Imagine, I get daily letters from unknown soldiers who demand money for having saved my life— — —When I die, a crowd of people will probably show up bragging that they have taken my life! (*He reads on.*) No, that is too much!— — —The story of David and Uriah, whom he sent to war— — —Uriah is supposed to be Emanuel— — —Ugh!

He rolls the correspondence up into a ball.

All of life is like this ball — a tissue of lies, mistakes, misunderstandings. Damn it to hell! — Forgive my swearing.

He tosses the ball into the nearest fire. Pause.

I cannot fight against lies and the father of all lies— — —My own sister . . . (*Pause.*) I was no angel, but I was never so satan-black as all that!— — —Let the people amuse themselves. The Sabbath was over at six o'clock.

The saraband is being played.

Who is playing my saraband?— — —Is there someone behind the masking there?— — —Come out fiddler!

*

DWARF (*steps forward.*)
THE KING Luxembourg! No! Where on earth have you been? Eh? You ran away from me after Stralsund!
DWARF (*on his knees.*) Your majesty, I didn't leave. I was dismissed . . .
THE KING Never by me! I have asked after you various times, but everything was going at such a rush. — Did you think that I threw you out?
DWARF Yes, your majesty . . .
THE KING There, you see. In the meantime you have gone and slandered me, I imagine . . . And maybe — maybe organized that mischief that was done to my house down in Lund?
DWARF Your majesty! Grace!
THE KING How miserable. — Go to the baggage train and play, you little blackguard!— — —Syllogismus perversicus: I have *not* kicked out my musical dwarf, ergo he goes and slanders me! March!
DWARF (*moves to speak.*)
THE KING No! You may not speak! March!

DWARF (*walks toward the back.*)

*

THE KING (*to SWEDENBORG.*) Such is life. What's death like then?
SWEDENBORG Nature makes no leaps.
THE KING (*looking about.*) Are they shooting from the fortress — or what is it that's buzzing around my ears?
SWEDENBORG It's most likely the night wind . . .
THE KING The lantern's glass is broken . . . They must be shooting.
SWEDENBORG We ought to have heard it.
THE KING (*rises in anxiety.*) I don't know . . . but I would like to have a glass of wine! . . . Hultman!— — —You see! Now he's gone! Just when he is needed— — —No, don't go— — —Feif!— — —Never mind.

*

The ADJUTANT enters with a dispatch.

The KING reads and sinks into himself: goes to GÖRTZ and shows him the dispatch, which he hands to him.

GÖRTZ makes a gesture of despair.

Pause.

THE KING (*to SWEDENBORG.*) Good night, Emanuel. Now I'm going to the assault.
SWEDENBORG Your majesty. For heaven's sake . . .
THE KING Good night.

He waves, walks to the rear, and out to the right.

*

SWEDENBORG (*to GÖRTZ.*) What was it?
GÖRTZ I can't say it.

He is besieged with questions.

SWEDENBORG (*goes to FEIF.*) What do you think, Feif?
FEIF Something has gone wrong again.
SWEDENBORG But what?
FEIF Look there. All he needs to do is turn his back, and everything
  falls to pieces. — Just look, baggage and men and camp followers!
  Counselors and generals!

*

SPARRE (*enters, approaching the ADJUTANT.*) Where is the King?
ADJUTANT He has gone up to the first trench!
SPARRE Lord Jesus!

He exits to the right.

*

DE LA GARDIE (*enters, approaches the ADJUTANT.*) Has the King
  gone?
ADJUTANT The King went to the first trench in order to . . .
DE LA GARDIE But they are shooting from the fortress!

He exits to the right.

*

MÖRNER (*enters.*) Where in Christ's name is the King?
ADJUTANT He is in the first trench.

A fireball from the fortress lights up the stage at the back. The KING is now visible in the trench above, waving with his yellow glove at someone below.

ADJUTANT There's the King!
MÖRNER Lord in heaven preserve us!

Exits.

*

FEIF Do you see him?
SWEDENBORG Yes! He is down on his knees, as if he were praying!
FEIF Praying? What's he after up there?
SWEDENBORG What's he after!— — —That strange man!
FEIF Have you ever understood how he's come to his fate?
SWEDENBORG No, and perhaps we'll never understand it. I have never understood the fate of any human being, let alone my own insignificant fate.
FEIF You notice that we're talking as if we were standing over a dead man?
SWEDENBORG He is dead.

A fireball lights up the stage, and goes out with an explosion. It is deathly silent on the stage, and everyone looks up toward the fortress. The MAN and the MALCONTENT are looking at GÖRTZ.

FEIF Now I have the feeling we are standing here waiting for something.
SWEDENBORG But not the assault?
FEIF No.
SWEDENBORG God's will be done.

Pause.

*

SHOUT *(from above.)* The King has been shot!
SHOUT *(from below.)* The King has been shot!

*

THE SAILOR Sweden's greatest king is dead! God save us!
THE MAN Is the crook dead?
MALCONTENT He's dead. And now I forgive him.
THE MAN To think, I really couldn't be angry at that fellah! In
  any case — he was one hell of a fellah!
SWEDENBORG God have mercy on his soul. — But where did the
  bullet come from?
FEIF *(points up at the fortress.)* Up there.
SWEDENBORG *(points heavenward.)* Up there.
FEIF Let us think that.
SWEDENBORG And if it didn't come from there, it's from there it
  should have come.

*The scene breaks up. The MAN and the MALCONTENT throw them-
selves on GÖRTZ and drag him out. Everyone rushes out in confusion. The campfires go out. Torches and lamps are carried off. It
becomes dark on the stage. But now, up in the far trench, a great
lamp is seen glowing.*

Curtain.

End.

––––––––––––––––––––

THE DANCE OF DEATH

A Drama

(1900)

CHARACTERS

EDGAR, Captain of the fort artillery
ALICE, his wife, previously an actress
KURT, the Quarantine Master

Secondary characters: Jenny, the Old Woman, the
Sentry (silent)

THE SCENE

The interior of a round granite tower in a fortress.

At back the large entrance, a pair of glass doors, through which can be seen a beach, a battery—artillery fortifications—and the sea.

On either side of the door a window with flowers and birds.

To the right of the doors an upright piano; farther downstage a sewing table and two armchairs.

To the left, center stage, a desk with a telegraph apparatus. Farther down a bric-a-brac shelf with photo portraits. Nearby a long chaise longue. At the wall a sideboard.

From the ceiling hangs a lamp. On the wall by the upright piano hang two large laurel wreaths with ribbons, one on either side of a portrait of a young woman dressed in a theatre costume.

At the door a free-standing coatrack with paraphernalia for a uniform, sabers and so on. Close by, a chiffonnier.

To the left of the doors hangs a barometer. [A porcelain stove.[1]]

It is a mild autumn afternoon. The doors stand open and out on the battery on the shoreline a SENTRY is visible. He is wearing a plumed helmet; his saber glitters now and again in the red glow of the setting sun. The sea lies dark and silent.

The CAPTAIN is sitting in the armchair to the left of the sewing table and fingers an extinguished cigar. He is dressed in worn-out fatigues and riding boots with spurs. He looks tired and disgusted.

ALICE is sitting in the armchair to the right doing nothing. She looks tired and expectant.

CAPTAIN Aren't you going to play for me?
ALICE *(indifferent, but not harsh.)* What should I play?
CAPTAIN What ever you want!

---

[1] Strindberg leaves out the stove here, which is used near end of the play.

ALICE You don't like my repertoire.

CAPTAIN And you don't like mine.

ALICE (*switches the subject.*) Do you want to keep the doors open?

CAPTAIN Whatever you want. I think it's warm.

ALICE Let them stay open, then!— — —(*Pause.*) Why aren't you smoking?

CAPTAIN I'm starting to have problems with strong tobacco.

ALICE (*almost friendly.*) Smoke milder tobacco then. It is, after all, your only pleasure, as you say!

CAPTAIN Only pleasure? What do you mean by that?

ALICE Don't ask me. I know as little about it as you!— — —Would you like a whiskey then?

CAPTAIN I'll hold off on that.— — —What's for dinner?

ALICE How should I know? Ask Kristín.

CAPTAIN Shouldn't we be having mackerel soon? It's autumn already!

ALICE Yes, it's autumn.

CAPTAIN Outside and in! But despite the cold that fall brings with it, outside and in, I'd have nothing against a grilled mackerel with a slice of lemon, along with a glass of burgundy, *blanc.*

ALICE You've certainly become eloquent!

CAPTAIN Do we have any Burgundy left in the wine cellar?

ALICE I don't think we've had a wine cellar in five years . . .

CAPTAIN You never keep stock of things. Meantime, we've *got* to supply ourselves for our silver anniversary . . .

ALICE Are you really thinking of celebrating that?

CAPTAIN Yes, of course.

ALICE It would be more natural to keep a lid on our misery. Our twenty-five years of misery . . .

CAPTAIN Alice, darling. It may have been misery, but we've had our good times now and again! And we must enjoy the short time left, before it's gone!

ALICE Will it be gone? If so, good riddance.

CAPTAIN It *will* be gone. All that'll be left is enough to wheel out on a barrow and dump in the garden plot.

ALICE And so much to-do, all for a garden plot!

CAPTAIN Yes, that's how it is. I didn't make it that way.

ALICE *So much* to-do! (*Pause.*) Did you get the mail?

CAPTAIN Yes.

ALICE Did the butcher's bill come?

CAPTAIN Yes.

ALICE How much was it?

The CAPTAIN draws some papers from his pocket and puts on his glasses, but quickly takes them off.

CAPTAIN Read it for yourself! I can't see anymore . . .

ALICE What's wrong with your eyes?

CAPTAIN I don't know!

ALICE Age.

CAPTAIN Oh, nonsense! Me?

ALICE Yes. Not me!

CAPTAIN Hm!

ALICE (*looks at the bill.*) Can you pay this?

CAPTAIN Yes. But not now.

ALICE Later, then! In a year, when you're retired with a little pension, and it's too late! Later, when your illness returns . . .

CAPTAIN Illness? I have never been sick. Just indisposed once! I'll live another twenty years!

ALICE That wasn't the Doctor's opinion.

CAPTAIN The Doctor!

ALICE Yes. Who else would have a sound opinion on an illness?

CAPTAIN I am not sick, and I've never been sick. And will not get sick either. Because my death'll come out of the blue, like an old soldier.

ALICE Speaking of the Doctor. You're aware that the Doctor is having a party tonight?

CAPTAIN (*agitated.*) Yes, so what! We're not invited, since we don't associate with the Doctor and his wife, and we don't associate with the Doctor and his wife because we do not want to, because I despise the both of them! They're trash!

ALICE That's what you say about everybody.

CAPTAIN Because everybody's trash.

ALICE Everyone except you!

CAPTAIN Yes, because I have conducted myself decently, whatever has come my way in life. That's why I'm not trash.

Pause.

ALICE Would you like to play cards?

CAPTAIN Why not.

Alice takes a deck of cards from the sewing table drawer, and begins to shuffle.

ALICE Imagine — the Doctor getting the band to play for a private affair.

CAPTAIN (*angry.*) It's because he sucks up to the Colonel in town. He sucks up to him, see? — He was able to do that.

ALICE (*deals.*) I was friends with Gerda. But she deceived me . . .

CAPTAIN They are liars, the whole pack!— — —What's trump? I can't see over there.

ALICE Put on your glasses.

CAPTAIN It doesn't help!— — —Come on!

ALICE Spades are trump.

CAPTAIN (*annoyed.*) Spades?— — —

ALICE Yes, you may be right. But the new officers' wives, in any case, have cut us out.

CAPTAIN (*deals and takes up his hand.*) So what? We never hold any parties, so it's not noticed! I can be alone . . . just as I've always been.

ALICE Me too. But the children! The children are growing up without any companionship.

CAPTAIN They'll have all they need in town!— — —That was my trick! Do you have any trumps?

ALICE I have one. That's mine!

CAPTAIN Six and eight make fifteen . . .

ALICE Fourteen. Fourteen!

CAPTAIN Six and eight give me fourteen . . . I think I've forgotten how to count too! And two makes sixteen . . . (*Yawns.*) You deal!

ALICE Are you tired?

CAPTAIN Not at all.

ALICE (*brightens.*) You can hear the music all the way over here!

Pause.

ALICE Do you think Kurt was invited?

CAPTAIN He got in this morning. So he's had time to get into his dress suit, though he had no time to visit us!

ALICE He's Quarantine Master? Will there be a quarantine station here?

CAPTAIN Yes . . .

ALICE He is my cousin, in any case. And we once bore the same surname . . .

CAPTAIN That was certainly no honor . . .

ALICE Listen, you . . . (*Sharp.*) Leave my relations in peace, and yours shall be left in peace too!

CAPTAIN All right! All right! Do you want to start up again?

ALICE Is a Quarantine Master a doctor?

CAPTAIN No. He's just a sort of civil servant, an official or a bookkeeper. And Kurt certainly never became much of anything.

ALICE He was . . . poor man . . .

CAPTAIN Who has cost me a sum . . . And when he left his wife and children, it was dishonorable behavior.

ALICE Not quite so harsh, Edgar!

CAPTAIN Yes! That's what he was!— — — Whatever he may have done in America! Yes! I can't say that I've been missing him! But he was charming as a boy and I liked to talk about things with him.

ALICE Because he was so indulgent . . .

CAPTAIN (*haughty.*) Indulgent or not, he was in any case someone you could talk to . . . Here on the island there is not *one* single person who understands what I'm talking about . . . It's a society of idiots . . .

ALICE It is strange that Kurt should come just in time for our silver anniversary . . . whether we're celebrating it or not . . .

CAPTAIN Why should it be strange? . . . Well, yes, he was the one who brought us together, or married you off, as they all said.

ALICE Well, didn't he?

CAPTAIN Yes, of course . . . It was this idea he got into his head . . . Whether it was such a good one I leave you to judge!

ALICE A frivolous inspiration . . .

CAPTAIN And we've had to sweep up the debris, not him!

ALICE Yes. Imagine if I had stayed on at the theatre! All my friends are big names now!

CAPTAIN *(gets up.)* Right you are!— — —Now I'm going to have my grog! (*Goes to the sideboard and mixes brandy and soda which he drinks standing.*) There should be a rail here to put your foot on. Then you might imagine yourself in Copenhagen at the American Bar!

ALICE We'll have a bar rail made, just so we can be reminded of Copenhagen! Those were always our best times!

CAPTAIN *(drinks deeply.)* Yes! Do you remember the *navarin aux pommes* at Nimb restaurant! Ahhh—mmm!

ALICE No. But I remember the concerts at Tivoli!

CAPTAIN You have such cultured tastes.

ALICE It ought to make you happy, to have a wife with taste.

CAPTAIN Actually, it does . . .

ALICE Now and again, when you need to show her off.

CAPTAIN They must be dancing down at the Doctor's . . . I hear bass tubas playing three-four time — Boom — boomboom!

ALICE I hear the melody to the "Alcazar Waltz." Yes — the last time I danced a waltz — wasn't just yesterday . . .

CAPTAIN Think you'd still be able to handle it?

ALICE Still?

CAPTAIN Ye-es? Aren't you past your dancing days — you like me?

ALICE I am, after all, ten years younger than you!

CAPTAIN Then we are equally old, since it's said the wife should be ten years younger.

ALICE For shame! You're an old codger, but I am in my peak years!

CAPTAIN Oh yes, quite true. You can certainly be charming — to other people — when you are so moved!
ALICE Shall we light the lamp now?
CAPTAIN If you like.
ALICE Ring then!

The CAPTAIN goes slowly to the desk and rings.

*

JENNY enters from the right.

CAPTAIN Jenny, would you be so kind as to light the lamp.
ALICE (*sharply.*) Light that ceiling lamp!
JENNY Yes, Your Ladyship!

She lights the ceiling lamp, while the CAPTAIN watches her.

ALICE (*curtly.*) Have you wiped the glass thoroughly?
JENNY Yes. Somewhat.
ALICE What kind of answer is that!
CAPTAIN Now . . . now . . .
ALICE (*to JENNY.*) Get out! I'll light the lamp myself! I think that's best!
JENNY I think so too.

She starts to go.

ALICE (*rises.*) Get out!
JENNY (*stops.*) I wonder what you'd say if I did get out, Ma'am.
ALICE (*is silent.*)

JENNY goes.

*

The CAPTAIN *goes up and lights the lamp.*

ALICE (*uneasy.*) Do you think she'll leave?

CAPTAIN It wouldn't surprise me. But then we'd be in a jam . . .

ALICE It's your fault, because you spoil them!

CAPTAIN Oohh no! You can hear how they are always respectful of me.

ALICE Because you crawl for them! You crawl, for that matter, before all your subordinates. Because you're a despot with a slavish soul!

CAPTAIN Really!

ALICE Yes, you crawl before your crew and your petty officers, but you can't be comfortable around your peers and your superiors.

CAPTAIN Ugh!

ALICE That's what all tyrants do!— — —Do you think she'll leave?

CAPTAIN Yes. If you don't go out and say a kind word to her.

ALICE Me?

CAPTAIN If I do, you'll say that I'm flirting with the maids.

ALICE Imagine, if she leaves! Then I'll have to do all the chores like the last time, and ruin my hands.

CAPTAIN That's not the worst of it. If Jenny moves out, then Kristín will move out. And after that we'll get no more servants to come here to the island! The pilot on the steamer scares away all the new people who come looking for jobs . . . And if he forgets to, then my gunners do it.

ALICE Yes, your gunners, who I'm supposed to serve in my kitchen. And you don't dare show them out . . .

CAPTAIN No, because, come sign-up time for the next tour of duty, they'll leave too— — —and then we'll have to close up the cannon shop here.

ALICE That would ruin us!

CAPTAIN That's why the officer corps has plans to make a request to the Crown for a special expenses fund . . .

ALICE For whom?

CAPTAIN For the gunners.

ALICE (*laughs.*) You've got to be crazy!

CAPTAIN Yes. Laugh a little for me. I could use it.

ALICE Soon I'll have forgotten how to laugh . . .

CAPTAIN (*lights his cigar.*) That's something we should never forget
. . . It's so tedious as things are.

ALICE It's no fun!— — —Do you want to play some more?

CAPTAIN No, I'm tired of it.

Pause.

ALICE Do you know, it annoys me that my own cousin, the new
Quarantine Master, goes first to visit people who are no friends
of ours.

CAPTAIN Well, it's not worth getting bothered about.

ALICE Did you see in the paper, in the list of new arrivals, that he
was listed as a *rentier*? He must have come into some money
then!

CAPTAIN *Rentier!* Ohhhh? A wealthy relative. That's actually the
first one in this family.

ALICE In your family, yes. But in mine we've had many who were
wealthy.

CAPTAIN If he has come into money, he's probably on his high horse.
But I will keep him in check. And he'll never get a peek at the
cards in my hand.

The telegraph begins tapping.

ALICE Who is it?

CAPTAIN (*stands still.*) Hush a minute, please!

ALICE Well, go closer to it.

CAPTAIN I hear. I can hear what they're saying. — It's the children!

*He walks over to the apparatus and taps out an answer. Then the
telegraph continues for a moment, and then the CAPTAIN answers.*

ALICE We-elll?

CAPTAIN Wait a minute!— — —(*He taps out the signal to terminate the message.*)— — —It was the children! They're at artillery head-quarters in town. Judith is ill again, and she's staying home from school.

ALICE Again? What else?

CAPTAIN Money, of course.

ALICE Why should Judith be hurrying so much? It would suffice if she took the exam next year.

CAPTAIN Tell her that! You'll see if it helps.

ALICE You should tell her.

CAPTAIN How many times haven't I told her! But you know very well that children will do as they please.

ALICE Here in this house, at least!— — —

CAPTAIN (*yawns.*)

ALICE You yawn in your wife's face?

CAPTAIN What am I supposed to do?— — —Don't you notice that every single day we talk about the same things? When you just gave your good old reply: "Here in this house, at least," I should have responded with my old: "It's not *my* house alone." But as I have already answered that way five hundred times, I yawn instead. My yawn could mean, then, that I'm not up to answering. Or: "You are right, my angel." Or: "Let's stop right there."

ALICE You are truly engaging tonight.

CAPTAIN Isn't it about mealtime?

ALICE Did you know that the Doctor ordered the dinner from the Grand Hotel in town?

CAPTAIN No! Then they have hazel-hens! Ahhh-mm! You know, the hazel-hen is the finest fowl, but it's barbarism to fry it in pork fat! . . .

ALICE Ugh! Are we going to talk about food?

CAPTAIN About wines, then? I wonder what those barbarians are drinking with their hazel-hens?

ALICE Shall I play something for you?

CAPTAIN (*sits at the desk.*) The last recourse! Yes, if you'll leave out your funeral marches and laments— — —which seem to have some intent behind them. And I'm always finding a subtext. "Hear how unhappy I am!" Meow! Meow! "Hear what an awful husband I have." Badum, badum, badum! "Oh, if he'd only die soon." Drum rolls of joy. Fanfares! The last bars of the "Alcazar Waltz"! The "Champagne Trot"! Apropos of champagne, there are definitely two bottles left. Shall we bring them up and pretend like we have guests?

ALICE No, we won't, because they're mine. I got them myself.

CAPTAIN Always so economical.

ALICE And you are always stingy, at least toward your wife.

CAPTAIN Then I don't know what I shall come up with! — Shall I dance for you?

ALICE No thanks. Your dancing days are past.

CAPTAIN You should get a female companion to live in the house.

ALICE Thanks! — You should have a male companion in the house!

CAPTAIN Thanks! It was tried. And to everyone's dissatisfaction. But there was something interesting in the experiment. As soon as an outsider came into the house we became so happy— — — at the beginning . . .

ALICE But later!

CAPTAIN Yes, don't let's talk about it!

There's a knocking on the door, left.

*

ALICE Who can it be so late?

CAPTAIN Jenny doesn't usually knock.

ALICE Go and open the door. And don't yell "Come in!" as if we were in some kind of workshop!

CAPTAIN (*goes toward the door, left.*) You don't like workshops!

The knocking is repeated.

ALICE Will you open the door!

The CAPTAIN *opens the door, and a calling card is handed to him.*

CAPTAIN It's Kristín! — Has Jenny left! (*After a reply, which is not audible, he turns to Alice.*) — Jenny has left!
ALICE So now I'm a maid again!
CAPTAIN And I'm the hired hand.
ALICE Couldn't we take one of your men to help in the kitchen?
CAPTAIN Not these days.
ALICE But it couldn't be Jenny who sent her calling card?
CAPTAIN (*examines the card with his glasses, and hands it to* ALICE.) Read it, I can't.
ALICE (*reads the card.*) Kurt. It's Kurt! Go out and invite him in!
CAPTAIN (*goes out to the left.*) Kurt! Well, good to see you!

*

ALICE arranges her hair, and appears to come to life.

*

CAPTAIN (*enters from the left with* KURT.) Look, here he is! The traitor! Welcome, old boy! Give us a hug!
ALICE (*going to* KURT.) Welcome to my house, Kurt!
KURT Thank you.— — —It's been a long time since we saw one another.
CAPTAIN What's it been? Fifteen years? And we've all grown old . . .
ALICE Oh! Kurt is just like he was, I'd say!
CAPTAIN Sit down! Sit down! — And first of all: your schedule. Have you any plans for this evening?
KURT I'm invited to the Doctor's. But I've made no commitment.

ALICE Then stay with your relatives!

KURT That would seem to be the natural thing to do. But the Doctor is like my supervisor, and it may cause me some trouble later.

CAPTAIN What kind of talk is that! I've never been afraid of my supervisors . . .

KURT Afraid or not, it'll cause some trouble in any case.

CAPTAIN Here on this island it's me who's boss! Stick close to me and no one will mess with you.

ALICE Hush, now Edgar. (*Takes KURT's hand.*) Never mind bosses and supervisors. You stay with us. That will be seen as only right and proper.

KURT So be it then! — Particularly since I feel so welcome here.

CAPTAIN Why shouldn't you be welcome— — —There's no damage done . . .

KURT (*cannot hide a certain embarrassment.*)

CAPTAIN Why would there be! You were a bit reckless, but you were young. And I've forgotten all that. I hold no grudges!

ALICE (*is upset.*)

All three sit at the sewing table.

ALICE Now you've traveled all round the world?

KURT Yes, and now I've ended up here, with you . . .

CAPTAIN The two you brought together twenty-five years ago.

KURT It wasn't that way at all, but no matter. It's nice to see you've stuck together twenty-five years.

CAPTAIN Yes, we drag along. From time to time it has been only so-so, but as you said, we've stuck together. And Alice has wanted for nothing — our cup has been full, and the money came streaming in. Perhaps you don't know that I'm a famous writer, an author of textbooks . . .

KURT Yes, I remember when we went our ways in the world that you had published a rifle manual that did well. Is it still used in the military schools?

CAPTAIN It's still around, and it's still number one, even though they tried to push it aside for an inferior book . . . which in fact they read now. But it's completely worthless!

A painful silence.

KURT You've travelled abroad, I understand!

ALICE Yes, we've been in Copenhagen — five times, I think!

CAPTAIN Yes! You see, when I took Alice from the theatre . . .

ALICE You *took* me?

CAPTAIN Yes, I took you, like one takes a wife . . .

ALICE So bold you are!

CAPTAIN But since I later had to swallow the guilt for hindering her brilliant career . . . hm! . . . to make it up I had to promise to take my wife to Copenhagen . . . And I have kept it — faithfully! Five times we've been there. Five! (*Holds up the fingers of his left hand.*)— — —Have *you* been in Copenhagen?

KURT (*smiles.*) No. For the most part, I've been in America.

CAPTAIN America? Isn't that an awful rowdy place?

KURT (*gloomily.*) Well, it's not Copenhagen.

ALICE Have you . . . heard anything . . . from your children?

KURT No!

ALICE My dear, forgive me, but it was surely thoughtless to leave them like that . . .

KURT I didn't leave them. It was the court that gave custody to their mother— — —

CAPTAIN We are not going to discuss that now! I think now that it was good for you to get away from that whole mess!

KURT (*to ALICE.*) How are your children?

ALICE Well, thank you. They're going to school in the city. They'll soon be adults.

CAPTAIN Yes, they're clever kids, and the boy has a brilliant head on his shoulders! Brilliant! He'll make it to the General Staff . . .

ALICE If they'll have him.

CAPTAIN Him? He's material for Defense Minister!

KURT To change the subject— — —There's going to be a quarantine station here— — —plague, cholera, and that sort of thing. And the Doctor's going to be my superior, as you know . . . What sort of guy is the Doctor?

CAPTAIN Guy? He's no sort of guy! He's an ignorant bastard.

KURT (*to ALICE.*) That's unpleasant news for me.

ALICE It's not as dangerous as Edgar's saying. But I can't deny that I find him unappealing . . .

CAPTAIN He's a bastard! And so are the others too: the customs officer, the postmaster, the telephone operator, the pharmacist, the pilot— — —what's he called — pilot station master — bastards the whole bunch, and therefore I don't associate with them!

KURT Are you at odds with everybody?

CAPTAIN Everybody!

ALICE Yes, it's the truth — that we *can't* associate with these people!

CAPTAIN It's as if all the country's tyrants have been sent to be interned on this island.

ALICE (*ironic.*) Yes, right!

CAPTAIN (*in a good humor.*) Hm! Was there any reference to me in that? I'm no tyrant, at least not in my home.

ALICE You take care!

CAPTAIN (*to KURT.*) Don't believe a word she says. I am a very decent married man, and this old girl is the best wife in the world!

ALICE Kurt, would you like a drink?

KURT Thank you, not now.

CAPTAIN Have you become . . .

KURT Only in moderation.

CAPTAIN . . . an *American*?

KURT Yes!

CAPTAIN I say be immoderate, or don't do it at all! A man should stick up for his pleasures!

KURT To return to your neighbors here on the island. My position will put me in contact with everyone . . . And it'll certainly be hard sailing — because whether or not you want to avoid being drawn into other people's intrigues, you get drawn in anyway.

ALICE Go on then, go. You can always come back here to us. Be cause here you have your true friends.

KURT Isn't it awful to sit here alone, surrounded by enemies this way?

ALICE It's not pleasant.

CAPTAIN It's not so awful. All I've had is enemies all my life, and they have helped prod me on rather than hurting me. And the day I die I'll be able to say: I owe nothing to anybody and I've taken no gifts. Every bit I own, I've had to fight for as mine.

ALICE Yes, Edgar's path has not been strewn with roses . . .

CAPTAIN A path over thorns and stones and flint . . . by relying on my own strength. You know what I'm talking about!

KURT (*simply.*) Yes. I learned how inadequate that was ten years ago.

CAPTAIN Then you are a poor slob!

ALICE (*to the CAPTAIN.*) Edgar!

CAPTAIN Yes, he's a poor slob if he can't be master through his own strength! It's certainly true that when the machine shuts down, then it comes down to a wheelbarrow dumping you in the garden plot. But as long as the machine holds together, then it's kick and thrash with your hands and feet for all your worth! That's my philosophy!

KURT (*smiles.*) You are amusing to listen to . . .

CAPTAIN But you don't think I'm right?

KURT No, I don't.

CAPTAIN Well, I am right anyway.

The wind has begun to blow during the last scene, and now one of the doors at back slams.

CAPTAIN (*rises.*) A storm's rising. I could feel it.

He goes to close the doors, and taps on the barometer.

ALICE (*to KURT.*) You'll be staying for dinner?

KURT Yes, thanks.

ALICE But it will be very simple, because our housemaid's left us!

KURT That's fine with me.

ALICE Dear Kurt. You are so easygoing.

*

CAPTAIN (*at the barometer.*) If you could see how the barometer's falling! I could feel it coming.

ALICE (*to KURT, secretive.*) He is nervous!

CAPTAIN It should be dinnertime soon!

ALICE (*gets up.*) I shall just run in and put something together. Sit down, you two, and talk philosophy. (*Secretly to KURT.*) But don't contradict him, it'll put him in a bad humor. And don't ask why he never became a major!

KURT (*nods agreement.*)

ALICE goes out, right.
The CAPTAIN sits at the sewing table with KURT.

CAPTAIN Make us something good, old girl.

ALICE Give me money, and you'll have it.

CAPTAIN Always money.

ALICE goes.

*

CAPTAIN (*to KURT.*) Money, money, money! The whole day I run about with the purse at the ready, till in the end I feel like I'm an open purse! Know what I mean?

KURT Oh yes! The only difference in my case is I thought I was a wallet!

CAPTAIN Haha! Well, so you've had to smoke the same stuff I have! Those women. Haha! And you picked out a good one!

KURT (*patiently.*) Let's leave that. It's over and buried.

CAPTAIN You had a real jewel!— — —But at least I've had — despite everything — had a good woman. Because she is solid, despite everything.

KURT (*smiles good-naturedly.*) Despite everything!

CAPTAIN Don't laugh, you.

KURT (*as before.*) Despite everything!

CAPTAIN Yes, she has been a loyal wife . . . A very fine mother, extraordinary . . . But — (*he looks toward the doors at right*) — she has a hellish temper. You know, there've been times when I've cursed you for saddling me with her!

KURT (*good-natured.*) But I didn't! Listen, my dear man . . .

CAPTAIN Tsk, tsk, tsk! You talk rubbish and forget everything that's unpleasant to remember. Don't take it the wrong way. I am used to commanding and blustering, you see. But you know me, and won't be angry!

KURT Not at all! But I didn't get you a wife. On the contrary!

CAPTAIN (*without allowing a break in his flow.*) Don't you think life is strange in any case?

KURT It certainly is that.

CAPTAIN And getting old — it's not funny, but it's interesting. Well, I'm not old, but I'm beginning to feel age. All the people you know die off, and you're left so alone!

KURT A man who has a wife to grow old with is lucky.

CAPTAIN Lucky? Yes, it's a lucky thing, although the children also leave you. So you should not have left yours!

KURT But, I didn't. They were taken from me . . .

CAPTAIN Now, you shouldn't be angry when I tell you . . .

KURT But it just wasn't so . . .

CAPTAIN Whatever happened, in any case, it's forgotten. But you're alone.

KURT One gets used to everything, my friend.

CAPTAIN Can one . . . can one get used to . . . being absolutely alone as well?

KURT Here I am — living proof!

CAPTAIN What have you been doing these fifteen years?

KURT What a question! These fifteen years!

CAPTAIN It's said you've come into money! And are rich!

KURT Rich, I am not . . .

CAPTAIN I've no intention of borrowing . . .

KURT If you did, I'm prepared to . . .

CAPTAIN Thanks very much. But I have a debit-and-credit account to pay my debts. You see — (*looks toward the doors, right*) — here in this house nothing can be lacking. And the day I run out of money . . . she'd go her way!

KURT Oh, no.

CAPTAIN No? I *know* she would. — Can you believe it — she's always taking special note of the times I'm broke, simply to have the pleasure of proving to me that I cannot support my own family.

KURT But I recall you saying you had a large income.

CAPTAIN Of course I have a large income— — —but it does not suffice.

KURT Then it's not large, in the usual sense . . .

CAPTAIN Life is strange, and so are we!

The telegraph begins tapping.

KURT What's that?

CAPTAIN It's just a time signal.

KURT Don't you have a telephone?

CAPTAIN Yes, in the kitchen. But we use the telegraph since the telephone girls repeat everything we say.

KURT You must have a dreadful social life out here at sea.

CAPTAIN Yes, it's absolutely horrid! All of life is horrid! And you who believe in an afterlife, do you think there'll be peace when it's all over?

KURT There'll be strife and storms there too.

CAPTAIN There too — if there *is* any "there." Better that it be annihilation!

KURT Do you know if annihilation can be painless?

CAPTAIN When I die, it'll be out of the blue, and painless!

KURT Really? Do you know that?

CAPTAIN Yes, I know it!

KURT You don't appear to be content with your existence.

CAPTAIN (*sighs.*) Content? The day I die, I'll be content!

KURT (*gets up.*) You don't know that!— — —But tell me, what is going on in this house? What's happening here? The wallpaper smells of poison, and you feel sick the moment you walk in here! I'd prefer to go my way, if I hadn't promised Alice to stay. There are bodies under the floor. And here there is so much hate that it is hard to breathe.

CAPTAIN (*collapses in his chair and stares straight ahead.*)

KURT What's wrong with you? Edgar!

CAPTAIN (*motionless.*)

KURT (*slaps the CAPTAIN on the shoulders.*) Edgar!

CAPTAIN (*comes to.*) Did you say something? (*He looks around.*) I thought it was . . . Alice! . . . Ah! It's you! — Listen . . . (*He goes blank again.*)

KURT This is horrible! (*He crosses to the door, right, and opens it.*) Alice!

*

ALICE enters with a kitchen apron on.

ALICE What is it?

KURT I don't know! Look at him!

ALICE (*calmly.*) He sometimes loses his faculties like this!— — —I can play. Then he'll wake up.

KURT No. Don't do that. Don't!— — —Let me try!— — —Can he hear? Can he see?

ALICE Right now he can't hear or see.

KURT And you say this so calmly! . . . Alice, what is going on in this house!

ALICE Ask that man!

KURT That man?— — —That's your husband!

ALICE To me he's a strange man. Just as strange as he was twenty years ago! I know nothing about this man . . . other than . . .

KURT Stop! He can hear you!

ALICE Now he hears nothing!

A bugle call outside.
The CAPTAIN jumps up, takes his saber and uniform cap.

CAPTAIN Excuse me! I've just got to inspect the guard!

He goes out through the doors at back.

*

KURT Is he sick?

ALICE I don't know!

KURT Has he lost his mind?

ALICE I don't know!

KURT Does he drink?

ALICE He brags about it, more than actually drinking.

KURT Sit down and tell me. But calmly and truthfully.

ALICE (*sits.*) What shall I say? — That I have sat imprisoned in this tower for ages, guarded by a man whom I've always hated, and now hate so infinitely that the day he died I'd laugh out loud!

KURT Why haven't you separated?

ALICE Good question! We separated when we were engaged twice. Since then we've tried to separate every passing day . . . But we are welded together and couldn't come loose! Once we were separated — in the same house — for five years! Now it's only death that can separate us. We know that, and so we wait for it like a liberator!

KURT Why are you so alone?

ALICE Because he isolates me. First he "cleansed" all my brothers and sisters from the house — he himself calls it "cleansing" — and after that all my friends and anybody else . . .

KURT But *his* relatives? Have you cleansed them out?

ALICE Yes. Because they were trying to deprive me of my life, after they'd taken my honor and my good name. — Finally I had to maintain contact with the world and people through that telegraph there — since the telephone girls monitored our calls— —I have taught myself to use the telegraph, and he knows nothing about it. You mustn't mention it, because then he'd kill me.

KURT This is horrible! Horrible!— — —But why does he blame me for your marriage? Let me tell you now how it was!— — — Edgar was my friend when I was young! When he got a look at you, he fell in love immediately. He came to me and asked me to be go-between. My first response was: no! And — my good Alice, I knew your tyrannical and harsh mind-set. So I warned him— — —and when he kept after me, I sent him to find your brother to propose for him.

ALICE I believe what you say. But he's been fooling himself all these years, so that now you'll never get him to think it was any different.

KURT So let him blame me then, if it makes it easier for him . . .

ALICE That's really not right . . .

KURT I am used to it . . . But the thing that gets my goat is his unjust accusation that I deserted my children . . .

ALICE That's how he is. He says what he thinks, and then he believes it. But he seems to like you, mostly because you don't contradict him . . . Now try not to get tired of us . . . I think that you came at a fortunate time for us. I take it, clearly, as a good omen . . . Kurt! You mustn't get tired of us, because we are the unhappiest people in the whole world! (*She cries.*)

KURT I've seen *one* marriage up close . . . and that was horrifying. But this is almost worse!

ALICE Do you think so?

KURT Yes.

ALICE Whose fault is that?

KURT Alice! The moment you cease asking whose fault everything is, you will find relief. Try to accept it as a fact, as a test which you must go through . . .

ALICE I can't do that! It's all too much! (*She gets up.*) There's no way out!

KURT You poor people! . . . Do you know why you hate each other?

ALICE No! It's the most irrational hate, there's no reason for it, there's no purpose, and there's also no end to it. And do you have any idea why he fears death the most? He's afraid I'll remarry.

KURT Then he loves you!

ALICE Possibly. But that doesn't prevent him from hating me!

KURT (*as if to himself.*) It's called love-hate, and it's from Hell!— — — Does he like you to play for him?

ALICE Yes, but only ugly tunes . . . For example that ghastly "March of the Boyars." When he listens to that, it's like a case of possession, and he wants to dance.

KURT Does he dance?

ALICE Yes, at times he's so funny.

KURT One thing . . . Forgive me for asking. Where are the children?

ALICE You might not know that two are dead?

KURT You've been through that too?

ALICE What haven't I been through?

KURT But the two others?

ALICE In the city. They couldn't stay at home! Because he was turning them against me . . .

KURT And you turned them against him!

ALICE Yes, of course. And so it came to taking sides, politicking and bribes . . . And so that it would not destroy the children, we sent them off. The thing which should have been the bond between us became the wedge. What should have been a blessing on our home became a curse . . . Yes, I believe our line is cursed!

KURT After the Fall, yes. That's how it is!

ALICE (*with a poison look and cutting voice.*) Which Fall?

KURT The first man and woman.

ALICE Ah. I thought you meant something else!

Embarrassed silence.

ALICE (*wringing her hands.*) Kurt! My cousin, my childhood friend!
    I haven't always been so good to you as I should. But now I've
    been punished, and you've had your revenge.
KURT Not revenge! There's no talk of revenge here. Hush!
ALICE Do you remember one Sunday, when you were engaged. I
    had invited you to lunch! —
KURT Hush!
ALICE I've got to talk. I need someone to understand!— — —Well
    . . . when you arrived, we were gone, and you had to turn back.
KURT You yourselves were called away. We need not discuss that!
ALICE Kurt! When today, just now, I invited you to dinner . . . I
    thought there was something in the cupboard! (*She hides her face
    in her hands.*) And there is nothing there, not even a bit of
    bread!— — —

She cries.

KURT Alice, you poor thing.
ALICE But when *he* gets here, and wants to eat, and there's nothing
    here . . . then he'll be angry. You have never seen him angry!—
    — —Oh God, this humiliation!
KURT Will you let me go out and take care of this?
ALICE There's no place to get anything here on the island!
KURT Not for my sake, but for his and yours . . . Let me think up
    something . . . something . . . We've got to make light of the mat-
    ter, joke about it . . . I'll propose that we have a drink, and I'll
    think of something while we buy time . . . Get him in a good
    humor. Play something for him—whatever the hell he wants. . .
    Sit down at the piano and be ready!
ALICE Look at my hands, as if they were hands to play music! I
    have to scour the brass and dry the glasses, make the fire and
    clean . . .
KURT But you have two servants!
ALICE That's what we have to say, because he's an officer . . . But

the servants come and go, so at times . . . most of the time, we
have none at all!— — —How am I going to get out of this . . .
this supper thing! Oh, if only the house would catch fire . . .

KURT Hush, Alice! Hush!

ALICE If only the sea would rise and sweep us away!

KURT No, no, no. I can't listen to you!

ALICE What's he going to say! What's he going to say!— — —Don't
go Kurt. Don't leave me!

KURT No, my poor friend . . . I *will not* go! . . .

ALICE Yes, but after you leave . . .

KURT Has he struck you?

ALICE Me? Oh no, he knows that I would leave if he did. One
must retain some pride.

Audible outside: "Halt! Wer da? *– Pass, sir!"*

KURT *(gets up.)* Is it him?

ALICE *(frightened.)* Yes, it's him!

Pause.

KURT What in the world are we going to do?

ALICE I don't know. I don't know!

*

The CAPTAIN *enters from the back doors.*

CAPTAIN *(upbeat.)* That's it. Now I'm free!— — —Well, now she's
been able to make her complaints! Isn't she unfortunate, eh?

KURT How is the weather out there?

CAPTAIN It's almost a storm.— — —*(Sets one of the doors ajar.
Jokingly:)* Sir Bluebeard with the maiden in the tower. And out
there paces the sentry with his saber drawn to guard the beautiful

maiden . . . And then come the brothers. But the guard goes for them. Look at it! One two! He's a fine guard! Look at him! Melitám-tamtá melitá-lialáy! Let's have the sword dance! Kurt has got to see that!

KURT No. Let's have the "March of the Boyars" instead.

CAPTAIN Do *you* know that one?— — —Alice, in your apron, come and play! Come on, I say!

ALICE goes reluctantly to the piano.
The CAPTAIN pinches her arm.

CAPTAIN You've been slandering me!

ALICE Me!

KURT turns away.
ALICE plays the "March of the Boyars."

The CAPTAIN performs some sort of Hungarian dance, behind the desk: clicking and jangling his spurs. Then he sinks to the floor, unseen by KURT and ALICE, and the latter plays the piece to its end.

ALICE (*without turning.*) Shall we take it one more time?

A silence.

ALICE turns and sees the CAPTAIN lying senseless, who's been hidden from view behind the desk.

ALICE Lord Jesus!

She remains standing with her arms over her chest, giving out a sigh as if of thankfulness and relief.
KURT turns around, and hurries over to the CAPTAIN.

KURT What is it? What is it?

ALICE (*in a high state of tension.*) Is he dead?

KURT I don't know! Help me!

ALICE (*stands in place.*) I can't touch him . . . Is he dead?

KURT No! He's alive!

ALICE (*sighs.*)

KURT helps the CAPTAIN *up and places him in a chair.*

*

CAPTAIN What is it?

A silence.

What is it?

KURT Well, you fell down.

CAPTAIN Did anything happen?

KURT You fell on the floor. How are you now?

CAPTAIN Me? There's nothing wrong with me! What are you standing there gaping at?

KURT You are sick.

CAPTAIN What kind of talk is that? Play, now, Alice . . . Oh! Now it's coming back . . . (*He holds his head.*)

ALICE You can see that you are sick!

CAPTAIN Stop yelling! It's just a dizzy spell.

KURT We've got to get a Doctor. — I'll go use the telephone! . . .

CAPTAIN I don't want any doctor!

KURT You need one. We'll have to call him for our sake. Because otherwise we're responsible!

CAPTAIN I'll shove him out if he comes in here! . . . I'll shoot him down!— — —Oh! It's coming on again! (*Clutches his head.*)

KURT (*goes to the door, right.*) Now I'm going to telephone!

He exits.

*

ALICE takes off her apron.

CAPTAIN Will you get me a glass of water!
ALICE I suppose I'll have to.

Gives him a glass of water.

CAPTAIN How kind of you!
ALICE Are you sick?
CAPTAIN Forgive me for not being in perfect health.
ALICE Will you take care of yourself, then?
CAPTAIN Well, you don't seem to want to.
ALICE That you can be sure!
CAPTAIN The time has come, that you've waited for so long.
ALICE Yes, and which you thought would never come!
CAPTAIN Don't be angry with me!

*

KURT enters from the right.

KURT What a miserable . . .
ALICE What did he say?
KURT He clicked off, without saying a word.
ALICE (*to the* CAPTAIN.) There you have the consequences of your
  boundless arrogance.
CAPTAIN I think I'm getting worse!— — —Try to get a doctor from
  town!
ALICE (*goes to the telegraph.*) I'll have to wire them then.
CAPTAIN (*half standing, amazed.*) Can — you — use — the tele-
  graph?
ALICE (*sending.*) Yes, I can!

CAPTAIN Really!— — —Go on then!— — —She's so full of deceit! (*To KURT.*) Come and sit by me.

KURT sits beside the CAPTAIN.

CAPTAIN Hold onto my hand! I am sitting and still I am falling. Can you figure that? Descending, somehow. It's strange.
KURT Have you had these attacks before?
CAPTAIN Never!— — —
KURT While we're waiting for an answer from town, I'll go to the Doctor's place and talk to him. Has he treated you before?
CAPTAIN That he has!
KURT Then he knows your condition!— — —

He heads out to the left.

ALICE The answer will come back in a little while. It's kind of you, Kurt. But come back soon!
KURT As soon as I can!

He goes.

*

CAPTAIN He's kind, Kurt. And so changed.
ALICE Yes, and for the better. But I'm sorry for him — that he should be getting mixed up in our misery right now.
CAPTAIN And it's lucky for us!— — —I wonder how things are going for him, actually. Did you notice that he will not talk about his own situation?
ALICE I noticed. But I don't think anyone asked him, either.
CAPTAIN Just think: his life!— — —and ours! I wonder if all people's lives are this way?
ALICE Maybe, though they don't talk about it, the way we do.

CAPTAIN Sometimes I've thought that misery loves company: and that those who are happy shun unhappiness! That's why we never see anything but misery!

ALICE Have you known any happy people?

CAPTAIN Let me think! . . . No! . . . Yes . . . The Ekmarks.

ALICE What are you saying! She had that operation last year . . .

CAPTAIN That's right! Well then, I don't know . . . Yes, the von Kraffts.

ALICE Yes, the whole family lived in an idyll: well-off, well-respected, lovely children, good marriages, for almost fifty years. Then the cousin came along and committed a crime, with a jail sentence and all the rest. And so that was the end of their peace. The family name was smeared in the newspapers . . . The "Krafft Murder" made it impossible for that previously esteemed family to show their faces in public. The children had to be removed from school— — —Oh God!

CAPTAIN I wonder what illness I've got?

ALICE What do you think?

CAPTAIN The heart. Or the head! It's as if my soul wanted to fly out, and disperse like a cloud of smoke.

ALICE Do you have an appetite?

CAPTAIN Yes. How's supper coming?

ALICE (*paces uneasily.*) I'll ask Jenny!

CAPTAIN She has left!

ALICE Yes, yes, yes!

CAPTAIN Ring for Kristín, so I can have some fresh water!

ALICE (*rings.*) Imagine . . .

She rings again.

ALICE She doesn't hear!

CAPTAIN Go out and look . . . What if she's gone too!

ALICE (*goes and opens the door, left.*) What's this? Her trunk is standing in the corridor — packed!

CAPTAIN Then she's gone!

ALICE This is hell! . . .

She breaks out in tears, falls to her knees and puts her head on a chair, sobbing.

CAPTAIN And everything at once! . . . And then Kurt comes along to witness how we've botched everything! If there is any other humiliation left, now's the time for it. Now, right now!

ALICE Oh — you know what I suspect! Kurt went, and he's not coming back again.

CAPTAIN That I can believe of him.

ALICE Yes, we are cursed . . .

CAPTAIN What do you mean by that?

ALICE Don't you see how they all shun us?

CAPTAIN Damn them all!

The telegraph begins tapping.

CAPTAIN There's the reply! Quiet, I'm listening!— — —Nobody has the time! Excuses!— — —Pack of scoundrels!

ALICE That's what you get for damning your doctors . . . and neglecting to pay them!

CAPTAIN That's not so.

ALICE Even when you could, you wouldn't pay their fees, because you despised their work, just as you've despised my work and everybody else's work!— — —They will not come! And the telephone is cut off, because you didn't think it was worth anything either! Nothing is worth anything anymore but your rifles and cannons.

CAPTAIN Don't stand there blabbing . . .

ALICE Our acts come back to us!

CAPTAIN Bloody superstition . . . That's the sort of thing you hear from the old hags.

ALICE You'll soon see!— — —Do you know that we owe Kristín six months wages?

CAPTAIN Yes, it matches the amount she has stolen!

ALICE But I, meanwhile, have had to borrow cash from her!

CAPTAIN I believe you would!

ALICE You are so ungrateful! You know that I borrowed for the children's trip to town.

CAPTAIN Kurt sure came back to us — in fine fashion. Scoundrel. Him too! And a coward! He didn't dare say he'd had enough, and that it was more pleasant at the Doctor's ball. Seems he expected to get a poor supper from us!— — —The wretch is very much himself!

*

KURT enters quickly from the left.

KURT Well, my dear Edgar! Here's the way it is!— — —The Doctor knows your heart by memory . . .

CAPTAIN Heart?

KURT Yes, you've long had a calcified heart . . .

CAPTAIN Petrified heart!

KURT And . . .

CAPTAIN Is it serious?

KURT Yes. That is to say . . .

CAPTAIN It is serious!

KURT Yes.

CAPTAIN Fatal?

KURT You've got to take a great amount of care. First of all: the cigars have got to go!

CAPTAIN (*throws away his cigar.*)

KURT And then: The whiskey's got to go!— — —And then: to bed!

CAPTAIN (*frightened.*) No, *that* I will not do! Not to bed! Then it's all over! Then you never get out of bed again. I'll spend the night on the sofa. What else did he say?

KURT He was very friendly, and will come as soon as you call him!

CAPTAIN He was friendly, was he? That hypocrite. I don't want to see him!— — —May I eat, then?

KURT Not tonight! And for the next few days, only milk.

CAPTAIN Milk! I can't stand the stuff!
KURT You'll have to learn to like it.
CAPTAIN No, I'm too old to learn!— — —(*Holds his head.*) Ah!
There it goes again!

He sits still and stares into space.

ALICE What did the Doctor say?
KURT That he *could* die!
ALICE God be praised!
KURT Watch yourself, Alice. Watch yourself!— — —And now, go
in and look for a pillow and a blanket. I'll put him here on the
sofa. Then I'll stay here in the chair through the night!
ALICE And me?
KURT You go to bed. Your presence seems to worsen his condition!
ALICE Command, and I'll obey. Because you mean well by both of
us!

She goes off to the left.

KURT Both of you. Remember that. And I will not take sides!

He takes the water carafe and goes out to the right.

*

*The wind can be heard blowing outside. Then the backdoors blow
open and a shabby and unpleasant-looking OLD WOMAN peeks in.
The CAPTAIN wakes up, rises, looks around.*

CAPTAIN Well, so they've left me, the bastards! (*He spots the OLD
WOMAN and becomes frightened.*) Who is it? What do you want!
OLD WOMAN I just wanted to close the door, kind sir.
CAPTAIN What for? What for?

OLD WOMAN Because it blew open, just as I was going past!
CAPTAIN You were thinking of stealing something!
OLD WOMAN There's not much worth taking! In Kristín's opinion.
CAPTAIN Kristín!
OLD WOMAN Good night, sir. Sleep well!

She closes the door and goes.

*

ALICE enters from the left with pillows and blankets.

CAPTAIN Who was that in the door? Was there anybody there?
ALICE Yes. It was old Maja from the shelter who walked past.
CAPTAIN Are you sure?
ALICE Are you scared?
CAPTAIN Me, scared? Oh no!
ALICE Since you won't go to bed, lie down here.
CAPTAIN (*lies down on the sofa.*) This is where I'll sleep!

He tries to take ALICE's hand, but she pulls it away.
KURT enters, with the water carafe.

CAPTAIN Kurt, don't leave me!
KURT I'll stay with you through the night. Alice is going to bed.
CAPTAIN Good night then, Alice.
ALICE (*to KURT.*) Good night, Kurt.
KURT Good night.

*

KURT takes a chair and sits at the side of the CAPTAIN's bed.

KURT Don't you want to take off your boots?

CAPTAIN No! A soldier must always be ready.

KURT You're expecting a battle, then?

CAPTAIN Perhaps!— — —(*He sits up in bed.*) Kurt! You are the only person I have confided in before! Listen to one thing!— — — If I die tonight . . . look after my children!

KURT I will.

CAPTAIN Thank you. I can depend on you!

KURT Can you explain why you can depend on me?

CAPTAIN We have been friends, although I don't believe in friendship. And our two families were born enemies and have always been at war . . .

KURT And still you can depend upon me?

CAPTAIN Yes! And I don't know why!

A silence.

*

CAPTAIN Do you think I'm going to die?

KURT You, like everyone else! No exception will be made for you.

CAPTAIN Are you bitter?

KURT Yes! . . . Are you afraid of death? The wheelbarrow to the garden plot?

CAPTAIN What if that were not the end?

KURT Many think it's not.

CAPTAIN So afterwards?

KURT Nothing but surprises, I'd guess.

CAPTAIN But no one knows anything for certain.

KURT No, that's exactly it. That's why we have to prepare ourselves for anything.

CAPTAIN You are not so childish as to believe in — hell?

KURT Don't you believe in it — you who live in the middle of it?

CAPTAIN Only metaphorically.

KURT As realistically as you've portrayed it, poetry or not, metaphor is out of the question!

*

A silence.

CAPTAIN If you only knew the pains I'm suffering.
KURT Physically?
CAPTAIN No, they are not physical!
KURT Then they must be spiritual. There's no third kind!

Pause.

CAPTAIN (*sits up in bed.*) I don't want to die!
KURT A while ago you wanted annihilation!
CAPTAIN Yes. If it's painless!
KURT But of course, it's not.
CAPTAIN Is this annihilation, then?
KURT The beginning of it!

*

CAPTAIN Good night!
KURT Good night!

Curtain.

[I.2]

The same set: but the lamp is in the process of going out. Through the window and the panes of the back doors the cloudy morning can be seen. Rough water out at sea. The sentry is out on the battery as before. The CAPTAIN is lying on the chaise-longue sleeping. KURT is sitting close by in an armchair: pallid and sleepless.

ALICE *(enters from the left.)* Is he sleeping?

KURT Yes, since about sunrise.

ALICE How was the night?

KURT He slept for periods. But he has talked so much!

ALICE About what?

KURT He has been debating religion like a schoolboy, but has pretensions to having solved the riddles of the universe! Finally, toward morning, he discovered the immortality of the soul.

ALICE He'll take the credit for that!

KURT Exactly!— — —He is truly the most arrogant person I have ever met. "I am, therefore God exists."

ALICE Now you see!— — —Look at those boots! With those he would have trampled the world flat, if he'd had the chance. With those he has trampled on other people's fields and plots. With those he has trampled on other's toes and on my skull!— — — Killer bear, now the bullet's found you!

KURT He would be comic if he wasn't tragic — and there are traces of greatness in all his pettiness. Can't you say a single good word about him?

ALICE *(sits.)* Yes! Only he can't hear it. Because if you say an encouraging word, he gets a swollen head.

KURT He doesn't hear anything. He's had morphine.

ALICE Brought up in a home with many siblings, Edgar early on had to support the family by giving lessons, while the father was a bum—or worse. It is certainly hard for a boy to have to give up all the pleasures of being young and slave for a bunch of ungrateful kids, which he didn't bring into the world. I was a little girl when I saw him as a young man with no overcoat in the winter, with the temperature far below freezing— — —his little sisters had woolen duffel coats— — —That was a fine thing and I admired him, but I shrank from his ugliness. Isn't he unusually ugly?

KURT Yes, and he can even become hideous. Every time we were on bad terms with each other, I noticed it most. And when he was not around his image began to swell in my mind. He took on grotesque sizes and shapes, and he literally haunted me!

ALICE Think of how it's been for me then!— — —In any case, his younger years as an officer were sheer martyrdom. But he received help here and there — from wealthy people. This he would never admit, and he has accepted everything that he could get like tributes that were his due, without any thanks!

KURT We were supposed to be speaking well of him.

ALICE After he is dead! Yes, well— — —I don't remember any more.

KURT Have you found him cruel?

ALICE Yes — and he can still be both kind and sensitive! — As an enemy he is simply horrifying!

KURT Why didn't he ever make major?

ALICE You ought to see why! They didn't want to have someone like that over them — someone who was already a tyrant when he was under them! But you must never mention that you know about this. He himself says he didn't want to be a major.— — — Did he talk about the children at all?

KURT Yes. He's longing to see Judith.

ALICE I can believe that. Oh! Do you know what Judith is to him? She's his own image, and he has trained her to incite me! Can you imagine, that my own daughter . . . has raised her hand against me!

KURT No. That is too much!

ALICE Hush! He's moving!— — —What if he heard us!— — —He's

also cunning!

KURT He's just now waking.

ALICE Doesn't he look like a troll? I'm afraid of him!

A silence.

The CAPTAIN *stirs, awakens, sits up and looks around.*

CAPTAIN It's morning. Finally!— — —

KURT How are you feeling now?

CAPTAIN Poorly.

KURT Do you want a doctor?

CAPTAIN No— — —I want to see Judith. My child!

KURT Wouldn't it be prudent to put your house in order, before —
or, in case — something should happen?

CAPTAIN What do you mean? In case what should happen?

KURT The thing that happens to everyone.

CAPTAIN Oh, nonsense. I won't die as easily as you think! Don't
celebrate prematurely, Alice.

KURT Think of your children. Make out your will so that at least
your wife will be able to keep the furniture!

CAPTAIN So she should inherit it while I'm alive?

KURT No. But if anything should happen, she ought not be cast out
on the street! Since she has cleaned, polished and dusted this
furniture for twenty-five years, she ought to have the right to keep
it. May I call the judge-advocate?

CAPTAIN No!

KURT You are a cruel man. Crueler than I thought!

CAPTAIN (*falls back on the bed.*) It's coming on again! (*He is
unconscious.*)

*

ALICE (*heads off, right.*) There are people in the kitchen. I've got to
go out there!

KURT Go on. There's not much to be done here.

ALICE exits.

*

CAPTAIN (*wakening.*) Now Kurt. How are you thinking of establishing the quarantine station here?

KURT I'm sure it'll go fine.

CAPTAIN No. I am commanding officer here on the island, and you have to deal with me. Don't forget that!

KURT Have you ever seen a quarantine station?

CAPTAIN Have I . . .? Yes, before you were even born! And I'll give you a piece of advice: don't set the disinfection ovens too close to the shore.

KURT I thought that was the idea, to locate them close to water. . .

CAPTAIN I can see how much you know about your field. Water is the element of the bacilli: the element in which they thrive.

KURT But salt water from the sea is necessary to cleanse out impurities.

CAPTAIN Idiot!— — —Now, once you've settled into your quarters, you'll have to bring your children over.

KURT Do you think they'll come?

CAPTAIN Naturally, if you're any kind of man! It would make a good impression on the neighbors here to see that you're faithful to your duties, in that area . . .

KURT I have always fulfilled my duties in that regard!

CAPTAIN (*raises his voice.*) . . . in that area which is your weakest point!

KURT Did I not tell you . . .

CAPTAIN (*continuous.*) . . . Because one does not leave one's children in that manner . . .

KURT You go right on!

CAPTAIN I feel as your relative, an elder relative, I have a certain right to speak the truth to you, even if it is bitter . . . And you mustn't be offended . . .

KURT Are you hungry?

CAPTAIN Yes, I am!— — —

KURT Would you like something light?

CAPTAIN No, a solid meal!

KURT That will do you in.

CAPTAIN Is it not enough to be sick, without having to starve too?

KURT That's how it is.

CAPTAIN And no drinking, and no smoking! Then it's no life much worth living!

KURT Death demands sacrifice. Otherwise he comes at once!

*

ALICE enters with some bouquets of flowers, some telegrams and letters.

ALICE These are for you!

She throws the flowers on the sewing table.

CAPTAIN (*flattered.*) To me!— — —May I see them please!— — —

ALICE Yes. They're only from the N.C.O.s, the band and the gunners.

CAPTAIN You're jealous!

ALICE Oh no! If they were laurel wreaths . . . that would be something else again. But you'll never be getting those.

CAPTAIN Hm! . . . Here's a telegram from the Colonel . . . Read it Kurt! The Colonel is a gentleman, anyhow— — —even though he's a bit of an idiot! . . . Here, from . . . What's it say? It's from Judith!— — —Please cable her to come out on the next boat! — — —Here . . . Yes! — You're never without friends, after all. And it is a fine thing that they think of a man when he's sick, a man who deserves more than his rank, who's without fear and above reproach.

ALICE I don't understand. Are these congratulations that you are sick?

CAPTAIN Hyena!

ALICE (*to KURT.*) You know, we had a doctor here who was so hated, that when he left the island they held a banquet — not *for* him, but *after* him.

CAPTAIN Put the flowers in vases . . . I'm certainly not gullible, and people are scum. But this simple tribute is sincere, by God . . . It can't be anything but sincere.

ALICE Ass!

KURT (*reads a telegram.*) Judith says that she cannot come, as the steamboat's been held up by the storm.

CAPTAIN Is that it?

KURT No-ooo! — There's something more.

CAPTAIN Out with it!

KURT Well, she begs Papa not to drink so much.

CAPTAIN What insolence! — That's children for you! That's my only belovéd daughter . . . My Judith. My very idol!

ALICE And your very image.

CAPTAIN That's life. And its greatest blessings. Damn it all!

ALICE Now you are reaping what you've sown. You raised her to be against her mother. Now she's turning against her father. Tell me there isn't any God!

CAPTAIN (*to KURT.*) What's the Colonel say?

KURT He's granted you a leave of absence, without further notice.

CAPTAIN Leave of absence? But I haven't requested one.

ALICE No. But I've requested one.

CAPTAIN I don't accept it!

ALICE The arrangements have already been made.

CAPTAIN That's no concern of mine!

ALICE You see, Kurt. For this man there are no laws, no rules that apply to him, no human order that is valid . . . He stands above everything and everyone. The universe is created for his private use. The sun and the moon revolve to carry his praises to the stars. Such is my husband! The insignificant captain, who couldn't even make it to major! At whose pompousness every-body laughs, while he imagines himself to be feared! This milksop who's afraid of the dark and believes only in barometers, and all this comes together in the final curtain: a barrow full of manure! And not even prime quality!

The CAPTAIN *fans himself with the flower bouquet, complacently, without listening to* ALICE.

CAPTAIN Have you invited Kurt to breakfast?

ALICE No!

CAPTAIN Then go right away and make two fine steaks! Two chateaubriands!

ALICE Two?

CAPTAIN I'm having one as well.

ALICE But we are three people.

CAPTAIN Shall you have one too? Well, make it three then!

ALICE Where am I going to get them? Yesterday afternoon you invited Kurt to supper, and there was not a crust of bread in the house. Kurt has had to stay up all night on an empty stomach, and hasn't had a cup of coffee, as there is none, because our credit's been withdrawn.

CAPTAIN (*to* KURT.) She's mad at me because yesterday I didn't die.

ALICE No. Because you didn't die twenty-five years ago, Because you didn't die before I was born!

CAPTAIN (*to* KURT.) Listen to her.— — —That's what happens when you get into matchmaking, my dear Kurt! This match wasn't made in heaven, that's for sure!

KURT *and* ALICE *look at each other meaningfully.*

The CAPTAIN *gets up and goes to the door.*

CAPTAIN In the meantime! Say what you will. Now I'm going on duty!

He puts on an old-fashioned artillery helmet, fastens his saber at his waist and puts on his cape.

If anyone is looking for me, they can find me at the battery.

KURT and ALICE try to stop him, but in vain.

Out of my way!

He goes.

ALICE Yes, go! You always go, turn your back, when the battle turns against you. And then you let your wife cover your retreat — hero of booze, big braggart, big liar! I spit on that!

*

KURT There's no bottom to this.
ALICE Yes, you don't know everything yet.
KURT Is there more?
ALICE But I'm ashamed . . .
KURT Where's he going now? And where'd he get the strength?
ALICE Well may you ask! Well, now he's going down to the N.C.O.s to thank them for the flowers . . . And then he'll eat and drink with them! And then he'll slander the rest of the officer corps . . . If you knew how many times he's been threatened with dismissal. They've only kept him here out of compassion for the family. And he imagines it's because they fear him and his superiority. And those poor officers' wives who've put themselves out for us, he hates and slanders them.
KURT I must confess that I applied for this posting to find peace out at the sea . . . and I knew nothing about your circumstances . . .
ALICE Poor Kurt!— — —How will you get food?
KURT Oh, I'll go to the Doctor. But you? Let me take care of this

matter for you.

ALICE As long as he doesn't find out — because then he'd kill me!

KURT (*looks out the window.*) Look. He's standing in the middle of the gale out on the ramparts.

ALICE It's a pity about him . . . that he should be like he is.

KURT It's a pity about both of you! . . . What can be done?

ALICE I don't know!— — —A packet of bills came in too! Which he didn't notice . . .

KURT It's sometimes a blessing not to see.

ALICE (*at the window.*) He has opened up his cape and is exposing his chest to the wind. Now he wants to die.

KURT I don't think he wants to. Because just a while ago, when he felt his life running out, he clung on to mine and began nosing into my affairs, as if he wanted to creep into me and live my life.

ALICE *That* is his vampire nature— — —to seize upon other people's fates, suck what's of interest out of other people's existences, to order and arrange things for others, since his own life is completely uninteresting to him. And, remember Kurt: never let him in on your family life. Never let him know your friends, because he'll take them from you and make them his. . . He is a real wizard in that regard!— — —If he should get to your children, you would soon find they'd be the dearest things in the world to *him.* He would advise them and raise them according to his mind, and above all *against* your wishes.

KURT Alice. Wasn't he the one who took my children from me, when I was divorced?

ALICE Since that's all in the past now: yes, it was him!

KURT I've suspected as much. But I didn't know for sure. It was him!

ALICE When you, with full confidence in my husband, sent him as peacemaker to your wife, he commenced a flirtation with her, and coached her on how she could get the children.

KURT Oh God!— — —Oh God in heaven!

ALICE There you have another facet of the man!

A silence.

KURT You know that last night— — —when he thought he was going to die— — —he made me promise him that I would look after his children!

ALICE But you wouldn't want to take revenge through my children?

KURT Through keeping my promise. Yes! I shall look after your children!

ALICE That is really the harshest revenge you could take. Because there is nothing he disdains more than generosity.

KURT So I'll feel avenged, without taking revenge.

ALICE I love it when justice is vengeance! And it inspires me to see evil punished!

KURT That's still your position?

ALICE That will always be my position. And the day I forgive or love an enemy is the day I'd be a hypocrite!

KURT Alice! At times we have a duty not to say everything, not to look at everything. As they say — "to overlook" some things. And we all need that.

ALICE Not me! My life is open and clear. And I've always laid my cards out on the table.

KURT That's quite a claim.

ALICE No, it's not nearly enough! Because what I have innocently suffered, for this man's sake, whom I never loved . . .

KURT Why did you get married?

ALICE Well may you ask! . . . Because he took me! Seduced me! I don't know! And then, I wanted to rise, to be someone in society . . .

KURT And abandoned an artistic career.

ALICE Which was held in contempt! — But, you know, he swindled me. He held out the promise of a good life . . . a fine home! And then there was nothing but debts— — —the only gold was on his uniform, and that wasn't gold either! He swindled me!

KURT Hold on a moment! When a young man falls in love, he looks to the future with hope . . . The fact that the hopes are not always realized, that you must forgive him. I have the same deception on my conscience without regarding myself as a swindler.— — —What do you see out there on the ramparts?

ALICE I'm looking to see whether he fell.

KURT Did he fall?

ALICE No, unfortunately. He's always swindling me!

KURT Well, I'm going to find the Doctor and the Justice of the Peace.

ALICE (*sits by the window.*) Go on, Kurt dear. I'm going to sit here and wait. And I'm one who's learned to wait!

Entre-acte.

[II]

The same set in daylight. The SENTRY walks the battery as before.
ALICE is sitting in the armchair at right. She has gray hair.
KURT enters from the left, after having knocked.

KURT Good morning, Alice!

ALICE Good morning, my friend! Sit down.

KURT (*sits in the armchair at left.*) The steamboat's coming in!

ALICE Then I know what's in store, if he's onboard!

KURT He is onboard. I saw his helmet glint in the sun . . . What's
he been doing in town?

ALICE I can figure that out. As he was dressed in parade uniform,
he went to see the Colonel. And as he took his good gloves, he
was paying some visits.

KURT Did you notice how quiet he was yesterday? Since he put
aside his drinking, and is observing moderation, he's a different
person. Calm, reserved, considerate . . .

ALICE I feel that. And if that man had always been sober, he would
have been a danger to mankind. Maybe it's fortunate for
mankind that he rendered himself harmless and ridiculous with
his whiskey!

KURT The spirit in the bottle has trimmed his sails!— — —But have
you noticed that, since death has set its mark on him, it's brought
out a certain dignity in him. And it is possible, with his new
thoughts on immortality, that he has a new perspective on life.

ALICE You deceive yourself! He's up to no good! And don't believe
what he says, because he lies deliberately! And he knows the art
of intrigue like no one else.— — —

KURT (*gazes at ALICE.*) Alice! What's this? You've become gray-
haired over the last two nights!

ALICE No, my friend, I have had it for a long time. It's just that I left off darkening it, since my husband is a dead man. Twenty-five years in a fortress— — —Do you know that this was a prison in times gone by?

KURT A prison! The walls do look that way.

ALICE And my complexion! Even the children became prison colored in here.

KURT It's hard for me to imagine little children chattering inside these walls.

ALICE And there wasn't much chatter, in fact! And the two that died, perished from the lack of light.

KURT What do you think will happen now?

ALICE The decisive blow, against the both of *us*! I saw a familiar gleam in his eye when you read the telegram from Judith. It should, of course, have been meant for her. But as you know, she gets off scott-free, and the hate settled upon you.

KURT What's he planning for me, do you think?

ALICE Hard to say. But he has the unbelievable power — or luck — to be able to nose out other people's secrets . . . And you noticed, of course, how all of yesterday it was like he was living in your quarantine station — how he sucked the interest in life out of your existence, ate your children alive . . . A cannibal, you see. I know him. His own life is abandoning him, or has already done so . . .

KURT I've had that impression too: that he's already on the other side. His face has a phosphorescence as if he were decomposing . . . and his eyes flame like the gaseous light over graves and swamps . . . Here he comes! Tell me, have you thought of the possibility he might be jealous?

ALICE No. He's too conceited!— — —"Show me the man whom I need be jealous of!" Those are his words.

KURT All the better. Even his faults also have certain merits!— — — Should I go out to greet him, anyway?

ALICE Don't be polite, or he'll think you're plotting something! And when he starts lying, let on that you believe him. I can easily translate his lies, and I always look up the truth in my personal dictionary!— — —I have a premonition of something terrible —

— —But Kurt, don't lose your command of the situation!— — —
My sole advantage in our long battle has been that I was always
sober and so I had presence of mind . . . He always fell back on
his whiskey! . . . Now we shall see!

*

The CAPTAIN *enters from the left, in dress uniform, helmet, cape,
white gloves. Calm, dignified, but pale and hollow-eyed. He stumbles
forward, and sits down in his helmet and cape far from* ALICE
and KURT *to the right. During the following dialogue he holds his
saber between his knees.*

CAPTAIN Good morning! — Forgive me for sitting down like this,
but I'm a bit tired.

ALICE AND KURT Good morning! Welcome back!

ALICE How are you feeling?

CAPTAIN Excellent! Just a bit tired! . . .

ALICE What's the news from town?

CAPTAIN A little of everything. Among other things, I visited the
Doctor there, and he said that there's really no problem. And
that I might live another twenty years, if I took care of myself.

ALICE (*to* KURT.) Now he's lying. (*To the* CAPTAIN.) That's splendid
news, dear.

CAPTAIN Yes, indeed it was!

A silence, during which the CAPTAIN *looks at* ALICE *and* KURT *as if
he wants to get them to talk.*

ALICE (*to* KURT.) Don't say anything. Let him speak first, so he'll
show his hand.

CAPTAIN (*to* ALICE.) Did you say something?

ALICE No. I didn't say anything!

CAPTAIN (*slowly.*) Listen, Kurt.

ALICE (*to* KURT.) You see, now it's coming out . . .

CAPTAIN I . . . I was in town, as you know.

KURT (*nods, acknowledging this.*)

CAPTAIN Oh — uh, I made the acquaintance . . . among others . . . of a young officer cadet — (*hesitates*) — in the artillery. (*Pause: during which* KURT *appears disturbed.*) As— — —we are lacking cadets here, I made arrangements with the Colonel for him to come here!— — —This ought to please you, especially you, when I inform you that it . . . was . . . your own son!

ALICE (*to* KURT.) That's the vampire! You see!

KURT Under other circumstances this would please a father. But in my situation, it is only painful.

CAPTAIN I don't understand.

KURT You need not understand it. It is enough that I do not want it.

CAPTAIN Really. Is that your opinion!— — —Then you should know that this young man has his orders to transfer here, and that from this minute he takes orders from me!

KURT Then I'll force him to seek a transfer to another regiment!

CAPTAIN You can't do that. Because you have no rights over your son!

KURT No?

CAPTAIN No. The court awarded them to his mother!

KURT Then I'll get in contact with his mother!

CAPTAIN You need not do that.

KURT I need not?

CAPTAIN No. Because I've done that already! So!

KURT (*starts to get up, but then falls back in his chair.*)

ALICE (*to* KURT.) Now he's got to die!

KURT He *is* a cannibal!

*

CAPTAIN So much for that matter! (*Directly to* ALICE *and* KURT.) Did you say something?

ALICE No. Are you having trouble hearing?

CAPTAIN Yes, a little.— — —But if you'll move a little closer, I'll tell you something, just between the two of us.

ALICE That's not necessary. And a witness can be advantageous to both parties.

CAPTAIN Right you are. A witness is always a good thing!— — — But first: have you put the will in order?

ALICE (*hands him a document.*) The judge-advocate drew it up himself.

CAPTAIN To your advantage!— — —Good! (*He reads the document, and then tears it carefully into strips, which he tosses on the floor.*) That takes care of that! So!

ALICE (*to KURT.*) Have you seen such a human being . . .

KURT That's no human being!

*

CAPTAIN Well, I have something I'd like to tell you, Alice!— — —

ALICE (*uneasy.*) Please do.

CAPTAIN (*calmly as before.*) On the basis of your long expressed wish to put an end to this wretched life and unhappy marriage, and on the basis of the loveless manner with which you have treated your spouse and children, on the basis of the irresponsible manner with which you managed the finances of the household, I have, during my stay in town, just submitted to the municipal court — an application for divorce.

ALICE Soo! And the grounds?

CAPTAIN (*calmly, as before.*) Outside of the grounds already mentioned, I have purely personal grounds. Since it has in fact been established that I may still live another twenty years, I have considered exchanging this unhappy union for one that better suits me. I'm thinking of uniting my fate with that of a woman, who, with some affection for her spouse, might bring into the house youth and, let us say — some beauty!

ALICE (*takes off her ring and throws it at the CAPTAIN.*) There you are!

CAPTAIN (*picks up the ring and stuffs it in his vest pocket.*) She's thrown away her ring. Would the witness be so good as to take note.

ALICE (*rises, enraged.*) And you dare toss me out, and put another woman in my house?

CAPTAIN Yes. So!

ALICE Well, then we'll do some plain talking!— — —Kurt, my cousin, this man is guilty of the attempted murder of his wife.

KURT Attempted murder!

ALICE Yes. He has shoved me into the sea!

CAPTAIN Without witnesses!

ALICE He's lying. Judith saw it!

CAPTAIN So what?

ALICE She will be my witness!

CAPTAIN No, she won't. Because she says that she saw nothing.

ALICE You've taught that child to lie!

CAPTAIN I didn't need to, as you'd taught her previously.

ALICE Did you go see Judith?

CAPTAIN Yes. So!

ALICE Oh God! Oh God!

*

CAPTAIN The fortress has been taken. The enemy is granted safe-conduct with ten minutes for evacuation! (*He places his watch on the table.*) Ten minutes. The watch on the table! (*He remains standing, with his hand on his heart.*)

ALICE goes to the CAPTAIN and grabs his arm.

ALICE What is it?

CAPTAIN I don't know!

ALICE Do you need something — do you want something to drink?

CAPTAIN Whiskey? No, I don't want to die! You!— — —(*He straightens up.*) Let go of me!— — —Ten minutes, or we raze the garrison. (*Draws his saber.*) Ten minutes! (*He exits through the back door.*)

*

KURT Who is this person!

ALICE It's a demon, not a person!

KURT What's he want with my son?

ALICE He wants him as a hostage so that he can rule you. He wants to isolate you from the authorities on the island . . . You know, the population of this island call it "Little Hell."

KURT I didn't know that.— — —Alice, you are the first woman to have awakened my compassion. All the others I felt deserved their fate!

ALICE Don't abandon me now! Don't leave me. He beats me!— — — He's beaten me for twenty-five years . . . and in front of the children . . . He has shoved me into the sea . . .

KURT Knowing that I must take an absolute stand against him! I came here with no ill will, without remembering the old humiliations and slanders from him. I even forgave him, by and by, after you told me that he was the one who cut me off from my children— — —because he was sick and dying . . . But now that he wants to take my son, I'll kill him — it's him or me!

ALICE Good! Don't surrender the fort! Instead, blow it up to the sky, with him in it! Even if we have to go down with him! I have access to some gunpowder!

KURT I wasn't angry when I came here. And I was thinking of getting out when I felt your hatred infecting me. But now I feel compelled to hate this man just as I hate evil itself!— — — What can we do?

ALICE He has taught me the tactics himself. Rally his enemies and seek allies!

KURT To think that he could search out my wife! Why didn't those two meet a generation ago! You'd have seen a tussle that would have made the earth tremble!

ALICE But now these soul mates have met . . . and we must split them up! I have a hunch I know his vulnerable point. I have long suspected it . . .

KURT Who is his most reliable enemy on the island?

ALICE It's the Ordnance Officer.

KURT Is he trustworthy?

ALICE Yes, he is.— — —And he *knows* what I— — —what I know too!— — —He knows what the Sergeant-Major and the Captain have been up to!

KURT What they have been up to . . . What do you mean?

ALICE Embezzlement!

KURT That's disgusting. No, I can't go along with this! To get involved in . . .

ALICE Ha! Man! Can you not strike back at your enemy!

KURT I used to be able to. But I can't anymore.

ALICE Why?

KURT Because, I discovered that . . . justice always comes around anyway.

ALICE And you want to wait for that? While he has taken your son from you! Look at my gray hair . . . Yes, feel how thick it is still! . . . He aims to get married again. And then I'll be free — to do the same! — I am free! And in ten minutes he'll be sitting down below, under arrest. Down there — (*stamping on the floor*) — down there . . . And I shall dance on his head, I shall dance the "March of the Boyars" . . . (*She does a few dance steps with her hands on her hips.*) Hahahaha! And I shall play the piano so he can hear it! (*She hammers on the keyboard.*) Oh! The tower opens up its doors! And the guard with his saber drawn shall not be my prison guard again — but *his*! . . . Melitám tamtá melitá lialáy! *His, his, his* prison guard!

KURT (*has watched her with fascination.*) Alice! Are you a devil too?

ALICE jumps up on the table and takes down the laurel wreaths.

ALICE These I'll take with me on our procession out of this place
... The laurels of victory and the waving ribbons! A bit dusty,
but eternally green. — Like my youth. — I am not old, Kurt!

KURT (*his eyes shining.*) You are a devil!

ALICE In Little Hell!— — —Listen, I'm going to fix myself up . . .
(*Lets down her hair.*) . . . be dressed in two minutes . . . two
minutes later we'll be with the Ordnance Officer . . . and then:
the fortress blows sky high!

KURT (*as before.*) You are a devil!

ALICE That's what you always used to say when we were children,
too! You remember when we were kids, and we got engaged!
Hahaha! You were shy, of course . . .

KURT (*seriously.*) Alice!

ALICE Yes you were! And it did suit you. You see, there are brash
women who like shy men, and there — — — also exist shy men
who like brash women! — — — You liked all of me then, a little!
Didn't you!

KURT I don't know where I am here!

ALICE With an actress, who is a free spirit, but otherwise a fine
woman! Yes! But now I am free, free, free!— — —Turn your
back. I'll change my blouse!

*She unbuttons her blouse. KURT rushes to her, takes her in both his
arms, lifts her high up and bites her on the throat so that she
screams. Then he throws her down on the chaise-longue and rushes
out to the left.*

Curtain.

[II.2]

The same set, in the evening. The SENTRY out on the battery is still visible through the windows of the back door. The laurel wreaths are hanging over the arm of a chair. The ceiling lamp is lit. Soft music.

The CAPTAIN, pale and hollow-eyed, unshaven, clad in dirty fatigues and riding boots, is sitting by the sewing table, playing solitaire. He has his glasses on.

The music from the scene change continues after the curtain rises up to the point that the next person enters.

The CAPTAIN *plays his game of solitaire, but gives a start now and then, then looks about and listens anxiously.*

It appears he is not able to get all the cards out; he becomes impatient and piles up the deck. Then he goes to the left window, opens it, and throws the pack out. The window remains open, but creaks on its hinges.

He goes to the sideboard, becomes frightened by the noises from the window, and turns about to see what it is. He takes out three dark, square whiskey bottles, looks at them for a moment — and tosses them out the window. He takes some cigar boxes, opens one and smells it, and throws them out the window.

Then he takes off his glasses, wipes them, and tests how well he sees with them on. Then he throws them out the window. He stumbles amid the furniture as if he can hardly see, and lights a candelabra with six candles on the chiffonnier. He catches sight of the laurel wreaths, picks them up and goes to the window, but turns back. Then he takes the cloth cover off the piano and wraps it carefully around the wreaths. He takes pins from the desk and fastens the corners of the cloth, and sets the whole thing on a chair.

He goes to the piano, bangs on the keys with his fists. He closes the piano lid and locks it, and throws the key out the window. Then he lights the candle on the piano. He goes to the bric-a-brac shelf; takes his wife's portrait, regards it, tears it to bits which he throws on the floor. The window creaks on its hinges and once again he becomes frightened.

Then, after he has calmed himself: he takes his son's and daughter's portraits, kisses them quickly and puts them in his breast pocket. The remaining portraits he sweeps down with his elbow, and shoves them into a heap with his boot.

Then he sits down at the desk, tired, and clutches at his heart. He lights the candle in the writing lamp and sighs; staring in front of him as if he were having terrible visions.— — —He gets up, and goes to the chiffonnier. He lifts the lid and takes out a pack of letters tied with a blue ribbon, and throws it in the stove. He closes the chiffonnier.

Now the telegraph makes one single tap and goes silent. The CAPTAIN *shrinks back, scared to death, and remains standing with his hand on his heart, listening. But when he hears nothing more from the telegraph, he begins listening at the door, left. He goes to it, opens it, takes a step in, and comes out with a cat in his arm which he strokes on its back. Then he exits to the right. [Now the music stops.]*

*

ALICE enters from the back door: in walking clothes, with dark hair, gloves and hat. She looks about, astonished at the many lights.

KURT enters from the left, nervously.

ALICE It looks like Christmas Eve in here!
KURT Well!
ALICE (*extends her hand to be kissed.*) Thank me!
KURT (*reluctantly kisses her hand.*)

ALICE Six witnesses, of which four are solid as rock. The report has gone through, and the response will come by telegraph here — here to my fortress!

KURT Ah!

ALICE Say thank you instead of "Ah!"

KURT Why has he lit so many candles?

ALICE Because he's scared of the dark, of course! . . . Look at the telegraph! Doesn't it look like the handle on a coffee grinder — I grind, I grind, and the beans crack like teeth being pulled . . .

KURT What's he been doing in the room here?

ALICE It looks like he was thinking of moving. Down there, Edgar! That's where you'll be moving!

KURT Alice, don't. I think it's disgusting . . . He was my childhood friend, and was often a help to me when I was down . . . It's a shame what's happened to him.

ALICE And what about me, who did nothing wrong, and had to sacrifice my career for that monster?

KURT What was your career like? Was it so brilliant?

ALICE (*furious.*) What kind of thing is that to say! Do you know who I am? Who I was?

KURT All right. All right.

ALICE Are you starting too? Already?

KURT Already?

ALICE flings herself around KURT's neck and kisses him.
KURT takes her by the arms and bites her throat so that she screams.

ALICE You're biting me.

KURT (*beside himself.*) Yes, I want to bite you, on the throat, and suck your blood like a lynx! You — you have awakened the wild animal in me which I have been trying to kill for years through denial and self-castigation! I came here, and I thought I was better than the both of you. But now I'm the most vile one of all! Since I have seen you in all your terrible nakedness, now that passion's distorted my vision, I know all the power of evil. The ugly becomes beautiful, and the good becomes ugly and weak! —

— —Come, let me choke you— — —with a kiss! (*He embraces her.*)

ALICE (*shows her left hand.*) You see the mark of the bond, which you broke. I was a slave, and am set free! . . .

KURT But shall I bind you . . .

ALICE You?

KURT Me!

ALICE I thought at one point you were . . .

KURT A pietist!

ALICE Yes, you talked about the Fall . . .

KURT I did?

ALICE And I thought you'd come here to preach . . .

KURT You thought that?— — —In one hour we'll be in town! Then you'll see who I am . . .

ALICE Then we'll go to the theatre this evening! To show ourselves in public! The shame will be his if I run away. You understand that?

KURT I'm beginning to understand. And prison is not enough for you . . .

ALICE No. It is not enough. There must be shame as well!

KURT Such a strange world. You commit the shameful act, and he has to bear the shame.

ALICE Since the world's such a stupid place!

KURT It is as if these prison walls have soaked in all the negativity of the criminals. And you need only breathe in here to be penetrated by it. You were thinking of theatre and dinner, I guess. I was thinking about my son!

ALICE (*strikes him on the mouth with her glove.*) Stuffed shirt!

KURT (*lifts his hand to box her ear.*)

ALICE (*shrinks back.*) Tout beau!

KURT Forgive me!

ALICE Okay. On your knees!

KURT (*falls to his knees.*)

ALICE On your face.

KURT (*puts his forehead to the floor.*)

ALICE Kiss my foot!

KURT (*kisses her foot.*)

ALICE And never do that again!— — —Get up!

KURT (*standing.*) Where have I come to? Where am I?

ALICE You know very well!

KURT (*looks around in terror.*) I'd almost think . . . I was in Hell!

*

The CAPTAIN enters from the right, looking miserable, supporting himself on a cane.

CAPTAIN May I speak with Kurt! Alone!

ALICE Is it about the safe-conduct?

CAPTAIN (*sits down at the sewing table.*) Kurt, would you be so kind as to sit with me a while. And Alice, could you spare us a moment's . . . peace?

ALICE What is it now, then?— — —New signals! (*To KURT.*) Please do sit down.

KURT (*sits reluctantly.*)

ALICE And listen to the voice of wisdom and age!— — —If a telegram should come . . . knock on my door.

She goes off to the left.

*

CAPTAIN (*after a pause, dignified.*) Have you been able to understand the fate of people like me — like us?

KURT No. Just as little as I understand my own.

CAPTAIN What is the meaning of this huge jumble?

KURT In my better moments I've thought that was just the idea — that we'd never get to know the meaning, and still have to submit . . .

CAPTAIN Submit! Without some fixed point outside of myself, I've got nothing to submit to.

KURT Exactly right. But as a mathematician, you should be able to seek this unknown point, when you have several known points as given . . .

CAPTAIN I have looked for it, and — I haven't found it!

KURT You have made miscalculations. Start over again.

CAPTAIN Me, start over!— — —Tell me, where did you acquire your resignation.

KURT I have none anymore. Don't overestimate me.

CAPTAIN As you have perhaps noticed, my understanding of the art of living involves this: to wipe things out! That is: cross it out, and carry on! Early on I made myself a sack, which I stuffed all of my humiliations into. And when it was full, I threw it in the sea! — I think no other person has suffered as much humiliation as me. But when I crossed them out and passed on, they didn't exist anymore.

KURT I've noticed how you've made up your life through your imagination, and have made up your world the same way.

CAPTAIN How else would I be able to live? How would I have held out? (*Puts his hands up to his heart.*)

KURT How are you?

CAPTAIN Bad! (*Pause.*) Then comes a moment when the ability to make things up, as you call it, ceases. And then reality stands forth in all its nakedness!— — —It is terrible! (*Now he speaks with the voice of an old man, with a tearfulness, and his lower jaw hangs open.*) You see, my dear friend . . . (*He pulls himself together and speaks with his usual voice.*) Forgive me! . . . When I was just in the city and spoke with the Doctor — (*the tearfulness returns*) — he told me that I was finished — (*with his usual voice*) — and that I didn't have long to live!

KURT He said that?

CAPTAIN (*tearful voice.*) Yes. That's what he said!

KURT It wasn't true then?

CAPTAIN What? Oh yes . . . No, that wasn't true.

Pause.

KURT Was the other thing not true as well?

CAPTAIN What thing . . . my friend?

KURT About — that my son was to be ordered here as a cadet?

CAPTAIN I never heard any talk of that.

KURT You know, your ability to cross out your own evil acts knows no bounds!

CAPTAIN I don't understand what you're saying, my friend.

KURT Then you *are* finished.

CAPTAIN Yes, there's not much left of me.

KURT Listen. Is it possible you didn't file for that divorce to disgrace your wife?

CAPTAIN Divorce? No, there was no talk of that.

KURT (*rises.*) Will you admit that you were lying then?

CAPTAIN My friend, you use such strong language! We all need friends who *overlook* our faults.

KURT You've had that insight?

CAPTAIN (*firmly, in a clear voice.*) Yes, I've had that insight!— — — So forgive me, Kurt! Forgive everything!

KURT Spoken like a man! — But there's nothing for me to forgive. And I am not the man you think I am! Not anymore! Least of all the one who is worthy to receive your confession.

CAPTAIN (*with a clear voice.*) My life was so strange! So contrary, so malicious, ever since childhood . . . And people are so malicious, so I became malicious too . . .

KURT paces the floor nervously, and looks at the telegraph.

CAPTAIN What are you looking at?

KURT Is it possible to turn off a telegraph?

CAPTAIN No, not easily.

KURT (*increasingly nervous.*) What kind of man is Sergeant-Major Östberg?

CAPTAIN He's an honest fellow. Though he does a bit of business of his own.

KURT What's the Ordnance Officer like then?

CAPTAIN He is my enemy, definitely. But I have nothing bad to say about him.

KURT (*looks out the window where a lantern appears to be moving.*) What are they doing with that lantern out on the battery?

CAPTAIN Is there a lantern?

KURT Yes. And people moving about!

CAPTAIN It must be fatigue duty, as we call it.

KURT What is it?

CAPTAIN Some men and a gunner. There's most likely some poor wretch they're going to lock up.

KURT Oh!

Pause.

CAPTAIN Now that you know Alice, what do you think of her?

KURT I can't really say . . . I don't understand people at all. To me she is just as inexplicable as you and myself! I've come to that age, in fact, when wisdom concedes: "I know nothing, I understand nothing!" — But when I see something happen, I'm curious to know the reasons for it.— — —Why did you shove her in the sea?

CAPTAIN I don't know. When she was standing on the pier, for me to push her in seemed a natural thing.

KURT Have you never regretted that?

CAPTAIN Never!

KURT That is strange!

CAPTAIN Yes, of course it is! So strange that I don't believe it was me who committed such a base act.

KURT Have you never thought that she would get revenge?

CAPTAIN She has had it, a sufficient amount! And I find that just as natural!

KURT How did you arrive at this cynical resignation so quickly?

CAPTAIN Since I looked death in the eye, life appears to me in a different perspective.— — —Listen, if you were to judge between Alice and me, who would you say was in the right?

KURT Neither! But I feel deep compassion for you both. For you
  perhaps a bit more.

CAPTAIN Give me your hand, Kurt!

*KURT extends one hand to him, and places the other on the
CAPTAIN's shoulder.*

KURT Old friend!

*

ALICE enters from the left, now carrying a parasol.

ALICE No! How intimate! Ah, that's friendship!— — —Hasn't the
  telegram come?

KURT (*coldly.*) No!

ALICE This delay is making me impatient. And when I get impatient, I hurry the situation along!— — —Watch now, Kurt. Now
  I'm going to fire the last round at him. Now he'll go down!— —
  — First I load — I know the rifle manual, the famous rifle
  manual, which never sold five thousand copies— — —and then
  I aim: Fire! — (*She aims with the parasol.*) — How's your new
  wife doing? That young, beautiful and secret wife? You don't
  know! But I know how my lover's doing! (*She puts her arms
  around KURT's neck and kisses him. He shoves her away from
  him.*) He's doing fine, but he's still shy!— — —You, wretched
  man, whom I've never loved — You who were too conceited to
  be jealous. You never saw how I led you by the nose!

*The CAPTAIN draws his saber and staggers toward her, slashing at
her, but making contact only with the furniture.*

ALICE Help! Help!

KURT (*stands motionless.*)

CAPTAIN (*falls with the saber in his hand.*) Judith! Avenge me!
ALICE Hurrah! He's dead!
KURT (*draws away toward the back door.*)
CAPTAIN (*gets up.*) Not yet!

He sheathes the saber and goes over to sit in the armchair by the sewing table.

CAPTAIN Judith! Judith!
ALICE (*goes toward KURT.*) Now I'm leaving — with you!

KURT pushes her away from him so that she falls on her knees.

KURT Go back to the abyss you came from! — This is farewell! For good!

He starts out.

CAPTAIN Don't leave me, Kurt. She'll kill me!
ALICE Kurt! Don't abandon me! Don't abandon us!
KURT Goodbye!

He exits.

*

ALICE (*complete change of attitude.*) What a wretch! That's a friend for you!
CAPTAIN (*softer tone.*) Forgive me Alice, and come here. Come quickly!
ALICE (*to the CAPTAIN.*) He was the biggest wretch and hypocrite I've ever met in my life! — You know, at least you're a man!
CAPTAIN Alice, listen!— — —I don't have long to live!
ALICE Wha-at?

CAPTAIN The Doctor has told me.

ALICE Then was the rest of it untrue also?

CAPTAIN Yes!

ALICE (*beside herself.*) Oh! What have I done?— — —

CAPTAIN We can fix everything again.

ALICE No! It can't be fixed!

CAPTAIN Nothing is unfixable. You just have to cross it out and carry on!

ALICE But the telegram! The telegram!

CAPTAIN What telegram?

ALICE (*on her knees beside the* CAPTAIN.) Are we condemned? Is this going to happen? I have blown myself up — blown us both up! Why did you do all that bluffing? And why did this man come and tempt me!— — —We are lost! Everything could have been fixed, your generous side would have forgiven everything.

CAPTAIN What is it that can't be forgiven! What haven't I forgiven you?

ALICE You're right . . . but this we cannot fix!

CAPTAIN I can't guess what you mean. Despite the fact that I know your inventiveness when it comes to cruelty . . .

ALICE Oh, if I could get out of this! If I could only get out of this, I would take care of you . . . Edgar, I would love you!

CAPTAIN Listen to that! Where am I?

ALICE Is there no one who can help us . . . No, not a human being alive!

CAPTAIN Who can then?

ALICE (*looks the* CAPTAIN *in the eyes.*) I don't know!— — —Imagine! What will become of the children, with the family name disgraced . . .

CAPTAIN Have you disgraced the family name?

ALICE Not me! Not me!— — —And then they'll have to leave the school! And when they go out into life, they'll be as lonely as us, and just as awful! Then, I'm to understand you didn't meet with Judith either?

CAPTAIN No! But cross that out!

The telegraph begins tapping. Alice jumps up.

ALICE (*screams.*) Now! The axe will fall! (*to the* CAPTAIN.) Don't
listen to it!
CAPTAIN (*calmly.*) I won't listen to it, my darling girl. Calm yourself!— — —

*ALICE stands at the telegraph and lifts herself on her toes to see out
the window.*

ALICE Don't listen! Don't listen!
CAPTAIN (*holds his ears.*) I'm holding my ears, Lisa, my girl!
ALICE (*on her knees with hands outstretched.*) God! Help us! — The
fatigue detail is coming — (*weeping*) — God in heaven!

She moves her lips as if in silent prayer.
*The telegraph taps a few more times, and a long strip of paper has
emerged. Then it goes silent.*
*ALICE rises, tears off the paper and reads in silence. Then she raises
her gaze upward. She goes over to the CAPTAIN and kisses him on
the forehead.*

ALICE It's all over! — It was nothing!

*She sits in the other chair and begins to cry violently in her handker-
chief.*

CAPTAIN What kind of secrets have you got there?
ALICE Don't ask! It's over now!
CAPTAIN As you wish, my girl!
ALICE You wouldn't have talked like this three days ago. What's
come over you?
CAPTAIN Well, my friend. When I fell that first time, I had put one
foot on the other side of the grave. What I saw I've forgotten.
But the impression remained!
ALICE What was it?

CAPTAIN The hope — of something better!

ALICE Something better?

CAPTAIN Yes. I've never really believed that this was life itself . . .
This is death! Or something even worse . . .

ALICE And we . . .

CAPTAIN Most likely we were put here for the purpose of tormenting
each other . . . so it seems.

ALICE Have we tormented each other enough?

CAPTAIN Yes, I think so. And what havoc we've wrought here. (*He
looks around.*) Shall we clean up after ourselves? And fix things
up?

ALICE (*gets up.*) Yes. If it is possible!

CAPTAIN (*looks around the room.*) It can't be done in a day. No it
can't!

ALICE In two days then. Many days!

CAPTAIN Let's hope so!— — —

Pause.

CAPTAIN (*sitting down again.*) So, you didn't break free this time!
But you didn't get me locked up either!

ALICE (*astonished.*)

CAPTAIN Yes, I knew you wanted to put me in prison. But I'll cross
that out!— — — After all, you've done worse things.

ALICE (*is speechless.*)

CAPTAIN And I was not guilty of embezzlement!

ALICE And now, is the idea that I'm supposed to be your nurse?

CAPTAIN If you wish.

ALICE What else is there for me?

CAPTAIN I don't know!

ALICE (*slumps down in despair.*) This must be the eternal fires! Is
there no end to it?

CAPTAIN Yes, if we are patient. Perhaps when death comes, life
begins.

ALICE If only that were so!

Pause.

CAPTAIN You think that Kurt was a hypocrite?
ALICE Yes I certainly do!
CAPTAIN I don't think so! But everyone who comes close to us finds themself growing evil and go their way.— — —Kurt was weak. And evil is strong!

Pause.

Think how banal life has become these days! In the old days we fought. Now we just shake our fists! — I am almost certain that in three months we'll hold our silver wedding anniversary. . . with Kurt as best man!— — —And the Doctor and Gerda will be there— — —the Ordnance Officer will propose the toast and the Sergeant-Major will lead the cheering — "Hurrah!" If I know the Colonel like I think I do, he will invite himself! — Yes, you laugh! But do you remember Adolf's silver anniversary . . . the man in the Army Rifles! His wife had to wear the ring on her right hand, since the husband, in a moment of tenderness, had chopped off her left ring finger with a machete.

ALICE holds the handkerchief over her mouth to suppress laughter.

Are you crying? — No, I think you're laughing! — Yes, my girl, it's part crying and part laughter! Which is more appropriate. . . don't ask me!— — —I read the other day in a newspaper that a man had been divorced seven times, accordingly was married seven times . . . In the end he ran off when he reached ninety years of age, and remarried with his first wife! That's love!— — — Whether life has meaning or is just random, I haven't got a clue! When it's a joke, that's the time it can be most painful, and when it's serious that's when it can be most pleasant and tranquil.— — — But when you finally take it all seriously, then somebody comes along and makes a fool out of you! For example: Kurt! — — —Do you want a silver anniversary party?

ALICE (*is silent.*)

CAPTAIN Come on, say yes! — They'll come to laugh at us. But so what! We'll laugh too — or take ourselves seriously! Whatever we like!

ALICE Yes, let's do it!

CAPTAIN (*serious.*) So a silver wedding anniversary it is!— — — (*He gets up.*) Cross it out, and carry on! — So! Let's go on!

Curtain!

End.

THREE ONE-ACTS

The Stronger

Pariah

Simoom

THREE ONE-ACTS:
INTRODUCTION

1.

STRINDBERG'S remarkable formal experimentation at the beginning of the twentieth century, and the *Weltanschauung* that went with it, certainly did not emerge completely out of the blue after his Inferno experiences. Even in the midst of Strindberg's famous naturalistic period his plays betrayed peculiar atmosphere. There was an element of the mysterious—though not mystic—and inexplicable in some of them. Most significantly: silences, in some of those plays, are a potent dramatic device.

Between 1888 and 1892 Strindberg wrote nine one-act plays.[1] The entire cluster represents an attempt to apply his new theoretical approach to the drama which are outlined in his article "On Modern Drama and Modern Theatre".[2] He was particularly influenced by the work which had just begun at André Antoine's Théâtre Libre in Paris, where the focus was on psychological action rather than on plot. Strindberg's own work would later provide the Théâtre Libre and the French naturalists with material for some of their vanguard productions. Antoine's theatre was at that time encouraging the writing of extremely short pieces, notably the *quart d'heure*, or fifteen-minute play.

The first three one-acts in the cycle were written in Holte, Denmark between December 1888 and March 4, 1889. They belong together not only because they were created during the same short period and exemplified Strindberg's new ideas on the drama—but the three plays were also written to help launch his Scandinavian Experimental in Denmark. The idea came partly as a result of many failed attempts to get his major naturalistic plays produced or published. *The Father (Fadren)* and *Marodörer (Marauders)*, later

developed into *Comrades (Kamraterna)*[3] had met with no success whatsoever since 1887, and in 1888 *Miss Julie (Fröken Julie)* and *Creditors (Fordringsägare)*, two more future Strindberg classics, met with the same resistance. After following Georg Brandes's reviews in the Danish daily *Politiken* (and perhaps those in *Figaro* in France) of the Théâtre Libre's work over the course of a year, he decided to create an experimental theatre on the same model. The limited resources of such a low-budget theatre—and the need to have productions that were portable enough for touring—would help to determine not only the length but the form of these plays. Writing to his—at that time—colleague, the author Gustaf af Geijerstam on November 18, 1888, Strindberg narrowed his artistic aims to the following formula: "Two characters, without plot, with sharp tension, in a Battle of the Brains, struggle between souls."[4]

For the account of the creation of these one-acts and their reception in the press, I am indebted to Gunnar Ollén's *Strindbergs dramatik*, and his commentaries in volume 33 of *Samlade Verk*, which contains all nine one-acts.

2.

The Stronger was probably written first—it was dated 1888 when it was published. It was a scant fifteen minutes, a *quart d'heure*, and required only one or two small tables and some chairs. Contrary to the reputation for elaborate sets the naturalistic theatre gained historically—usually a replica of a bourgeois living room or dining room, a seedy salon, or in our time the "kitchen sink" milieu—Strindberg's approach was actually to move in the other direction. "Here there are none of the superb sets which blind the eyes and get you to overlook a plot's emptiness; none of those famous works of virtuosity which, like a purple mantle, hide the poverty of a form.—Here we have simple *mise-en-scène*."[5]

The Stronger was written with his wife Siri von Essen in mind, who could have played the talkative Mrs. X in Swedish in Scandinavian countries, giving her a high profile, while she could have easily switched to the role of the silent Mlle. Y in other countries.

Ironically, neither Siri nor other available actors in Copenhagen were interested in the play, at first. It was suddenly given its chance when the production of *Miss Julie* at Dagmarteatret, with Siri in the title role, was banned by the censor at the last minute. In only a few days' time Siri learned the role of Mrs. X, and the piece was staged together with *Pariah* and the longer naturalistic drama *Creditors* on March 9, 1889. Siri's reception, especially after years away from the stage, went from bad to worse among the critics. Also working against her was the fact that she was playing in Swedish to a Danish audience and was only partly understood—while the other two plays were performed in Danish.

Strindberg always tended to give actors direction through the written word—a practice he would continue between 1907 and 1910 at his Intimate Theatre in Stockholm. Here Siri was no exception. His written advice to her was to play Mrs. X "as if she were an actress, not the typical proper family girl." She was to be the "stronger, that is to say, the more flexible. The stiffened one breaks, you see, but the pliable one bends back—and rises again." In his instructions Strindberg also gives the following paradoxical piece of advice—the kind that is a nightmare for all but the most advanced performers, and that illustrates the emphasis which Strindberg always placed on contradictions in roles and characters: "Study it terribly closely: but afterwards play it simply. That is, not 'simple.' Put about 50% charlatan behind it. . . . [A]nd imply chasm-like depth, which is not there."[6]

The criticism at the time of the première indicates that the critics by and large also perceived Mrs. X as the stronger. One critic for *Aftonbladet* wrote, though perhaps with irony: "It seems to me that she who had the most remarkable ability to stay quiet during all of this, actually is the strongest."[7] Strindberg had, in fact, written a piece in the Danish paper *Politiken* two months before in which he directly contradicted himself. He wrote there that the play's "heroine doesn't say a word."[8] Gunnar Ollén suggests that the production history of this remarkable one-act—which is now constantly being performed in many languages in all parts of the world—shows widely differing perceptions as to which of the two characters is in fact the stronger. This underscores an aspect of Strindberg's dramaturgy which has not been touched upon enough: his sense of contradiction—the ability to take any position and oppose it at the same time.

3.

Pariah (*Paria*), completed in January 1989, was also written to be a portable piece for possible touring. It fit many of the same requirements that Strindberg had set down for *The Stronger*, although it is more than twice as long. It was loosely based on a short story by his friend Ola Hansson, which Strindberg praised for traits it shared with the works of Edgar Allan Poe—whose prose was making a deep impression on Strindberg at that time. Other influences include Cesar Lombroso's criminal anthropology, which was related to the pseudoscience of phrenology—in that a criminal character could supposedly be determined, according to Lambroso's system, by external characteristics. There is also plenty of evidence of Nietzsche's influence.[9] Strindberg had already commenced his correspondence—most often in Latin—with the philosopher he believed to be his soulmate in the late 1880s. As always, these influences should be kept in perspective, for Strindberg transformed all ideas and artistic trends which he absorbed into something distinctively his own. In the case of Lombroso's theories, there is nothing in the play where Strindberg directly employs this "science," although he inserts it chillingly (and with a twist of irony) into a metaphor when Mr. X in *Pariah* says to Mr Y: "And the back of your head, then! It looks to me as if there were another face there. But a face of a different sort than yours. You are terribly narrow between the ears so that I wonder what race of men you belong to!"

The same can be said of Strindberg's application of Nietzsche's ideas in his plays. As in *Miss Julie*—where Strindberg's own notion of the Nietzschean "superior man" comes to mean the increasing superiority of the working classes, a highly un-Nietzschean notion in itself—the idea of the superior or stronger person here has nothing to do with some sort of *aryanism*, or class or race for that matter. It would be hasty to conclude that the play provides us with the non-

Christian moral (or any moral at all) as to the superior man's right to rule over the intellectually inferior. Even so, a fair number of critics have seen this two-man play as a depiction of a pariah pitted against an mental "brahmin," or an inferior man against an *über-mensch*. The play is not exactly set up that way. For both men, from the outset, are set up as pariahs. They have crimes in their pasts which place them outside of society. Pariahship can also be seen as a quality belonging only to the exceptional—though it may well belong to both the exceptionally dull or the exceptionally clever (Strindberg long felt himself to be a pariah in Sweden, after all). More to the point, the pariah of ruthless truth-seeking is set up against a pariah of ruthless lying. In the play, at first, they are hard to tell apart.

Strindberg had attempted to get Ola Hansson to dramatize the story himself. When the script was not forthcoming, Strindberg, who had come to the conclusion that the piece would provide the perfect opportunity to stage an "Edgar-Poer," set to work himself. In the Hansson story the traveling entomologist from America confesses the story of how he forged his signature on a bill of exchange—the victim of a compulsion which came over him as if from outside of himself. In the Strindberg stage version, the story itself is a ruse, a fiction created by an imagination fired into action during what Strindberg called a "battle of the brains" or "battle of souls" (*hjärnornas kamp*). Mr. Y is not in fact as stupid as Mr. X makes him out to be. A performance of the play cannot be nearly as interesting if Mr. Y is never permitted to get the upper hand. But like Poe's Dupin, Mr. X is the detective who is at the same time the true *artist*—the man who is capable of seeing the whole instead of the parts. It is that which, in the end, makes him the stronger.

Pariah has certain features in common with Strindberg's novella *Tschandala*, which he'd completed in December 1888.[10] It is widely accepted that the battle of minds in *Tschandala* is at least partly a product of Strindberg's own battles with Ludvig Hansen, the caretaker of the estate at Skovlyst in Denmark, where the Strindbergs lived in the summer of 1888. Strindberg's garrulous camaraderie with Hansen had quickly turned to open enmity.[11] Hansen's accusations about Strindberg—to the effect that he had seduced his supposedly "underaged" sister—were lapped up by several Swedish papers, who did not miss the value in a potential scandal involving Sweden's most famous pariah, a married man, cheating on his wife. This is an example of the ways myths were constructed around Strindberg, and how he in fact was partly responsible. In this case the facts were: the girl was not underage, Strindberg and Siri were no longer living as a married couple, he informed her of the affair—and the girl in question, when asked how it happened, answered: "I liked him a lot."[12] On the other hand, Strindberg suspected Hansen of being a thief and had him reported to the police.

In the story *Tschandala*, in which Master Törner is in a position similar to that of Mr. X in *Pariah*, and the character Jensen (i.e., "Hansen") in one like that of Mr. Y, Strindberg is at pains to show certain contradictions in the "inferior" man: "[I]n his admiration lay a bit of compassion with this person who didn't have sufficient discernment to see through another man's deceit. And true to his thief's nature, he couldn't resist fooling his unselfish benefactor and friend."[13] So the dishonest man is not without admiration or pity for the man of integrity.

The première of *Pariah* was to take place on the same program with *The Stronger* and *Creditors* in Denmark. Hans Riber Hunderup played Mr. X and Viggo Schiwe was Mr. Y. *Pariah* achieved considerable success, despite the hasty preparation after the sudden banning of *Miss Julie*. The reviewer for *Nationaltidende* found an "undeniable and charming genius" in the script. Carl Behrens wrote in *Ny Jord*, comparing the play with Hansson's short story, that Strindberg had "deepened the subject matter and written a sequence of absolutely superb speeches which contain a lot of witty and intriguing observations." *Morgenbladet* was impressed by Mr. X's "paradoxes," which were "portrayed half-ironically and thereby have a double effect." The paper's critic suggested that Strindberg should "apply the weapon of irony" and dispense with devices like "the razor in *Miss Julie* and the epilepsy in *Creditors*." In Sweden, however, the publication of *Pariah* provided an occasion for an attack on the movement of naturalism in general (which Strindberg was still championing). This came from the pen of Arvid Axelsson in *Nya Dagligt Allehanda* in April of 1890: "Naturalistic drama deals with phenomena that are examples of the abnormal, preferably criminals, murderers, idiots, disturbed and depraved souls that have fallen victim to nauseating diseases or the retribution of the law. The characters in 'Pariah' are a forger and a murderer . . ." Nevertheless, there were voices in Sweden which took a very different tone, such as that of Axel Krook in *Göteborgs-Posten* in March: "It is undeniable that there is something daring in the mental experiment of combining these two men, both of whom are actually outside of society . . . something original, which sets it apart from the usual wish-washy stuff . . ."[14]

4.

Simoom (Samum) fits into this triptych of plays as another take on the theme of the "battle of brains" or souls. It is obvious that something wildly different has occurred to Strindberg here. Naturalistic form is thrown out the window, for an attempt at stylization and a storm of bizarre imagery seizes hold of the play. It's as if his later formal experimentation after the Inferno years, emerges incompletely hatched in this puzzling *quart d'heure*. The play seems to have been completed on March 4, 1889 after a gestation period of several months. On February 27 Strindberg wrote to Siri that he had sketched out a play "in which you will be an Arab girl who soul-murders a French officer (with song, among other things)."[15]

The idea may have come to him considerably earlier. Arab motifs had been in the air for a decade. Verner von Heidenstam had written a sequence of poems praising the beauty of the East, and the poet Snoilsky had, in 1880, written a lush poem about the oasis of *Biskra* in Algeria. In 1889 an international congress of "orientalists" was planned for Stockholm. Strindberg wrote to Hansson on March 9: "[H]ave written a brilliant Edgar-Poer—called *Simoom* (in one act of course) in which I've employed the desert wind's ability to call forth terrifying visions which drive French soldiers to suicide."[16] Strindberg had once again drawn on his fascination with Poe. Added to this was his own peculiar brand of Nietzscheanism in which the oppressed have the potential to become the superiors. This, combined with works he was reading on hypnosis and suggestion emerging from the experiments of the "Nancy School" in France—which actually figures strongly in almost all the so-called naturalistic plays he wrote—pushed him in the direction of a formal experiment. Then as now it is an experiment which can probably only succeed under a strong directorial conceit, and with an actor who can move "over the top" with great fluidity.

The final product from Strindberg's hand ran entirely against the grain vis-a-vis the fad for things Eastern during the time. Goethe's *East-West Divan* had glorified the lyric ghazals of Hafez half a century before. Lesser minds perceived the East through the rose-colored lenses of travel writing. All was beauty and exoticism of the sort that would later emerge in the genre known as "guide-book." *Simoom* is no hymn of beauty—to either the European or Arab world. It is a struggle between oppressor and oppressed, a battle of minds, as well as a collision of cultures (one of which Strindberg knew only through reading) all wound together in a fifteen-minute format. Strindberg tried to sell his publisher Bonniers on the play, this "dramatic-poetic-arabic-psychologismic bit" with the suggestion that "There could be an unexpected market for Arab subjects after the congress."[17] The play was not produced until March 1890, when it was the opener for *Creditors* at Svenska teatern. The première received a universally negative response from the critics that time round—though a number of them suggested that Anna Lundberg in the role of Biskra was not the right actress to be able to drive it through with the right whirl-wind of passion. J.A. Runström in *Stockholms-Tidningen* wrote:

> This play is dominated by a wild power, but the nature of the subject is not such that justice can be done to it on the stage when all that is left of it is, for the most part, the awkward elements. The least that is required is acting talent of the highest caliber, to bring out the fantastically ghastly atmosphere, and in that regard, the whole play could clearly tolerate a wild allegro furioso. At Svenska Teatern it went instead at a moderato sustenato.

Aftonbladet's Georg Nordensvan saw it as a "strange and difficult poem" in which "the strong Bedouin race wins and triumphs over effete Europeans. . . . The play is sustained by a wild power. . . ." He adds, however: "The spectator knows nothing about these people . . . and therefore remains cold to their fate."[18]

Today it is safe to say that this is not quite so much the case—in a time when the tangled history of colonialism has made its way into schoolrooms, and the mass media has brought the daily struggles of distant peoples into the homes of Westerners. It might also be said that the Europeans in the age of colonialism had a stake in knowing "nothing about these people," and even more, not being so "distasteful" as to suggest that European massacres (which of course didn't happen) might justify for survivors the taking of European lives. Strindberg, as was so often the case, was out of step. Seventy years later Jean Genet would go deeply into similar themes in his most expansive play, *The Screens (Les Paravents)*, as colonial rule finally crumbled. There is a similarity in spirit between Strindberg's tiny play and Genet's epic that is striking.

By the turn of the century, this problem-child of a play would succeed in getting a better response. The first success came in 1902, when one of Scandinavia's best remembered actors took the part of the avenging Arab girl, Biskra: Harriet Bosse, Strindberg's third wife, for whom he had been writing another "Eastern" role—Indra's Daughter in *A Dream Play*.

Strindberg apparently had done some research: enough to know about the geography, about the fragile state of French colonial rule. He also knew of the existence of *marabouts*, shrines to holy men (which were also the sites of mystic schools in the Maghreb, suppressed by the French). He seems to have been particularly interested in the phrases used by Islamic mystics, drawn from the ritual prayer *Lâ ilâha ill'allâh* ("There is no God but God") which—though he was at that time agnostic or atheist—would have appealed to his distaste for idolatry, which belonged to his youthful religious ideals, and would fit with his later post-*Inferno* mystical ideas.[19] He also seems to have been aware that such phrases—including the two opening lines of the *Koran*—were used to attain certain "states" by

Islamic mystics in the marabout "schools." It is a curious fact, as these things were very little known by any Europeans, even those living in Arab countries. He was not correct about the state these phrases were supposed to achieve. In any case, he was both mixing it with hypnosis and indulging in a theatricalization of "oriental magic" to fit the trend.

It might be worth examining an anecdote which Strindberg included in his collection *Vivisections (Vivisektioner,* 1894) on his effort to find music for *Simoom*. It tells us something revealing about Strindberg's "naturalist" period—or his instincts for the theatrical despite it.

> I was looking for a melody to a one-act, *Simoom*, which takes place in Arabia [*sic*]. To do so, I tuned my guitar haphazardly, loosened the tuning pegs arbitrarily until I found a chord which gave me the impression of something exceptionally bizarre, but which nevertheless did not overstep the boundaries of art.
>
> The actor in the lead role thought the melody was suitable, but the director, an ultra-realist, saw that it wasn't genuine and decided he was going to have authentic music. I had a collection of Arab songs brought over, and showed them all to the director, who threw them out, and in the end considered that my tune was more Arabic than the real Arab ones.
>
> The melody was performed, and achieved a certain success.[20]

Almost another decade would pass before Strindberg would foster another movement in the theatre world with his play *To Damascus*: the epic pilgrimage drama which sowed the seeds of expressionism. In *Simoom* Biskra manipulates the inner world of the French officer's mind through suggestion, ventriloquism, and the use of props and objects in the real world, which change their significa-tion in Guimard's confused brain. She exploits a "theatre magic"—a semiotic flux—which Strindberg would later employ in works like *A Dream Play*, where a lime tree can become a coat rack and a church organ a grotto with stalactites. Already in *Simoom*, at the peak of his naturalist phase, Strindberg attempted to demonstrate how the inner world can be "staged" in the outer world. Strindberg would employ the technique extensively in his dramas after the turn of the century, in both pilgrimage plays and chamber plays—and most notably in the play where Eastern philosophy meets Western society, the drama of appearance and illusion: *The Ghost Sonata. Simoom* might be seen as a first awkward step, leading toward a modern theatre that was yet to be born. Strindberg, however, was to be present at the birth.

THE STRONGER

A Play in One Scene

(1888)

CHARACTERS

MRS. X, an actress, married
MLLE. Y, an actress, unmarried
[A WAITRESS]

THE SCENE

A corner in a café which caters to ladies; two small iron tables, a red shag sofa and some chairs.

MRS X enters, dressed for winter in a hat and coat, with a fine Japanese basket on her arm.

MLLE Y is sitting before a half-finished beer bottle and is reading an illustrated magazine, which she later exchanges for others.

MRS X Hello Amelie, dear! — You're sitting here so alone on Christmas Eve, like some poor bachelor.

MLLE Y *(glances up from the magazine, nods, and goes on reading.)*

MRS X You know, I'm really sorry to see you this way. Alone, alone at a café, and even on Christmas Eve. I feel as sorry as that time in Paris when I saw a wedding reception in a restaurant, and the groom played billiards with the witnesses. Hunh! I thought. With a start like that, how will they go on, and how will it end!

He was playing billiards on his wedding night! — And she was reading a comic book, you're thinking. Well, it's not exactly the same thing!

A WAITRESS enters and places a cup of chocolate in front of MRS X, and goes out.

MRS X You know what, Amelie? I think now you would have been better off to stay with him! You remember, I was the first to tell you: forgive him! Do you recall? — You could have been married now, with a home. You remember last Christmas, how happy you were when you were out with your fiancé's parents in the country? How you praised the joys of family life, and really longed to get away from the theatre! — Yes, Amelie dear, a home is by far the best there is — next to the theatre — and children you see — Well, you wouldn't understand that.

MLLE Y (*gives her a contemptuous look.*)

MRS X takes a few sips from the cup, then opens the basket, revealing her Christmas presents.

MRS X   Look at what I've bought for my little sweeties.— — (*She takes out a doll.*) Look at that! Lisa will get that one. You see, her eyes can roll and her neck twists around! Eh! — And here is Moe's cork-gun — (*Loading and firing the cork, attached by a string, at MLLE Y.*)

MLLE Y (*makes a gesture of horror.*)

MRS X   Were you scared? Did you think I'd shoot you? Eh? My Lord! I can't believe you'd think such a thing! It would surprise me less if you wanted to shoot *me* for getting in your way — And I know that you can't ever forget — although I was absolutely innocent. You still think that I conspired to make you lose your job at the theatre, but I didn't! I did not, even though you think so! — Well, it makes no difference what I say, because you still think it was me. (*She takes out a pair of embroidered slippers.*) And these are for my old man. With tulips on them that I embroidered myself — I loathe tulips, of course, but he likes to have tulips on everything.

MLLE Y (*looks up from her magazine ironically, and with curiosity.*)

MRS X (*slides a hand into each slipper.*) You see what small feet Bob has, eh? And such an elegant stride. You should see it! You've never seen him in slippers! (*MLLE Y laughs aloud.*) Look, I'll show you.

She walks the slippers across the table top.

MLLE Y (*laughs aloud.*)

MRS X   And then when he's mad, you see, then he stamps his foot like this: "What! Those goddamned maids! They can't even learn to make coffee! Ugh! Now the cretins have trimmed the lamp wicks wrong!"

And then there's a draft coming under the door, and his feet are freezing: "Jeesh! It's freezing here. And those thick-headed dolts can't even keep a fire going in the stove!"

She rubs the slippers together with the sole of one against the top of the other.

MLLE Y (*roars with laughter.*)

MRS X And then when he comes home and will be searching for his slippers, which Marie put under the bureau . . . Oh, but it's shameful to make fun of one's husband this way. He's a sweetheart really — a doll, actually. You should have had a man like that Amelie! — What are you laughing at? What! What! — And then I know, you see, that he is faithful to me. Yes, I know that. Because he himself has told me . . . what are you grinning at! — that while I was traveling in Norway, that nasty little Frédérique came around and tried to seduce him — Imagine, what gall! (*Pause.*) But I would have torn the eyes out of her head, I would, if she'd come around while I was home! (*Pause.*) It was fortunate that Bob brought it up himself, so that it didn't come out by way of gossip. (*Pause.*) But Frédérique was not the only one, I'll have you know! I don't know why it is, but girls go really crazy for my husband. They must think that he has some say about hiring at the theatre because he's in the ministry! — Perhaps you've been in there making passes at him too! — I wasn't sure if I wouldn't put it past you — but now I know that he didn't care about you, and it's always seemed to me that you've borne some grudge against him.

Pause.
They regard each other with some embarrassment.

MRS X Come over to our place this evening, Amelie, and show us that you're not angry with us — not angry with me anyway! I think it's awful to be on bad terms, especially with *you*. Perhaps it's because I got in your way that once — (*slowing gradually*) — or — I don't know why at all — actually.

Pause.

MLLE Y (*looks hard at* MRS X, *with curiosity.*)

MRS X (*in thought*) It's so strange, how we came to know one another. — When I first saw you I was afraid of you. So afraid that I didn't dare to let you slip out of my sight. So in all my comings and goings I still found a way to be near you. — I didn't dare become your enemy, so I became your friend. But there was always a disharmony when you came to our place because I saw that my husband couldn't stand you — and then things felt askew to me, like when your clothes aren't fitting properly — and I did everything possible to get him to show you some courtesy, but without success — Not until you went and got engaged! Then you became fast friends, so that for a time it seemed as if you both would show your real feelings for the first time, now that you had some security — and then — What happened next? — I wasn't jealous — how strange! — And I recall that at the baptism, when you were godmother, I made him kiss you — and he did, but you were so confused — that is to say I didn't notice it then — didn't think about it later either — haven't thought about it before — now!

She rises abruptly.

Why are you silent? You haven't said a word the whole time — just let me sit here talking! You've sat there with your big eyes and wound all of these thoughts out of me. Like raw silk from a cocoon — thoughts — suspicions perhaps — let me see — Why did you break off your engagement? Why didn't you ever come to our house after that? Why won't you come to see us tonight?

MLLE X (*makes a move to speak.*)

MRS X Quiet! You don't have to say anything because now I see everything! — So that's why you and why you and why you — Aha! — Now it all adds up! So that's it! — Ugh! I won't sit at the same table with you!

She moves her things to the other table.

That was why I had to embroider tulips, which I hate, on his slippers — because you liked tulips! That's why *(casting the slippers on the floor)* we had to live at lake Mälaren in the summer — because you couldn't stand salt water! That's why my boy had to be named Mauritz, because that's your father's name. That's why I had to wear your colors, read your authors, eat your favorite dishes, drink your drinks — your chocolate, for example! That's why — Oh my God — It's awful to think of it. Awful! — Everything. Everything came from you to me, including your passions! Your soul crept into mine like a maggot in an apple, ate and ate, dug and dug, until it was nothing but a shell on a bit of black meal! I wanted to flee from you, but I couldn't. You bewitched me like a serpent with your black eyes — I'd feel my wings lifting me, only to be dragged down. I was in the water with my feet bound, and the harder I swam with my arms, the deeper I worked my way down, down, till I'd sunk to the bottom, where you were waiting like a giant crab to grip me in your claws — and — that's where I am now!

Ugh, how I hate you, hate you, hate you! But you, you just sit there, silent, calm, indifferent — indifferent if it be new moon or full, Christmas or New Year's, if others are happy or miserable, unable to hate or love, motionless like a stork at a rat hole — You couldn't get your prey yourself, you couldn't pursue it, but you could wait it out! Here you sit in your corner — you know they call it the rat-trap in your honor — reading your papers to see whether anyone's suffered misfortune, if anybody's come to grief, if anybody's been fired at the theatre. Here you sit checking out your prey, calculating your chances for causing wrecks like a ship's pilot, receiving your payments of tribute!

Poor Amelie! You know, it makes me sorry for you just the same. Because I know that you're unhappy, unhappy like someone who has been hurt. And *evil* because you've been hurt. — I can't be mad at you, although I'd like to be — because you're still that little — and, well, that thing with Bob, I'm not concerned about that. — What's it to me, really? — And so what if you taught me to drink chocolate or if someone else taught me? It's all the same in the end!

She takes a sip from the cup — puts on an air of wisdom:

Chocolate is quite healthy as a matter of fact! And if I learned to dress from you — well, *tant mieux* — it's only made my husband all the more firmly attached to me — That's where your loss is my gain — Yes, judging from certain signs, I believe you've lost him already! — But it was obviously your intention that I would go my way, as you did — and like you, be sitting here now with my regrets — But you see I'm not! — Why be petty? And why would I want to have something no one else wants?

Maybe — now that it really comes down to the fact that at this moment I am the stronger of us — you never got anything from me, but only gave away — And now I am like the thief — when you awoke, I owned what you were missing!

Otherwise, why is it that everything becomes worthless and sterile in your hands? You couldn't keep any man's love — with all your tulips and your passions — as I have. You couldn't learn the art of living from all your authors like I've learned it. You've never had a little Moe, even though your father's name is Moe!

And why do you stay silent — always and forever silent, silent? Well, I thought it was strength, but maybe it was only that you had nothing to say! Because you couldn't think of anything.

She stands, and picks up the slippers.

Now I'm going home — and I'm taking the tulips with me — Your tulips! You couldn't learn anything from others. You couldn't bend — and so you broke like a dry reed — but I didn't!

Thank you Amelie, for all the things you've taught me so well. Thanks for teaching my husband how to love! — Now I'm going home to love him.

She goes.

End.

PARIAH

A Play in One Act

Freely, after a short story by Ola Hansson

(1889)

CHARACTERS

MR X, archeologist

MR Y, traveler from America

} Middle-aged men

THE SCENE

A simple room in the country: door and window at back, looking out into the countryside. In the middle of the floor, a large dining table with archeological relics, writing materials on one side: a microscope, a case holding an insect collection and glass bottles with preserving fluids.

To the left a bookshelf. Otherwise, the furnishings of a well-to-do farmer.

MR Y enters with a butterfly net and a botanical tin, dressed in his shirtsleeves; goes straight to the bookshelf and takes down a book, situating himself to read.

The bells from mass ring out in the country church. The landscape and room are starkly lit by the sun.

The cackling of hens can be heard outside now and again.

MR X enters in his shirtsleeves.

MR Y pulls himself together abruptly, places the book back upside down; gives the appearance that he is looking for another book on the shelf.

MR X What oppressive heat! I think we're clearly going to have thunder.

MR Y We-lll! What makes you think so?

MR X The chiming of the bells is so dry, the flies are biting and the hens are cackling. I intended to go out fishing, but I couldn't find a worm. Don't you feel nervous?

MR Y (*reflecting.*) Me? — Go on!

MR X You always look like you were expecting a thunderstorm, for that matter.

MR Y (*with a start.*) Do I?

MR X Well, you're going to be leaving tomorrow, so it wouldn't be odd if you had a bit of suitcase fever.

What's new! — There's the mail!

He picks up some letters from the table.

MR X Oh! I get palpitations every time I open a letter — nothing but debts, debts!

Have you ever been in debt?

MR Y (*ponders.*) Na-aah.

MR X Well, then you don't understand how it feels when unpaid bills arrive —

He reads a letter.

Rent not paid — landlord making a stink — the wife desperate! And me, up to the elbows in gold!

He opens a strongbox which is on the table, at which point they sit, one on either side.

You see, here I have six thousand crowns worth of gold, which I've dug up the last couple of weeks. I'd only need this bracelet here to get the three hundred fifty crowns I need! And with the whole thing I should be able to start up a brilliant career. Of course, I'd quickly have sketches and woodcuts made for my research study, have it printed — and move on. Why don't I do it, do you think?

MR Y You're afraid of being found out, of course!

MR X Perhaps that too! But don't you think that an intelligent person like myself could arrange things so that it wouldn't be found out?

I go out there alone — without witnesses — and poke around in the hills. Would it be so strange if I stuffed a little into my pockets?

MR Y Yes, but disposing of it is said to be the most dangerous part.

MR X Ah! Naturally I should melt it all down, and then mold gold ducats — up to official standards, naturally —

MR Y Naturally.

MR Y Of course, you understand! Because if I had merely wanted to forge money, then — I wouldn't need to dig up gold first!

Pause.

It is remarkable, in any case, that if another person were guilty of doing the thing that I can't get myself to do, I would have him acquitted. But myself, I would never be able to acquit. I would be able to present a brilliant defense for the thief — prove that this gold was *res nullius,* or no one's, since it was left in the earth at a time when there were no rights of ownership. That it didn't belong to anyone now either, other than the first comer, as the owner of the property had not taken it into account as part of his property value, and so on.

MR Y And you would be able to do this all the more easily if — hm! — the thief had not stolen out of need, but rather, for example, out of collecting mania. Out of scientific interest. Out of ambition to be able to possess a discovery. Right?

MR X You mean that I wouldn't be able to have him acquitted if he'd stolen out of need. No, for that is the one instance the law will not excuse. That is *theft,* pure and simple!

MR Y And that you would not excuse?

MR X Hm. Excuse! Of course I couldn't, since the law doesn't excuse it. And I must confess it would be hard for me to accuse a collector of theft if he took from another's land a newly discovered relic which wasn't already in his collection.

MR Y And so vanity, ambition, should excuse what need could not excuse.

MR X And, all the same, *need* should be the stronger, the only excuse. Yes, that's the way it is. I can change that just as little as I can change my own intention *not* to steal under any circumstances.

MR Y You count that as a great virtue, that you can't — hm — steal!

MR X With me it's just as irresistible as the urge to steal is irresistible for some other people, and therefore it is not a virtue. I can't steal, and he can't stop stealing! — You must grasp the fact that I don't lack the desire to own this gold! Why don't I take it, then? I can't! It is my inability. And a deficiency is not a virtue! So!

He slams the box shut.

Rain clouds have drawn over the landscape, and have now and then darkened the interior of the cabin. It now darkens as if a storm were gathering.

MR X It's so stuffy. I believe we're going to have thunder!
MR Y (*rises and closes the doors and windows.*)
MR X Are you afraid of thunder?
MR Y One should take precautions.

They sit at the table again.

MR X You are a curious fellow. You arrive here like a bomb out of the blue fourteen days ago, introduce yourself as a Swedish American who is out bagging flies for a little museum —
MR Y Oh, don't bother about me.
MR X That's what you always say when I get tired of talking about myself and start devoting some attention to you. Maybe that's why you seemed so appealing to me. Because you let me speak about myself so much!

 We were like old acquaintances right away. You had no edges that I could hurt myself on, no needles to stick me. There was something so mild in your whole character. You were so full of consideration, which only the most cultivated people can display. You never made a racket when you came in late, didn't make a stir when you got up in the morning, overlooked small annoyances, bowed out when things headed towards conflict — in a word, you were perfect company! But you were altogether too compliant, altogether too negative, too quiet, for me not to reflect upon it after a while — And you are extremely fearful and cautious — it seems as if you were someone's ghostly *double*. Do you know that, sitting here in front of the mirror and seeing your back — it's as if I were seeing another person.

MR Y turns and glances into the mirror.

MR X Yes, you can't see your own back! From the front you look like a forthright man, who faces his fate with bared breast. But from the back — Well, I don't want to be rude — but it looks as if you were carrying a burden. As if you were ducking from a blow with a stick. And when I see your red suspenders crisscrossing on that white shirt— — —it looks like a huge mark, a trademark on a crate— — —

MR Y (*rises.*) I think I'm going to suffocate — if the thunderstorm doesn't break soon.

MR X It will come shortly, just relax. — And the back of your head, then! It looks as if there were another face there. But a face of a different type than yours. You are terribly narrow between the ears so that I sometimes wonder what race of men you might belong to!

There is a flash.

MR X That looked as if it struck down at the district police office.

MR Y (*uneasy.*) At the d-district police office.

MR X Yes. It only looked like it. But those thunder clouds out there have blown over. Sit down now and let's talk, since you leave tomorrow. —

It is strange that you, who I grew close with right away, are one of those types whose image I cannot summon up when they're not present. When you are out in the fields and I try to recall you, I always see another person I know, who doesn't really resemble you, but with whom you share a certain likeness.

MR Y Who is that?

MR X I won't mention names! In any case, I ate dinner at the same place during a period of several years, and there I met a little blond man at the smörgåsbord — a man with light, agonized eyes. He had an uncanny ability to pass through the worst crowds without jostling others, and without being jostled. Though he was standing by the door he could get hold of a slice of bread from a distance of two yards. He always looked content to be among people. And when he saw someone he knew he fell into a guffaw of delight, embraced him and thumped him on the back as if he hadn't met a human being in years. If somebody trampled on his foot he laughed as if to be forgiven for getting in the way.

For two years I saw him and amused myself by trying to guess about his occupation and character. But I never asked anyone who he was, because I didn't want to know, since as soon as I did my little amusement would come to an end.

This man had the same quality as you — of being indefinable. At times I made him out to be a teacher without a degree, a lower officer, a pharmacist, a county clerk, or secret police. And he seemed, like you, to be made up of two different parts, because his front didn't fit with his back.

One day I happened to read in the paper about a scandalous case of forgery committed by a known public official. — I then found out that my indefinable friend had been the business partner of the forger's brother, and that his name was Strawman. And then I was informed that the aforementioned Strawman had previously been conducting business for lending libraries, but that he was now police reporter for a large daily. Where, then, do I find a connection between forgery, the police, and my indefinable friend's strange sort of behavior? I don't know. But when I asked a friend whether Strawman had ever been sentenced and punished for anything, he answered neither yes or no — He did not know!

Pause.

MR Y We-elll? Was he — punished?
MR X No! He was not punished!

Pause.

MR Y So that's why you think he stuck close to the police, and was
so afraid of offending people.

MR X Yes!

MR Y Did you get to know him later?

MR X No, I didn't want to.

Pause.

MR Y Would you have made his acquaintance if he had been —
punished?

MR X Yes, gladly.

MR Y (*rises and walks a few paces across the floor.*)

MR X Sit still! — Why can't you sit still!

MR Y Where have you gotten this tolerant view of human behavior?
Are you a Christian?

MR X No. You should know that by now.

MR Y (*gives him a look.*)

MR X Christians require forgiveness, but I require punishment in
order to restore *balance*, or whatever you'd like to call it. And
you, who have been locked up, ought to know about that.

*MR Y stops, is immobile, regarding MR X with a wild, scornful look,
then with amazement and admiration.*

MR Y How — can — you — know — that?

MR X I can see it, of course.

MR Y How? How can you see it?

MR X I have taught myself. It's an art, like so many others! But
that's not the issue at hand!

*He looks at his watch, sets out a paper for signing, dips the pen
and extends it to MR Y.*

MR X I have to think about my muddled finances. Be so good as to witness my signature on that loan application, which I'll be dropping at Malmö Bank tomorrow morning when I head out with you.

MR Y I don't intend to travel via Malmö.

MR X Not via Malmö!

MR Y No!

MR X But you can witness my signature in any case.

MR Y N-no! — I never sign my name to any papers —

MR X — anymore! That's the fifth time you've refused to write your name. The first was on a post office receipt — that was when I began to watch you. And since then I've noticed you have a fear of holding an ink pen. You haven't sent a single letter since you came here, but one postcard — and that you wrote with blue pencil. Do you see now that I've taken note of every false step!

Furthermore! It is the seventh time you have refused to join me to Malmö. You haven't been there during your entire stay here. And yet you have come here from America just to see Malmö. And each morning you walk south several miles to the mill grounds to be able to see the rooftops of Malmö. And when you're standing there at the right-hand window and peer out through the third pane to the left, roughly, you can see the spires of the castle and the chimneys of the county jail.

You see that it's not so much that I'm so quick, but that you are so stupid!

MR Y You must despise me now.

MR X No.

MR Y Yes you do. You must!

MR X No! — Here's my hand on it!

MR Y (*kisses his outstretched hand.*)

MR X (*pulls his hand back.*) Why are you acting like a dog!

MR Y Forgive me, sir. But you are the first person who has reached a hand to me *after* finding out! —

MR X And now you're getting formal with me! — It's frightening to me, that after having undergone punishment, you don't feel that you're rehabilitated, equal, cleansed — just as good as the next person. Will you tell me how it happened? Will you?

MR Y (*fidgets.*) Yes. But you won't believe what I tell you. I will talk about it, and you will see that I am not any typical sort of criminal. You will be convinced that there are lapses that are involuntary, so to speak — (*fidgeting*) — that is, as if they come on you of themselves — spontaneously — without your willing it. And which are not your fault! — May I open the door a bit, I think the storm has passed.

MR X Please do!

MR Y opens the door. Then he sits at the table and narrates the following with dry enthusiasm, theatrical gestures and false emphasis.

MR Y Yes. You see. I was a student in Lund. And at one time I was supposed to get a bank loan. I had no debts worth worrying about, and my father had a bit of property — not much, to be sure! In any case, I had sent out the promissory note to the second guarantor to have it signed, and against all expectations I got it back with a refusal. — I sat there for a while stunned by the blow, since it was an unpleasant surprise. Very unpleasant! — The paper lay in front of me on the table and the letter beside it. At first my eyes wandered inconsolably over the fatal lines which contained my sentence — It was clearly no death sentence, since I could very easily find other guarantors. As many as I wanted, in fact — But as I was saying, it was very unpleasant as it was. And somehow I'm sitting there in my innocence, my glance gradually comes to rest on this signature on the letter which, in the right place, might have made my future. It was an unusual, calligraphy-like signature — You know how you can sit lost in thoughts and fill up blotting paper with the most meaningless words. I had my pen in hand — (*Picks up the pen*) — like so. And for whatever reason it begins to go — I won't claim that there was anything mystical-spiritistical behind it — because I don't believe in those things! — It was purely a nonconscious, mechanical process — as

I sat there copying that lovely autograph time after time — of course without any idea of getting anything out of it.

By the time the letter was completely covered with scribbling, I had acquired enough skill to sign the name —

He throws the pen away violently.

— and then I forgot the whole matter. That night I slept soundly and deeply — and when I woke I had the feeling that I had dreamed, but I couldn't recall my dream. — At times, though, it was like a door was opening, and I saw the desk with the promissory note like a memory — and when I got up, I was driven toward the table completely as if I, after careful consideration, had made the irrevocable decision to write this name at the bottom of that fatal paper. All thought of consequences, of risks, had vanished — It was almost like I were fulfilling a sacred duty — and I wrote!

He leaps up.

What can this be? Is it an inspiration from somewhere? "Suggestion," as they call it? But from whom? I was the only one sleeping in that room. Could it have been my primitive self, the wild part of me which couldn't hold out and resist? Which while my conscience was sleeping, took control with its criminal will, and its inability to consider the consequences of an act? Tell me what you think about that!

MR X struggles with his response.

MR X To tell the truth, your story doesn't satisfy me completely — there are holes. But that can arise from the fact that you can no longer recall all the details. — And I have been reading something or other about criminal compulsions — I'm trying to recall — hm! — But it's all the same anyway — you have gone through your correction — — and you have had the guts to confess your offense. We'll speak of it no further.

MR Y Yes, yes, yes. We will talk further about it! We will talk so that I will be fully conscious of my own innocence.

MR X Aren't you already?

MR Y No, I'm not.

MR X Yes, you see, that's what's bothering me! — Don't you think that every human being has a corpse on his conscience? Haven't we all lied and stolen as children? Yes, of course. Well now, there are people who remain children their entire lives, so that they can't gain control over their illicit desires. All it takes is for the opportunity to arise, and the crime is committed! — But I don't understand why you don't feel innocent. Since children are not considered responsible for their actions, the criminal should be considered in the same light.

It is remarkable — well, it's all the same — I might regret this later —

Pause.

I have killed a man — me — and I have never felt any scruples.

MR Y (*interested in the utmost.*) Have — you?

MR X Yes, right. Me! — Maybe you wouldn't want to take the hand of a murderer?

MR Y (*cheerfully.*) Ah, the way you talk!

MR X Yes. But I haven't been punished.

MR Y (*intimate, superior.*) All the better for you! — How did you slip out of it, then?

MR X There was no plaintiff, no suspicions, no witness. The matter went like this, you see. — A companion had invited me to go hunting outside of Uppsala one Christmas. He sends to me an old, drunken coachman, who falls asleep in the driver's seat, gets us stuck in the gate, and overturns in the ditch. I won't blame it on the fact that my life was endangered — But rather, in an attack of impatience I gave him a chop with my hand on the neck, to wake him up. But with the result that he never woke again. Instead he died on the spot!

MR Y (*cunningly.*) We-lll, and you didn't turn yourself in?

MR X No. On the following grounds. The man had no dependents or others for whom his life was necessary. He had lived out his vegetation period, his position could be taken immediately by someone who could make better use of it. Meanwhile, on the other hand, I was indispensible for the well-being of my parents, for myself and for science. Through the outcome of the incident, I was cured of my wishes to give other people chops to the neck. And I had no desire to ruin my parents lives and my own in order to satisfy an abstract justice!

MR Y Ah, so that's how you judge the value of a human life?

MR X In the case before us, yes.

MR Y But what about the sense of guilt? The balance?

MR X I had no sense of guilt, because I hadn't committed any crime. I had given and taken neck-chops of that sort as a boy. And it was only my ignorance of the effect that sort of thing has on older folks which brought about the fatal result.

MR Y Yes, but it is still two years hard labor for accidental man-slaughter — the same length of time as for — writing people's signatures.

MR X I have also thought of that, of course, you can imagine! And many's the night I've dreamt I was in jail. Ugh! Listen, is it so hard as they say to live under lock and key?

MR Y Yes, it *is* hard. — First they distort your appearance by cutting off your hair, so that if you didn't look like a criminal before, you do afterwards. And when you look at yourself in the mirror you become convinced that you're a bandit.

MR X Perhaps it's that the mask has been pulled off. Not so bad for a calculated effect!

MR Y You must be joking! — And then they cut down your diet so that with each day and hour you feel distinctly the dividing line between life and death! All life functions are repressed. You feel how you are shrinking. And your soul, which is supposed to have been cured, is prescribed a starvation diet. It's forced to regress a thousand years back in time. You are only allowed to read things that were written for savages during the time of the great migrations. You are only allowed to hear about what is never going to come to pass in Heaven, while what's happening on earth is kept a secret. You are torn loose from your surroundings. You're brought out of your class and are beneath them who are beneath you! Have visions of living in the bronze age — feel as if you were going around in animal skins — lived in a hole and ate from a trough! Oh!

MR X Yes, but there is a logic in it, since anyone who acts as if he were from the bronze age might just as well live in the costume of his period.

MR Y (*angered.*) And you can be so scornful! You who have acted like a person from the stone age! And yet can live in the golden age!

MR X (*searching, sharp.*) What do you mean by that last term — golden age?

MR Y (*insidious.*) Nothing at all.

MR X You're lying, because you're too cowardly to say exactly what you mean!

MR Y Am I cowardly? Do you think so? I wasn't a coward when I dared to take the steps which led me to the place that made me suffer as I have. — But do you know what you suffer from most when you're sitting in there? — Yes, my friend. It's the fact that the others are not sitting in there too!

MR X Which others?

MR Y The unpunished!

MR X Are you alluding to me?

MR Y Yes!

MR X I've never committed any crimes.

MR Y Ohhh no?

MR X No. An accident isn't any crime.

MR Y Really! It is an accident when you commit a murder?

MR X I have not committed murder!

MR Y *Soo* — it isn't murder when you kill a person?

MR X No, not always. There is homicide, manslaughter, assault with
fatal outcome, with the subcategories "with intent" and "without
intent." Meanwhile — now I am really afraid of you — because
you belong to the most dangerous category of my fellow human
beings — the stupid!

MR Y Really. You believe that I am stupid. Listen you! Would you
like some proof that I am quite astute?

MR X Let's hear this!

MR Y We'll see if you don't confess my reasoning logical and smart
when I put things in this way!

You have been caught up in an accident which could have
brought a sentence of two years hard labor down on you. You
have gotten out of facing your shameful punishment completely.
Now, here sits a man — who has been the victim of an accident —
an unconscious impulse — and had to suffer two years' hard labor.
Only through his important scientific credentials can this man wash
away the blot which he has unwittingly gotten on his life. — But
in order to get these credentials, he has to have money — a lot of
money — and money now, preferably!

Don't you think that the other — the one who hasn't been
punished — would restore balance to the human situation, if he
were sentenced to pay a reasonable restitution? Don't you think
so?

MR X (*calmly.*) Ye-ess.

MR Y Well. We understand each other then! — Hm! — (*Pause.*)
How much do you consider reasonable?

MR X Reasonable? The law sets restitution at a minimum of fifty
crowns. But as the deceased had no dependents, all discussion of
the matter is irrelevant.

MR Y You really don't understand! Then I will speak more plainly:
It is to me that you will pay restitution.

MR X I've never heard the like — for a murderer to pay restitution
to a forger! — And besides, there is no prosecutor here!

MR Y No? — Yes — I am here!

MR X Now it's beginning to come clear! — How much do you want,
to become an accomplice to the murder?

MR Y Six thousand crowns!

MR X That is too much! — Where am I going to get them?

MR Y (*points to the box.*)

MR X I won't do that. I will not be a thief.

MR Y Don't play games with me. Do you want to have me believe that you haven't grabbed anything out of that box before?

MR X (*as if to himself.*) To think that I could make such a capital mistake. But that's how it is with these soft sorts. We like soft personalities. And it's so easy to believe that we are being liked in return: and that's exactly why I have been on my guard against those I liked! — So you are fully convinced that I have already been taking from the box?

MR Y Yes, I'm sure!

MR X And now you will turn me in if you don't get six thousand crowns?

MR Y Most definitely! You can't get out of it, so it's not worth trying.

MR X You think that I would give my father a thief for a son, my wife a thief for a husband, my children a thief for a father, and my brethren in my field a thief as a colleague? That will never happen. — Now I'm going to the authorities to turn myself in.

MR Y leaps up and collects his things.

MR Y Wait a minute!

MR X What for?

MR Y (*stammering.*) I was only thinking — that since I'm not needed anymore — that I didn't need to hang around — and might just as well go.

MR X No you don't! — Now sit down at the table where you just were, and we'll chat a little first.

MR Y sits down after putting on a dark coat.

MR Y What. What next?

MR X (*looks into the mirror behind* MR Y.) Now it's all clear to me! Ah! —

MR Y (*uneasily.*) What do you see that's so remarkable?

MR X I see in the mirror that you are a thief! — Just now, as you were sitting there in your white shirt, I just noticed that there was something out of order on my bookshelf. But I couldn't figure out *what*, because I wanted to listen to you and observe you. Now, since I've started feeling my dislike for you, my eyes have grown sharper. And after you put on your black coat which makes a color contrast to that red book binding — which couldn't be seen before against your red suspenders — now I see that you've been reading about your forgery story in Bernheim's study on compulsion, and have put the book back upside down! So you stole that story as well!

On the basis of that fact, I'd consider it correct to conclude that you committed your crime out of need, or out of pure pleasure!

MR Y Out of need. If you knew —

MR X If *you* knew the kind of need I have lived in — and live in! But that's neither here nor there! — To continue! That you have been locked up — that is almost for certain, but it was in America. Because that was life in an American prison you described. Another thing almost just as certain is that you have not done your time *here*!

MR Y How can you say that!

MR X (*rises.*) Wait until the police arrive, and you'll find out!

MR Y (*gets up.*)

MR X You see that! The first time I mentioned the police in connection with the lightning, you wanted to run then too! And when a man has been in a jail, he would never walk to a mill every day just to have a look at it, or stand at the window pane —

In a word: you are both punished and unpunished. And that's why you were so unusually hard to figure out!

Pause.

MR Y (*completely beaten.*) Can I go now?

MR X Now you can go!

MR Y (*gathering his things.*) Are you angry with me?

MR X Yes! — Would you prefer I pity you?

MR Y (*sullen.*) Pity? Do you consider yourself better than me —

MR X Of course I do, since I am your better. I am smarter than you, and have here upheld the rights of common property.

MR Y You are quite shrewd, but not as shrewd as me! I am in check, but after the next move you may be in checkmate nonetheless.

MR X (*stares at Y.*) Shall we go another round? — What evil are you planning now?

MR Y That's my secret!

MR X Let me have a look at you. — You're thinking of writing an anonymous letter to my wife to tell about my secret!

MR Y Yes, and there's nothing you can do to prevent it! You don't dare put me in prison. So you've got to let me go. And when I have gone I can do as I please!

MR X Oh you devil! You've found my Achilles heel — you want to force me to be a murderer?

MR Y That you'll never be — poor thing!

MR X You see, no two people are the same. And you have the feeling that I'm not capable of the same type of thing as you, and that therefore you have the advantage. But just think, if you forced me to do to you what I did to the driver!

He lifts his hand as if to strike.

MR Y (*looks X hard in the face.*) You can't do it! Anyone who can't take his salvation out of a box, can't do that!

MR X So you don't believe that I've taken anything from the box.

MR Y You were too much of a coward. Just as you were too cowardly to tell your wife she was married to a murderer.

MR X You are a different sort of person than I am — whether stronger or weaker — I don't know — more criminal or not — don't touch me! — but that you are more stupid, that's for sure. Because you were stupid when you wrote another person's name instead of begging, which I am able to do. You were stupid when you went and stole from my book — didn't you think that I read my books? — You were stupid when you thought you were smarter than me and that you could trick me into becoming a thief. You were stupid when you thought it would create *balance* if the world got two thieves instead of one. And you were most stupid of all when you imagined that I'd gone and built my life's happiness without laying the cornerstone securely! Go ahead and write anonymous letters to my wife, that her husband's a killer — She already knew that when we were engaged.

Do you give up now?

MR Y   May I go?

MR X   Now you'd *better* go! This second! — Your things will follow! Out!

SIMOOM

(1889)

CHARACTERS

BISKRA, an Arab girl
YOUSSEF, her lover
GUIMARD, lieutenant in the Zouaves

In Algeria [Latter half of the 19th century.]

THE SCENE

An Arab Marabout (burial shrine) with a sarcophagus in the middle of the floor. Prayer rugs here and there. In the right-hand corner, an enclosure containing bones.

A door at the back with gates and curtains: window apertures on the back wall.

Small heaps of sand here and there on the ground: an uprooted aloe, palm fronds, and esparto grass in a heap.

SCENE I.

BISKRA enters wearing a burnoose with the hood drawn down over her face and a guitar on her back, casts herself down on a rug and prays with her arms across her breast.

Outside the wind is blowing.

BISKRA *Lâ ilâha ill'allâh!*

YOUSSEF enters quickly.

YOUSSEF Simoom is coming! Where's the Frank?

BISKRA He will be here any minute.

YOUSSEF Why didn't you cut him down on the spot?

BISKRA No! Because he must do it all himself! If I did it, the whites would kill all our tribe, because they know that I was the guide Ali, even though they don't know that I am the girl, Biskra!

YOUSSEF He's going to do it himself? How will that happen?

BISKRA Don't you know that Simoom dries up the whites' brains like dates? And that they get nightmare visions which make life look so ghastly that they flee out into the great unknown?

YOUSSEF I have heard these stories. And at the last encounter six of the French had taken their lives by their own hands before they made it through. But don't count on Simoom today, because snow has fallen on the mountains, and in half an hour it could all blow over. — Biskra! Can you still hate?

BISKRA Can I hate? — My hate is boundless as the desert, burns like the sun and is stronger than my *love*! Every moment of pleasure they have stolen from me since they murdered Ali, has gathered like the venom under the adder's tooth. And what Simoom can't do, *I* can!

YOUSSEF What you've said is right, Biskra. And you will succeed. My hate has faded like esparto at harvest, since you came into my sight. Take power from me, and be the arrow of my bow.

BISKRA Hold me Youssef! Hold me!

YOUSSEF Not here in the presence of the sacred. Not now — later, after! After you've earned your wages!

BISKRA Glorious shaikh. Glorious man!

YOUSSEF Yes — the woman that's to carry my child beneath her heart, she must show herself worthy of the honor.

BISKRA I — no one else — will bear Youssef's child. I, Biskra — despised, homely — but I have power!

YOUSSEF Well then. I'll go down below and sleep at the well! — You don't need me to show you the secret arts which you learned from the great Marabout Siddi-Shaikh, do you? — The ones you've been perfecting in the marketplace since you were a child!

BISKRA No, there's no need. — I know all the secrets I need to scare the life out of a cowardly Frank. The coward that creeps up on his enemy and sends lead bullets ahead of him. I can do everything — including throwing my voice. And what my arts can't do, the sun will do, because the sun is with Youssef and Biskra!

YOUSSEF The sun is a friend to Muslims. But you mustn't depend on using that. You might burn yourself, girl!

Have a drink of water first, because I see that your hands are wrinkling and— — —

He has lifted a rug, opened a hatch in the floor, and goes down for a bowl of water, which he hands to BISKRA.

BISKRA (*lifts the bowl to her mouth.*) — And my eyes are beginning to see red — my lungs are becoming dry — I hear — I hear — Do you see how the sand is already trickling through the roof — and the strings of the guitar are singing — Simoom is here! But not the Frank!

YOUSSEF Come down here Biskra, and let the Frenchman die — by himself!

BISKRA First *hell.* And afterwards death! Do you think I'd back out? (*She tosses the water on a sand pile.*) I will water the sand so revenge can grow! And I will dry out my heart. Grow hate! — burn sun! — choke wind!

YOUSSEF Praise be with you, Ibn Youssef's mother! Because you shall bear my son, the avenger. You!

The winds picks up, the curtain in front of the door flaps: a red glow lights the room but transforms during the following scene to yellow.

BISKRA The Frank is coming, and — Simoom is here! — Go!

YOUSSEF In a half an hour you'll see me again. There is the sand of your hour glass. (*He points to a pile of sand.*) Heaven itself will measure the length of the heathen's hell.

SCENE II.

BISKRA. GUIMARD enters staggering and pale, confused, speaking with a weakened voice.

GUIMARD The Simoom has started! — Which way do you think my people have gone?

BISKRA I directed your people to go from west to east.

GUIMARD West to — east! — Let me see! — That is due east, and
— west! — Could you get me to a chair, and give me some water?

*BISKRA leads GUIMARD to a mound of sand, lays him on the floor
with his head on the sand.*

BISKRA Are you sitting all right?
GUIMARD (*looking at her.*) I'm sitting a bit crooked. Put something
behind my head.

BISKRA piles the sand up under his head.

BISKRA There. Now you have a pillow under your head.
GUIMARD Head. That's my feet there! — Aren't those my feet
there?
BISKRA Yes, of course!
GUIMARD I thought so! — Give me a stool now for my — head!

BISKRA brings forth the aloe and places it under GUIMARD's knees.

BISKRA There. Now you have a stool!
GUIMARD And water! — Water!

*BISKRA takes the empty bowl, fills it with sand, and extends it to
GUIMARD.*

BISKRA Drink while it is cold!
GUIMARD It *is* cold — but even so, it doesn't quench your thirst! —
I can't drink — water disgusts me — take it away!
BISKRA There's the dog that bit you!
GUIMARD What dog! I've never been bitten by any dog.
BISKRA Simoom has dried up your memory — watch out for
Simoom's delusions! You remember the mad greyhound that bit
you at the hunt before last in Bab-el-Ouëd.
GUIMARD The hunt in Bab-el-Ouëd! That's right! — Was it a
beaver-colored —

BISKRA — bitch? Yes! That's it! And it bit you on the calf. Don't you feel the wound stinging —

GUIMARD (*grabs hold of his calf, and sticks himself on the aloe.*) Yes, I feel it! — Water! Water!

BISKRA (*hands him a bowl of sand.*) Drink! Drink!

GUIMARD No, I can't! Holy Mary Mother of God — I am scared out of my wits.

BISKRA Don't be afraid. I will cure you and drive out the demon with the power of music. Listen!

GUIMARD (*screams.*) Ali! Ali! Not music! I can't stand it! And what good is it to me?

BISKRA Music tames the serpent's deceitful spirit. Don't you think that it can manage a mad dog's? Listen!

She sings with the guitar.

BISKRA Biskra-Biskra, Biskra-Biskra, Biskra-Biskra.
Simoom! Simoom!

YOUSSEF (*from below.*) Simoom! Simoom!

GUIMARD What's that you're singing! Ali?

BISKRA Was I singing? Look, now I'll put a palm leaf in my mouth.

She takes a palm frond between her teeth. Singing is heard from above.

BISKRA Biskra-Biskra, Biskra-Biskra, Biskra-Biskra.

YOUSSEF (*from below.*) Simoom! Simoom!

GUIMARD What damned hocus-pocus!

BISKRA Now I'll sing. (*BISKRA and YOUSSEF together.*)
Biskra-Biskra, Biskra-Biskra, Biskra-Biskra.
Simoom!

GUIMARD (*rises.*) Who are you — devil that sings with two voices! Are you a man or a woman? Or both?

BISKRA I am Ali, the guide! You don't recognize me because your mind is confused. But if you want to save yourself from deliriums of sight and thought, then trust me. Trust what I say, and do as I tell you.

GUIMARD You don't need me to do that. Because I'm finding that everything *is* as you say it is.

BISKRA That's the way — idolater!

GUIMARD Idolater?

BISKRA Yes. Take out that idol you wear on your chest.

GUIMARD (*pulls out a medallion.*)

BISKRA Trample it under your feet. And praise God the One, the Compassionate, the Merciful!

GUIMARD (*hesitates.*) Saint Edward. My patron saint — my protector.

BISKRA Can he protect you now? Can he?

GUIMARD No, he can't! — (*Coming to.*) — Yes. Yes he can!

BISKRA Let's see then!

She opens the door, the curtains flap and the esparto grass begins to move.

GUIMARD (*hand to his mouth.*) Shut the door!

BISKRA Throw down the idol!

GUIMARD No, I can't!

BISKRA You see! Simoom doesn't touch a hair on my head. But you, unbeliever, he will kill! Throw down the idol!

GUIMARD (*tosses the medallion on the floor.*) Water! I'm dying!

BISKRA Pray to the One, the Compassionate, the Merciful!

GUIMARD How should I pray?

BISKRA Repeat my words!

GUIMARD Say them!

BISKRA God is One, there is no other God but He, the Compassionate, the Merciful.

GUIMARD "God is One, there is no other God but He, the Compassionate, the Merciful!"

BISKRA Lie down on the floor!

GUIMARD (*lies down reluctantly.*)

BISKRA What do you hear?

GUIMARD I hear the murmuring of a spring!

BISKRA You see! God is One, and there is no other than He, the Compassionate, the Merciful. — What do you see?

GUIMARD I see the murmuring of a spring — I hear a lamp being lit — in a window with green shutters — on a white street —

BISKRA Who is sitting at the window?

GUIMARD My wife — Elise!

BISKRA Who is standing behind the curtain putting his hand on her neck?

GUIMARD That is my son — Georges!

BISKRA How old is your son?

GUIMARD Four years old — on Saint Nicholas day!

BISKRA And can he already stand behind the curtain with his arms around the neck of another man's wife?

GUIMARD No he can't — but it *is* him!

BISKRA Four years old, with a blond mustache?

GUIMARD Blond mustache — you say! — Ah, that's Jules, my friend!

BISKRA Who is standing behind the curtain with his arms around your wife's neck!

GUIMARD Ah! Devil!

BISKRA Do you see your son?

GUIMARD No, not anymore.

BISKRA (*imitates the ringing of bells on her guitar.*) What do you see now?

GUIMARD I see bells ringing — and I feel the taste of a corpse — it smells like rancid butter in my mouth — ugh! —

BISKRA Don't you hear the Deacon singing out — "A child deceased!"

GUIMARD Wait a minute! — I can't hear that — (*gloomily*) — but if that's what you want? — then — now I hear it!

BISKRA Do you see the wreath on the coffin which they're carrying between them?

GUIMARD Yes —

BISKRA There are violet ribbons — and there, printed in silver letters — "Farewell my belovéd Georges — your father."

GUIMARD Yes, it says that! — (*Weeping.*) — My Georges! Georges! My darling child! — Elise my wife, comfort me! — Help me! (*He gropes about.*) Where are you? Elise! Have you gone from me? Answer! Call out the name you love!

A VOICE FROM THE CEILING Jules! Jules!

GUIMARD Jules! — My name is?— — —What is my name? — My name is Charles! — And she yelled *Jules*! — Elise — my dear wife — answer me, because your spirit is here — I can feel it — and you promised me that you'd never love any other —

The VOICE laughs.

GUIMARD Who is that laughing?

BISKRA Elise! Your wife!

GUIMARD Kill me! — I don't want to live any longer! Life nauseates me, like sauerkraut in sain-doux — Do you know what *sain-doux* is? Hogs' lard! (*He spits.*) I don't have any more saliva — water! Water! Or else I'll bite you!

Full storm outside.

BISKRA (*puts her hand to her mouth and coughs.*) Now you die, Frenchman. Write your last will while there's time! — Where is your notebook?

GUIMARD (*takes out his notebook and pen.*) What should I write?

BISKRA A man thinks of his wife when he is going to die — and of his children.

GUIMARD (*writes.*) "Elise, I damn you to hell! Simoom — I'm dying—"

BISKRA And so sign it, or your testament isn't valid.

GUIMARD What — sign?

BISKRA Write: *Lâ ilâha ill'allâh!*

GUIMARD (*writes.*) I've written it. Can I die now?

BISKRA Now you may die. Like a cowardly soldier who has deserted his people! — And you're likely to have a lovely burial, with the jackals singing hymns over your corpse.

She drums the "charge" on her guitar.

BISKRA Do you hear the drums playing the "charge" — the infidels who have the sun and Simoom with them sweep forward, from where they've been lying in ambush —

She strikes the guitar.

Shots go off all along the line — the Franks aren't able to reload — the Arabs shoot in scattered order — the Franks flee! —

GUIMARD (*rising.*) The French don't flee!

BISKRA (*plays a "Retreat" on a flute she has taken up.*) The French flee, when they hear the "Retreat!"

GUIMARD They're pulling out — that's the Retreat — and I am here —

He tears off his epaulets.

GUIMARD I am a dead man!

He falls to the ground.

BISKRA Yes, you are dead. — You don't know that you've been dead a long time! —

She goes to the bones and pulls out a skull.

GUIMARD Have I been dead?

He puts his hands to his face.

BISKRA A long time. A long time. — Look here in the mirror!

GUIMARD Ah! Is that me?

BISKRA Don't you see how your cheekbones are standing out — Don't you see how the vultures ate your eyes — can't you still feel the hole from the right molar you had pulled out — Don't you see the hollow on your chin where your pretty little imperial once grew, which your Elise liked to stroke — Don't you see where the ear once was which your Georges used to kiss in the morning at the coffee table — Don't you see here where the blade struck the back of your head — when the executioner put the deserter to death!— — —

GUIMARD, who has watched and listened in horror, falls lifeless.

BISKRA who has been kneeling, rises after she has examined his pulse. She sings.

BISKRA Simoom! Simoom!

She opens the doors. The draperies flutter: she puts her hands before her mouth and falls backwards.

BISKRA Youssef!

SCENE III.

BISKRA, GUIMARD. YOUSSEF climbs up from the cellar. YOUSSEF examines GUIMARD, looks for BISKRA.

YOUSSEF Biskra!

He catches sight of her, lifts her in his arms.

YOUSSEF Are you alive?
BISKRA Is the Frank dead?
YOUSSEF If he isn't, he will be. Simoom. Simoom!
BISKRA Then I will live! But give me some water.
YOUSSEF (*bears her toward the hatch in the floor.*) Here! — Now Youssef is yours.

BISKRA   And Biskra will be the mother of your son.   Youssef, glorious Youssef!

YOUSSEF   Your power Biskra.   More power than Simoom.

Curtain.

APPENDIX
TOTEN-INSEL: *Hades* (A Fragment)

Background: Boecklin's painting, *The Isle of the Dead*. The stage is empty. First whispering is audible, then soft voices, talking.

The GUARDIAN, on the upper terrace of the hill, comes forward and blows on a *lur*.

The TEACHER, a man completely clad in white with a Zeus-like head but white hair and beard, emerges from the grove of cypresses, going down to the dock.

A black boat with an oarsman clad in black comes in from the left, bearing a white coffin, beside which stands a figure in white.

*

TEACHER Who?

FIGURE Read this!

TEACHER (*takes the plate from the coffin and reads.*) I know him! — A poor human being who was tormented to death by life. . . . No, don't frighten him . . .

The coffin is pushed onto land.

Sixty-two years of toil, duties, sorrows . . . no flowers, no wreaths . . .

FIGURE Your orders!

TEACHER First the salutation!

INVISIBLE CHOIR "And God shall wipe away all tears from their eyes; and there shall be no more death, neither sorrow nor crying, neither shall there be any more pain: for the former things are passed away."

*

TEACHER (*to the DEAD MAN.*) Awake!

DEAD MAN (*sits up.*) What time is it, Anna? — I thought I heard ringing . . . Oh, I am so sleepy, so tired . . . if only I could sleep an hour more, just one hour . . . lessons at six thirty, yes, but I have fifty essay books to correct first, seventh form essays . . . What is it? Bills: the butcher, the tailor, the bookstore, we'll never get our heads above water this year. But I must have two guarantors for the loan by twelve o'clock, and I've only got one, and I've been thinking of . . . of Jansson, he'll sign, but his name doesn't carry much weight, might not work . . . Hummel is rich, but he has principles . . . the butcher'll have to wait, Oh I am so tired, only one hour until . . . and then there's the rent and Edvard's books, the girls need new boots, I promised Greta gloves . . . Could you please put on some coffee Anna, with two eggs, but for five minutes, I cannot look at raw egg-whites you know . . . I am so hungry, and so tired, but I sleep so soundly . . . only a half hour left, and I've never been late in forty years, it's shameful, but I've got to sleep, otherwise I'll die!

TEACHER (*passes his hand over the DEAD MAN, who lies back down.*)

DEAD MAN (*mumbles.*) Oh, how beautiful! Anna, wake me, so that I won't arrive too late at the school!— — —

TEACHER Poor child of humanity! — "And when they've done their best with all their strength, yet is their strength labor and sorrow." Sixty-two years! And with such a childhood. And such an adulthood!

*

DEAD MAN (*rises again.*) Hummel, you've got to sign, it's a bad principle not to help someone in need, I remember the dean who said: I never forget! That was well put! — I know that I've talked behind your back, I can't keep quiet, you must forgive that, in any case you have forgiven me, and it's so awful that I was forgetting my place. Dear Hummel, you can't turn me down, it's for the rent . . . yes, you think I live too expensively, but it's for the children, I own the shirt on my back, nothing more . . . I confess, I go out to celebrate once in a while, it gives me a shot in the arm, and also just to enjoy my friends, you are so hard . . . (*Pause.*) — The highest things! When was I supposed to have time to think about such things, me, who's always lived with the very lowest things . . . I've been sitting in hell all my life, so that's nothing new! What, you have more to say? I think I've had enough! Sign, please, you know I'm going to pay it off, if I can only keep up my health and my strength . . . I have life insurance! . . . Jansson's name won't do me any good. He's on the outs with all the banks . . . If I could only sleep a little more . . .

TEACHER "The day of death is better than the day of one's birth," and yet they carry the fear of death in them . . . He doesn't know yet where he is, and everything he says has full reality for him . . .

DEAD MAN (*rises.*) Don't be angry, Anna, but you have forgotten the salt-cellar, the eggs are raw, because you set them in cold water, I suffer from these raw eggs, I have been asking you for thirty years to spare me these raw eggs, I am not quarreling, I'm just asking to be spared something that makes me suffer — do you enjoy my suffering? I'd almost think so, because your laugh is so nasty — forgive me now if I get up and get a napkin, it's not a reproach, it's only because I have to dry my beard, when I eat raw eggs, I shall invite you for a carriage ride, if you don't get angry when I go now to open the register, because if we don't open the register, then the children will be freezing all day . . . Are you going to argue with me now because it's been snowing outside, it's not my fault, dear child, I won't fight with you even though you've wrecked my shaving razor to rip seams . . . (*Pause.*) It was so stupid of me to bring up the shaving razor, if you'll just forget what I said I'll take you to the theatre — forgive me for your having wrecked my shaving razor, look, there I go talking about it again, it's horrible that I really cannot shut up . . . I'll buy a new carving knife, you split birch wood with the old one, and I'll give you my black handbag . . . Oh, I simply can't be quiet anymore, but I have held my tongue for thirty years, in the end I grew so full of lies that I was about to explode, full of self-contempt . . . When you'd complain to me about how mean-spirited people were, it always seemed as if you were sitting there telling me off, and were angry at me, and when you cut your finger you got incensed at me . . . Is there no end to this — will I never get one full night's sleep? When you had nightmares, you'd wake me up to talk about your dreams! Why should you disturb my sleep when I had to go to work all day for you . . . Let me be in peace! I want to die!

He lies down.

TEACHER   O, for the waters of Lethe, and to drink down oblivion, a sleeping drug for the tired wanderer! Thus the foolish sigh of the Child of Humanity. But life's laws invite remembrance — for all that you have lived, the great things and the small things, the good and the bad, they're broken up in life's mill and are ground and ground, the husks are shredded off, seeds are sifted out and are blown away by a breath of air. Then what remains is the fine flour, which is baked into the snow-white bread of spirit for eternity. Whatever evil you've done is transformed in time to good, whatever ugliness you saw in yourself is turned to beauty — Your path passes through blame on the way to virtue, and the suffering of the flesh makes your spirit free. "They that sow in tears shall reap in joy."

Bring the tired one to his room in the tomb. And he must rest in the peace of silence, till the moment comes when we shall read the book of the spirit, he and I — And interpret the riddles in his fate — Peace, dead man, sleep soundly for once — Not even the school bells will wake you! Here it's the final bell! The term is over — The exam is approaching — And then begins the summer!

Curtain.

*

A white, Egyptian room.
The DEAD MAN, now called ASSIR (=man of earth) sits and corrects essay
books. He looks awake but delirious.

*

TEACHER (*enters.*) Have you had a thorough sleep?

ASSIR I have, master.

TEACHER Is it boring?

ASSIR I won't deny it.

TEACHER Shall we chat, the two of us?

ASSIR Gladly!

TEACHER What is that you're correcting?

ASSIR Essays! Here's one who has written on "Life Is a Dream."

TEACHER Really? What's he say about it?

ASSIR That life cannot be a dream, since then it would be nonsense.

TEACHER How so? Can't a dream be instructive? Have you never had an
    instructive dream?

ASSIR Yes, in fact! When I think about it!

TEACHER Tell it to me. We have plenty of time.

ASSIR Well: One day I received a long, anonymous letter. But as I found
    it sarcastic and intrusive, I tore it in pieces and threw it in the trash. But
    that night I dreamed I met a wise and learned man who had passed
    away, who held some writing up before me: "take it and read it!" he said.
    I read it, but found nothing remarkable. Then the wise man took the
    writing and held it up against the light, and like watermarks, another
    writing lit up through the paper. When I woke up I went straight to the
    trash basket and with great pains I reassembled the letter! On that letter
    were words of wisdom, which exercised a good influence on the direction
    of my life.

TEACHER That was one of those informative dreams! If life is that sort
    of thing, then life is not nonsense! Is that correct?

ASSIR That's correct.

TEACHER But you have had true dreams as well, which forecast future
    events, which warned and exhorted you, advised against things, recom-
    mended others, scared and punished you?

ASSIR Yes — if one could remember them.

TEACHER That's why memory is necessary for us to be able to make use
    of our true dreams or our experiences! Memory is our capital which we

should invest. And all the same, you wish to drink oblivion. If at some point you could lose your memory, you'd be a book with blank pages, less than a newborn baby, and would have to begin again! Is that what you want?

ASSIR No. Not begin again! Not for anything!

TEACHER Meanwhile, let the boy say life's a dream or it's not. It's only a term or a metaphor, and he really can't know anything about the matter, right?

ASSIR How so?

TEACHER No, even you know nothing about the matter. You only know things as you perceive them through sight and sound? And not even that, but only the way you perceive them through your eyes and ears . . . Not so?

ASSIR Certainly!

TEACHER Be a little careful, therefore, when you correct the essay — — *Pause.*

Do you want company?

ASSIR Yes, but not the accountant . . .

TEACHER Why not?

ASSIR I don't like him . . . He's the sort who holds the opinion of the last person he spoke to . . .

TEACHER But, friend, don't people always do that, in a way, out of pure humanity? After all, they call it courtesy, humility, without which human relations would be impossible.

ASSIR Perhaps. But we see our own faults in others, because we cannot see ourselves . . .

TEACHER Exactly right. Therefore it's good to see others now and again! Would you like to see the accountant?

ASSIR No. He also has the bad habit of taking what I say as a joke. Me! A quite serious man . . .

TEACHER So strange! He has remarked the same about you . . .

ASSIR But he's always trying to get me to share his jokes . . .

TEACHER That choleric accountant?— — —Then the two of you are quite in tune. But you're two steps ahead of him in that you like to give comic speeches . . .

ASSIR Me? As a schoolmaster I'm used to giving severe lectures, even when I raise a glass for a toast.

TEACHER Which they laugh at . . .

ASSIR Why?

TEACHER They were laughing at your double naiveté, when you spoke the brutal truth, all the while expecting those who were your targets to laugh ... It was you they were laughing to scorn, and not your speeches, which weren't that witty.

ASSIR Really? Really! — We know so little about ourselves and other people!

TEACHER You didn't love other people?

ASSIR How could I? They were not lovable ...

TEACHER That is the general opinion, so we'll let that pass . . . We are indifferent to people who are strangers to us. Only when we make their acquaintance do we begin to assess their value, according to the ego's gold standard. If you're a knot in the net, then you'll believe yourself to be, like every other one does, the main knot. When there's a change in temperature or humidity, they all tighten and tear, and each and every one blames the others . . .

ASSIR Is there no consciousness among people?

TEACHER They are not what they seem to be, and seem not to be what they are. They are therefore not . . .

ASSIR But character, then? There's such a thing as character . . .

TEACHER A presumptuous way to exist! You are not a comic, but that's how you were seen! You saw yourself as having strength of character, but you didn't . . .

ASSIR I didn't?

TEACHER No! — When an opportunity knocked you abandoned your principles and your teaching methods . . . You discredited co-educational schools, but when it became profitable you accepted it. You were conservative by nature, but when the government became liberal, then you changed sides to get ahead. For fifty years you thought it shameful to wear medals, but at sixty you took them . . .

ASSIR But that's how all people are . . .

TEACHER And therefore there's no such thing as character . . . Do you want to know who you are? What you are?

ASSIR Is this part of some kind of court proceedings?

TEACHER Not at all!

ASSIR Then it's school . . .

TEACHER Yes! School, upbringing, education all your life. And that was life's simple meaning, which you wanted to push away with empty talk about the riddles of the universe . . . Do you want to know who you are?

ASSIR   Yes, all right!

The TEACHER claps his hands. A curtain is drawn aside. People are seen sitting on benches. The WIFE of the deceased is among them.

TEACHER   Who is this man?

WIFE   The greatest tyrant who's ever lived!

ASSIR   Because I wouldn't obey her! But the Lord said: Because thou hast hearkened to the voice of thy wife . . . curséd is the ground for thy sake!

TEACHER   Let's go on! Who is this man?

DAUGHTER 1   Thou shalt honor thy father and thy mother . . .

TEACHER   (*nods.*)

DAUGHTER 2   His faults and his weaknesses shall be sealed over . . .

TEACHER   (*as before.*)

THE SON   He lived as he could, with his troubles and his duties . . .

COLLEAGUE   As a colleague and competitor he was like a savage animal: in personal company a lamb; as a superior full of humanity; as a teacher a model; as a subordinate a monster. As a husband, loyal, he loved only her, the bride of his youth; as a father he gave the children more than himself; as a master of the house, indulgent; as a citizen law-abiding of necessity; as a son he sacrificed for a father gone to seed; toward his mother he was respectful beyond what was due; toward his brothers and sisters he was always changing as they were too; false to the false, faithless to the faithless; loyal to friends, though not always!

TEACHER   Can you now put all of this together: A monster role model; a savage lamb; a humane tyrant; a faithful traitor; an unfaithful loyal friend? Which character shall we use to designate him? A, B, C, or D?

COLLEAGUE   I don't think the alphabet would cover it . . .

TEACHER   Then shall we designate him with a question mark? (*To ASSIR.*) Now do you know who you are?

ASSIR   No!

TEACHER   You don't know yourself, and others don't know either. Perhaps you simply don't exist?

ASSIR   Yes, I exist, because I react against others. And if I ceased doing that, then others would fill me with their own egos, with their opinions, their views. They'd kill me with their wills. I would cease to exist. And my whole life I struggled to defend my ego!

TEACHER   So let us leave that question, Assir.

ASSIR   Why are you calling me Assir? What's it mean?

TEACHER It means Man of Earth — for you are still tied to the world.

He claps his hands. The curtains are drawn in again.

*

TEACHER Would you like some entertainment? What do you like most?
  Traveling, plays, books, art?
ASSIR Plays, best!
TEACHER You preferred the play in the theatre over the play on the stage
  of life! But if life is a dream, then plays are a dream of a dream, although you treat it like reality.
ASSIR Me?
TEACHER Yes indeed! You discussed the phantom picture presented by
  the last play you wrote a review of. You struggled for or against things
  — exactly as if the phantasmagoria were reality. Meanwhile you'd like
  a play. As you will!

He goes out. ASSIR sits as a spectator.

[*Here the play is performed.*]

ASSIR What kind of play was that? I'm sure I've seen it before.
TEACHER Did you find it true to life?
ASSIR Ye-es, more than true. But it was so heavy, it was horrifying . . .
TEACHER Can you give a summary of what it contained?
ASSIR No. It was so dreadful that I struck it from my memory . . .
TEACHER Sort of worked it out of your mind!— — —
ASSIR Yes. My mind is lighter and I long to be out in nature.
TEACHER A little trip, a walking tour perhaps, after which you'll be rested
  up.
ASSIR Perhaps so, yes! Why not!
TEACHER You'll have company on the way!
ASSIR But I want good company and beautiful terrain . . .
TEACHER You'll have everything you want . . . so long as you want things
  within reason! — So: have a good trip!
ASSIR But light! Light! After all this darkness!
TEACHER Day follows night. Only in dark can light shine. The moon
  gives no light during the daytime, but the midnight sun gives its sunshine
  in the middle of the night!

Curtain.

Notes to the Introductions

ABBREVIATIONS IN THE NOTES:

SS: August Strindberg, *Samlade Skrifter [Collected Writings]*, 55 vols., ed. John Landquist (Stockholm: Bonniers, 1910–23).
SV: *August Strindbergs Samlade Verk [August Strindberg's Collected Works]*, 73 vols. (Stockholm: Norstedts, 1981–). This is the new national edition of Strindberg's works, published in collaboration with the State Council for Culture and Stockholm University.

PREFACE

1. On the script as a "score" for actors, Strindberg writes: "*Being* the character portrayed intensively is to act well, but not so intensively that he forgets the 'punctuation'; then his acting becomes flat as a musical composition without nuances, without piano and forte, without crescendo and diminuendo, accelerando, and ritardando. (The actor should know these musical terms and have them constantly in mind, because they say almost everything.)" *Open Letters to the Intimate Theatre [Öppna brev till intima teatern]*, trans. with introductions by Walter Johnson (Seattle: University of Washington Press, n.d.), 132.

STRINDBERG—A REVALUATION

1. Bentley also begins his remarks noting Shaw's donation of his Nobel Prize money to the cause of translating Strindberg's works, O'Neill's tribute to the "Master" in his own Nobel Prize acceptance speech—and even Ibsen's remark, "I am an enemy of his—but I cannot write a line except when this bold man with his mad eyes looks down on me." Eric Bentley, *The Playwright as Thinker* (New York: Harcourt Brace Jovanovich, 1946 & 1967), 159, 160, 158–80 passim.

2. *Ibid.*, 166.

3. One of those writers whose work is reduced by the labels used to describe it—*avant-garde* and *feminist*—such descriptions do apply to Løveid's work. There are not a few writers and theatre artists matching that description in Europe who claim a debt to Strindberg despite his "reputation." Cecilie Løveid, master

class, Department of Performing Arts, American University, Washington, D.C.: September 11, 1992.

4. This has been Lagercrantz's argument throughout his work on Strindberg, and is a core idea in his literary biography. In the early 1980s this very influential volume by one of the three most famous Strindberg "revisionists" (the others being Jan Myrdal and Björn Meidal) came out in Swedish, making squall waves in the Scandinavian literary and theatre circles. Olof Lagercrantz, *August Strindberg*, trans. Anselm Hollo (New York: Farrar, Straus, and Giroux, 1984), 263, 269, 276 and passim. It has the same title in Swedish. (Stockholm: Wahlstöm & Widstrand, 1979). For Evert Sprinchorn, another Strindberg "thinker" in a similar vein, see *Strindberg as Dramatist* (New Haven: Yale University Press, 1982.)

5. Myrdal takes alternately very personal perspectives on Strindberg, and sometimes very ideological ones. The latter emerged during his period as champion of the so-called ultra-left among the post-'68 intellectuals, and the former in recent times as he himself pushed controversial issues as an essayist in the Swedish press. To his credit, with the exception of a short Afterword, this book is strictly a compilation of Strindberg's diverse writings on politics, society and culture, fiction and essays: thus, straight from the horse's mouth. Giving credence to Myrdal's argument for Strindberg as advocate for the oppressed is the rather eye-opening essay: "August Strindberg's Little Catechism for the Underclass" ["August Strindberg's Lilla katekes för Underclassen"] from 1884. August Strindberg, *Ordet i min makt: Läsebok för underklassen*, ed. Jan Myrdal. (Stockholm: Pan/Norstedts, 1968). Myrdal's personal stake in shaking out the myths about Strindberg have had some interesting results. The following startling observation of the photographs of Strindberg in torment at his desk sums them up: "The man who lies head down in desperation on his desk has himself arranged the flower vase and himself has taken the photo of his desperation with a remote shutter release." (My translation.) See Jan Myrdal, *Strindberg och Balzac: Essayer kring realismens problem* (Stockholm: Norstedt, 1981), 17.

6. Gunnar Ollén's comprehensive work on all of Strindberg's seventy-two plays (including drama fragments) is a veritable encyclopedia on Strindberg as dramatist. Through the introductions to the plays in this volume, his work is one vital source for my comments on the plays, together with the commentaries in *Samlade Verk*. Gunnar Ollén, *Strindbergs Dramatik* (Kristiansand: Sveriges Radio förlag, 1982), 28–38.

7. Strindberg wrote to Edvard Brandes about *Son of a Servant* (27 May 1886): "It [will be] the story of how an author emerges, the story of the growth of a soul and its development during a specific period. . . . It seems to me literature should emancipate itself completely from art and become science. Authors must learn their craft through studying: psychology, sociology,

physiology, history and politics. Otherwise they're only dilettantes!" Included in the second volume, *Time of Ferment [Jäsningstiden]* in a recent edition: *Tjänstekvinnans son: En själs utvecklingshistoria*, vol. 2. (Stockholm: Litteraturfrämjandet, 1985), 5.

8. August Strindberg, *Getting Married*, trans. with an introduction by Mary Sandbach (New York: Viking Press, 1972), 44–48.

9. *Ibid.*, 46.

10. *Ibid.*, 48–50.

11. Lagercrantz, 75–77.

12. "Moses" in *The New Kingdom [Det Nya Riket]* in *August Strindberg's Samlade Verk* (Stockholm: Norstedts, 1983 —) vol. 12. This "national edition" of Strindberg's "Collected Works," in 73 volumes including all his literary production, restored to match Strindberg's final drafts, is still not complete. Referred to hereafter as *SV*.

13. A conflict between Strindberg and the Brandes brothers, after the story in *The New Kingdom*—of Jews ingratiating themselves with the wealthy and powerful in Sweden—erupted when Edvard Brandes wrote him a letter, returning his copy of the book. He wrote that it did not bode well for their friendship and would aid their enemies, adding, "You rightly complain of the insults to which your little daughters are subjected. That is what every Jewish boy or girl has to suffer, year in, year out, as my two little girls will find. . . . No article is ever written against my brother or me in which anti-semitism is not manifest." Edvard Brandes would have nothing to do with Strindberg for three years, until Strindberg published an open recanting of his anti-semitism in 1885. The letter is taken from *Edvard and Georg Brandes Brevveksling med nordiske Forfattere og Videnskabsmænd* as cited and translated by Michael Meyer, *Strindberg* (New York: Random House, 1985), 105.

14. SV, 27:70.

15. Lagercrantz, 185–91.

16. August Strindberg, *A Madman's Manifesto (Le Plaidoyer d'un fou)*, trans. Anthony Swerling (Alabama: University of Alabama Press, 1971), 228.

17. Børge Gedsø Madsen, introduction to *A Madman's Manifesto*, viii–ix.

18. *Ibid.*

19. "Mitt antisemitismen," *Tiden* (Stockholm: December 1984). Edvard Brandes wrote again to him in response to the piece: "You have erased all that could wound in *The New Kingdom*." But during the following months, crass remarks especially about his Jewish publishers and a theatre promoter show up in some letters, in one case with the caveat: "But hate them as reactionaries, not as Jews!" Meyer's biography, less literary and more of an *exposé* than Lagercrantz's, consumes more pages on Strindberg's erratic letters—in an effort to

present the evidence for Strindberg's alleged disingenuousness, callousness, anti-semitism and misogyny—than it does examining his massive and always changing literary statement. Meyer, 143–46.

20. Olof Lagercrantz, *Eftertanker om Strindberg [Afterthoughts on Strindberg],* (Stockholm: Författarförlaget, 1980), 19–22.

21. Strindberg writes on the Jewish household: "It is good to be here, thought Johan. They were liberated people, who took the best from the culture of every country, without being obliged to bring the worst with them. Here he met for the first time a breath of air from other places. They had travelled, had relatives abroad, spoke every language and received foreigners in their home. All of the country's great and small affairs were judged and illuminated by precedents abroad, by means of which one learned to broaden one's point of view and obtain a true basis for evaluating the adopted homeland." (My translation.) *Tjänstekvinnans son*, 2:64–65.

22. Some interesting reflections on Frida Uhl's book *Marriage with Genius* can be found in a brief essay and play about Strindberg's second marriage: Eivor Martinus, "The Misogynist," *Swedish Book Review: August Strindberg*, supplement issue SBR 2 (1986): 33–38.

23. Meyer's biography begins to enlighten when he discusses the reactions of Europe's artists and literati to Strindberg's works. He quotes Max Brod—in the Strindberg centenary issue of *Adam* (1949)—on Kafka's addiction to Strindberg's works. Kafka was "highly delighted with the realistic and satirical power with which Strindberg depicts his age and setting. . . . [Strindberg's works] had a powerful influence on him, and for a time he read nothing else." Meyer, 448.

24. *Inferno & From "An Occult Diary*," trans. and with an introduction by Mary Sandbach (Harmondsworth: Penguin Classics, 1979), 210–224; see also Lagercrantz, *August Strindberg*, 271–76; Emanuel Swedenborg, *Secrets of Heaven [Arcana Coelestia]*, 6 vols. (New York: Swedenborg Foundation, 1985), based upon a translation from the last century, *Arcana Coelestia*, trans. John F. Potts (New York: Swedenborg Foundation, 1873).

25. Göran Söderström, "Strindberg's Scenographic Ideas," *Strindberg on Stage: Report from the Symposium in Stockholm May 18–22, 1981*, ed. Donald K. Weaver (Stockholm: ITI and the Strindberg Society, 1983), 37–42.

26. Brecht is strangely quiet on the work of Strindberg throughout his writings. He has more to say about Ibsen, if only to react against his form of theatre. After his move to Berlin he viewed various Strindberg productions: some one-acts, *Miss Julie* and *A Dream Play*, and regularly attended lectures by Frank Wedekind who was clearly working in the wake of

Strindberg. Ronald Hayman, *Brecht: A Biography* (London: Weidenfeld & Nicolson, 1983), 42, 46, 85. Evidence suggests that Brecht could not have avoided—and probably attended—Leopold Jessner's production of *Gustav Adolf* at the Staatliches Schauspielhaus in Berlin in 1930. See Ollén, *Stindbergs Dramatik*, 328. Jessner was one of Berlin's major producers, had collaborated on Brecht productions, and was always being hounded by Brecht for more. Furthermore, Brecht's closest artistic collaborator, the designer Kaspar Neher, was working for Jessner on a regular basis in 1929–30. See John Fuegi, *Brecht & Co.* (New York: Grove Press, 1994), 241. The Berlin production of *Gustav Adolf*, according to Frankfurter Allgemeine Zeitung, revealed "the bestiality, destitution, suffering and degradation of war." Ollén, 328.

27. Esslin, however, mentions other plays by Strindberg that gave impetus to the Theatre of the Absurd, as "the first to put on the stage a dream world in the spirit of modern psychological thinking was August Strindberg. The three parts of *To Damascus* . . . *A Dream Play* . . . and *The Ghost Sonata* . . . are masterly transcriptions of dreams and obsessions, and direct sources of the Theatre of the Absurd." Martin Esslin, *The Theatre of the Absurd* (New York: Anchor, 1961; New York: Penguin, 1987), 352–53.

28. For those who can't read Swedish, the book contains a substantial English summary of its contents at the end, which demonstrates the spiritual/political synthesis, which can be found already in these plays, but which culminates later in the "Strindberg Feud." Björn Meidal, *Från Profet till Folktribun: Strindberg och Strindbergsfejden 1910—12.* (Stockholm: Tidens förlag, 1982). See also Meidal's short summary of Strindberg's career, in English: *August Strindberg: A Writer for the World* (Stockholm: The Swedish Institute, 1995).

29. Meidal, 44–47.

30. *Days of Loneliness (Ensam)*, trans. Arvid Paulson (New York: Phaedra, 1971), 41.

31. Gunnar Ollén, "Kommentarer," *SV*, 58:408.

32. 30 August 1906, quoted in Göran Lindström, ed., "Kommentar," *Spöksonaten* (Lund, Sweden: Gleerups förlag, 1964), 98.

33. *Ibid.*

34. Ollén, *Strindbergs Dramatik*, 520.

35. Lindström, 88–92. See also *Inferno*, trans. Mary Sandbach, 210–24 and the chapter "The Redeemer," 256–66.

36. Ollén, *SV*, 58:403–04.

37. Ollén, *Strindbergs Dramatik*, 520.

38. All quoted passages have been taken from an unpublished English translation of *Svarta Fanor [Black Banners]*, which is in the possession of the Strindberg Museum in Stockholm. This version bears the title: *Black Flags*, Don Deaver, trans. (Stockholm: Strindberg Museum, stencil, 1989). It is found in volume 41 of *Samlade Skrifter*, and vol. 57 of *Samlade Verk. SV*, 57:39.

39. *SV*, 57:49–51.

40. *SV*, 57:145–46.

41. *SV*, 57:7.

42. *SV*, 57:9.

43. *SV*, 58:188

44. *Ibid.*, 202.

45. *Ibid.*, 221.

46. Sandbach, *Inferno & from An Occult Diary*, 311–12, 361.

47. Ollén, *SV*, 58:415.

48. *Ibid.*

49. *Ibid.*, 417.

50. *Open Letters to the Intimate Theatre*, 297. See also Paul Walsh's essay "Textual Cues to Performance Strategies in 'The Pelican'," on the tension provided by the rhythm and textual cues for actors in the script, in Stockenström, *Strindberg's Dramaturgy*.

51. Ollén, *SV*, 58:418–21.

52. Ollén, *Strindbergs Dramatik*, 545.

53. Ollén, *SV*, 58:417–18.

54. Cited in Meidal, *SS*, 48:1033–35.

55. *SS*, 1:308–09.

56. *SV*, 48:415, 421—22; *Strindbergs Dramatik*, 541-42.

57. See *Toten-Insel*, the appendix in this volume, 360. *Samlade utrykte skrifter*, ed. Vilhelm C. Gyllensköld (Stockholm: Bonniers, 1919), 293-310.

58. I have rendered, in a few cases, the Swedish word *ond* as "sick" in the translation of the play. A typical dilemma of translation arises here where you have a word of high connotative value in one language, while the connotations are restricted in another. The first dictionary definition of *ond* is often "evil"—but it's also "bad," "mean," "wrong," "ill" and so on. In English when we refer to someone as evil, it means just that, period. To have the children constantly bemoaning the fact that their mother is "evil" is more ham-fisted in English. Therefore, "sick," with its modern negative connotations about people and attitudes, as well as illness, a disease, a misfortune—is as close as I think we can get to a word that can be *played*

by actors. *SV*, 48:287.

59. 15 October 1885. Ollén. *Strindbergs Dramatik*, 546. See also Harry Järv's article describing the younger Strindberg's anarchist and nihilist notions: Harry Järv, "Samhällskritikern: Den reaktionäre radikalen," *Strindberg* (Stockholm: Kulturhuset, exhibition catalogue, 15 May–4 October 1981), 78–86.

60. Included in the collection *Ordalek och Småkonst*: *SS*, 37:320–25.

61. Extensive use of draped linens and shrouds to negotiate the tensions between the *esoteric* (mystic) and *exoteric* (realist) levels of the piece have been used in two notable productions: the first in 1970 at Teatr Polski in Wroclaw, Poland, (directed by Bogdan Augustniak and designed by Wojciech Krakowski) in which the ceiling, walls and floors were draped in white shrouds. In 1975–76 the Mingey Theatre in Tokyo seems to have draped the set in white linen (directed by Mittsuya Miyauchi). Some directors' "concept" experiments with the play have been noteworthy. In Paris at *Petit-Odéon* in 1973 there was a neo-Absurdist staging by Henri Ronse, produced together with *L'île des morts (Toten-Insel)*. Ollén, 558-59.

Perhaps the most interesting deconstruction of the play (before that term came into vogue) was Per Verner-Carlsson's *2 x Pelikanen* at the Royal Dramatic Theatre in Stockholm in 1968. The play occured twice: once in the style of high intensity psychological realism. The second version was played on an empty stage, with walls of paper and mirror-like mylar. There was only a hanging lamp and a kettle of porridge on stage. The paper was used as graffiti walls, in which lines from the play, and slogans of the ex-ploited were written. (Beginning with "free", "air", "porridge" and "wall." Characters burst in and out through the paper.) It was the memory of the action of the play at the moment of death. The actors painted on white facial masks. The same text was used, but sometimes spoken and sometimes played, faster or slower, on a tape. Verner-Carlsson saw the action as being about "four or five people who were locked in by their limited capital." Far from underscoring the play's esoteric side, it was intended to reflect the abandonment of young generations by a complacent older one, that consumes all the resources. Verner-Carlsson, not a director known for half-measures, continued his exploration of the play with *Pelikanen 3* 1978, which was combined with Charles Marowitz's play *Artaud at Rodez*, which together he titled *Vita Rum* (White Room). All action took place in a world that was a madhouse. The use of graffiti and paper remained. After the Artaud play, the Son burst in through the paper wall, and *The Pelican* began in Artaud's visionary space. This time all the action was played by the two children, the other characters were voice-overs. The graffiti this time included: "All Power to the Imagination," "Bird Lives," "Mother is a snake," "Father is nice," accentuating the issues of the play and modern conscious-ness at the same time. The paper was burst apart by the end, but this time for the younger generation, or the forgotten class they represent, there was no bursting out of the trap: they were driven to ground—literally. The solid walls at right and left, and a ceiling panel, inconspicuously began moving in on the Son and Daughter, until the two were enclosed in the middle. The ceiling pressed them into the floor until they disappeared on the last lines of the play. Interestingly, through all this *theatre of cruelty* work, Verner-Carlsson tried to keep the text: "The language was interesting, so we kept it in various shapes and forms." Per Verner-Carlsson, interview by author, Stockholm, Sweden, 17 August 1989.

62. This was a relatively conservative realistic presentation for the television camera, until the final scene. (Stockholm: *TV Teater*, 17 September 1973). Far more interesting was the *TV Teater* version directed by Willgott Sjöman in 1982. The colors and light were high-contrast, neo-expressionist; the sense of bitter cold, winter and snow pervaded all the scenes; the acting had a terrifying edge (with flashbacks of the deceased father howling in the garden); Gerda always outside listening through the doors with focus on her face and her growing insight; the mother drawn toward the open windows in a sort of trance; and a finale with a cubist montage of the faces of the two children. (Stockholm: *TV Teater*, 17 March 1982).

63. Reflections on Shakespeare dominate two thirds of the *Open Letters to the Intimate Theatre*, though he takes the opportunity to help the company members gain an understanding of his own history plays. One of many examples: "My purpose was, as was my teacher Shakespeare's, to depict human beings both in their greatness and their triviality . . . to let history be the background and to compress historical periods to fit the demands of the theatre of our time . . ." *Open Letters*, 249.

64. Some remarkably clear essays on Swedenborg's life and philosophy were written by one of the *twentieth* century's best-known "mystics": D.T. Suzuki, one of those credited with bringing Buddhism to the West. Suzuki wrote about him for Japanese readers in the 1920s. D.T. Suzuki, *Swedenborg: Buddha of the North*, trans Andrew Bernstein (West Chester, P.A.: Swedenborg Foundation, 1996).

65. Meidal suggests that Strindberg was drawn into the great press debate, when his religious views transferred from the "everything serves" attitude of Paul, to the dualism (i.e., divine versus evil) in John. Thus he

opened fire with his article "Pharaoh Worship" in 1910 with a Swedenborg-inspired attack on Carl XII. Aside from the main theme, it began the critique of the poet Verner von Heidenstam and the explorer Sven Hedin. (58) Hedin's militarist pamphlet *A Word of Warning [Ett varningsord]* along with Heidenstam's appeal to nationalism glorifying Carl XII—*The Carolinians*—and the formation of the Carolinian League (Carolinska förbund) moved him to attack both the nature of the work for which they had received honors from the crown, and their politics. The beginning of the Strindberg feud marks Strindberg's final break with his Nietzscheanism as well. Meidal, 58–80 & 277–97.

66. Lagercrantz, 40.

67. These quotes are from two letters: 22 October and 11 December 1902. Hans Lindström, "Kommentarer" *SV*, *Dödsdansen*, vol. 44 (Stockholm: Norstedts, 1988), 247.

68. Susan Brantly, "Naturalism or Expressionism: A Meaningful Mixture of Styles in 'The Dance of Death,' " in Stockenström, *Strindberg's Dramaturgy*.

69. Esslin discusses throughout his famous work that finally defined the "Absurd" as a movement, the rejection of traditional linear plotting in favor of circular plots or even a "spiral," though he leaves out discussion of the circular plot in Sartre's play *No Exit*: a proto-absurdist play which turns the triangle game into a circular, game-based plot—where the characters unsuccessfully try to generate a sense of self in Hell. The so-called cyclical plot first appears with *Dance of Death*.

70. Friedrich Dürrenmatt, *Play Strindberg & Porträt eines Planeten* (Zürich: Diogenes Verlag, 1980).

71. Lindström, *SV*, 44:245.

72. Lindström writes that Strindberg made an open declaration of love to her, with her husband in the vicinity. Here I feel we're on the swampy ground of the myths about Strindberg and women, so it might be best to let this anecdote rest. *Ibid.*, 44:236.

73. *Ibid.*, 44:237.

74. *Ibid.*, 44:240.

75. *Ibid.*

76. "He had divided his brother-in-law from his children and let them go with a sodomite [greek letters] woman. Now he asks his brother-in-law to have compassion on his children" *ibid.*, 243–44.

77. *Ibid.*, 44:242–43.

78. *Ibid.*

79. *Ibid.*, 44:248–49.

80. *Ibid.*, 44:251. One may add that the tone of these reviews results from gut responses, by adherents of order and beauty, or ideology, to the general unruliness and provocative nature of Strindberg and his work—and as such they were to be expected, and still should be today. It is the same "gut" repulsion which informs the Meyer biography of Strindberg, and Meyer's own pronouncements in recent times have become almost as strident as that of Strindberg's culturally "correct" colleagues at the end of his life—and thus similarly distorted:

> I was negatively influenced by Olof Lagercrantz's biography, which I felt was less than totally honest in its glossing over of Strindberg's less pleasant characteristics, such as his vicious and repeated public abuse of former friends, his vehement and sustained racism, anti-black [*sic*] as well as anti-Semitic, and his extreme right wing attitude for over a quarter of a century until two years before his death when, as part of a general mellowing, he became again a *good* socialist [my italics]. . . . Strindberg died a good socialist, but, speaking as someone who has never voted anything but left-wing in my life, I think it the grossest travesty to suggest he was a good socialist or even a democrat between the ages of 34 and 61. Michael Meyer, "Strindberg and His Disciples," *Swedish Book Review: August Strindberg*, 1986:2, supplement issue, 5–6.

In light of these claims, in which Strindberg is depicted as a stubborn straight line, perverse and unwilling and unable to change—and "mellow" at the end, when he unleashed a national debate of unprecedented proportions for two years—it's interesting to note one of the issues Strindberg took up years prior to the "Strindberg Feud." Xenophobia against Asians and Asian cultures was one of the strongest strains of racism among Europeans at the turn of the century. Björn Meidal points out that Strindberg's critique of Sven Hedin, the explorer of Russia and Asia—aside from his broadside against Hedin for his jingoistic warnings to prepare for war with Russia after 1910—suggested that Hedin's claim of making it to Lhasa was a sham. More importantly, in *A Blue Book II* (*En Blå Bok II*, 1906-8), Strindberg excoriated Hedin for his attitude toward those people and places he did encounter around Tibet. Meidal writes: "Hedin had, in several of his works, described his efforts to reach Buddhism's religious center, Lhassa, and Strindberg now protests his lack of respect for religious values." He quotes

Strindberg: "Now a certain travel writer has visited Tibet, and portrayed the lamas as bizarre, unsympathetic figures; but that may be either lies or distorted perspective, deriving from a profane mind that sees everything exalted as ridiculous." Meidal, 60.

81. For all excerpts of reviews cited here, *ibid.*, 44:251.

82. *Ibid.*, 44:248.

THREE ONE-ACTS: INTRODUCTION

1. All nine one-acts are included in *SV, Nio Enaktare: 1888-1892*, vol. 33 (Stockholm: Norstedts, also Almqvist & Wiksell, 1984).

2. *SS*, 17:281ff.

3. *SV*, 28.

4. Ollén, "Kommentarer," *SV*, 33:331.

5. *Ibid.* 331–32.

6. *Ibid.*, 333.

7. 11 March 1889, *ibid.*, 334.

8. 26 January 1889, *ibid.*

9. Ollén's idea that the play portrays—and that Nietzsche himself advocates—the Aryan superior man's right to rule over the weaker would seem a bit too simple to anyone who has worked in staging it, *ibid.*, 336–37.

10. Strindberg was able to finish this fiction piece when Nietzsche sent him a copy of *Twilight of the Idols*, in which the rigid caste laws of the Indian *Manu* seem to call for the suppression of the *Chandala* caste. Evert Sprinchorn has pointed out that Strindberg very soon repudiated the novella, stating that he wished he had never written it, in a letter to Ola Hansson (3 April 1889). Evert Sprinchorn, "Strindberg and the Superman," *Strindberg's Dramaturgy*, 20.

11. Lagercrantz, 189–90.

12. *Ibid.*

13. *SS*, 12:250.

14. Ollén, *SV*, 33:340.

15. *Ibid.*, 341.

16. *Ibid.*

17. *Ibid.*, 342.

18. *Ibid.*, 343–44.

19. The explanation of terms in *Samlade Verk*, which states that Strindberg should have added the syllable *"hu"* to the end of the phrase,

making it *La ilâha illa'llâhu,* is misleading. *Hu* is a sacred syllable, used only in mystic rites of Divine love, which certainly doesn't fit here. Neither is the "o" ending as in "Allâho" needed. For purposes of pronunciation, the Arabic phrase is correct as Strindberg wrote it.

20. Ollén, *SV* 33:343.

Notes to the Texts

The following notes to the texts of the plays draw heavily on *Samlade Verk*—the new national edition of Strindberg's collected works. In particular I draw from a small portion of the lengthy textual commentaries offered in that edition—for these translations—primarily by Gunnar Ollén, but also, in the case of *The Dance of Death*, by Hans Lindström. In the case of *The Ghost Sonata*, Göran Lindström's annotations and commentaries in his edition of *Spöksonaten*, were of equal importance. There were many other sources used here and there on the periphery—but I lack space to mention them all.

THE GHOST SONATA

Page 59   WHITE LINENS: Sheets were customarily hung over the windows after a death. PUBLIC FOUNTAIN (*gatufontän*): These were water pipes with basins, with a spoon or ladle on a chain; common in Stockholm in the early 1900s. STREET REFLECTOR (*reflexionsspegel*): Mirrors were placed in the window at an angle so that people approaching the house from the street could be seen. (G. Lindström)

Page 65   SUNDAY CHILD (*söndagsbarn*): According to an old superstition children born on a Sunday would be clairvoyant. They might have the ability to heal; could see the invisible world and would be successful in life. FLAG OF THE CONSULATE: This indicates the flag of the country the consul represented.

Page 67   SPRUCE TWIGS (*granris*): It used to be the custom to strew spruce twigs on the path the deceased would take from home to burial.

Page 68   ENGLISH RIDING OUTFIT (*engelsk amasondräkt*): A popular term for riding clothes which included a skirt. (Ollén)

Page 74   THE ASS IN THE WELL AND THE CORN IN THE FIELD: The phrase refers to two separate references to the Sabbath in the Gospels, in which it is seen as permissible to do what is needed on the Sabbath: to save one's ox (*Luke* 14:5) or to reap ears of corn (grain) from the fields (*Mark* 2:23–28) as, "the Sabbath was made for man, and not man for the Sabbath." (Ollén)

Page 80   SPINNING HOUSE (*spinnhus*): A kind of prison for women in Sweden, actually before 1825, where the inmates worked spinning wool. The Mummy uses the word "*prästbetyg*" here, which is not exactly a modern birth certificate, but an extract from the parish register. (G. Lindström)

Page 84   MAIDENS FOUNDATION: The Fiancée is here referred to as a "foundation maid" (*stiftsfröken*). Unmarried aristocratic women were supported by a foundation (*jungfrustift*) set up by the nobility, providing living quarters and pensions. (G. Lindström)

Page 87   DEATHWATCH (*dödsur*): In Swedish this also refers to a beetle

(Abobium) that lives in dry wood, and gives off a ticking sound like a clock. In popular superstition the sound is a harbinger of death. (Ollén)

Page 90   "I SAW THE SUN . . .": The poem or lyric at the end of this scene—and the end of the play as well—is based upon stanzas from the Icelandic "Sólarljóð," the "Sun Song" from the 13th century. (G. Lindström)

Page 91   SHALLOT (*askalonlök*): A member of the onion family (Alium ascolonicum), this flower takes its Swedish name from the ancient city of Aschalon, in present day Israel north of Gaza. It has an edible bulb. The scene contains a series of references to flowers and other star-shaped things.

Page 92   SNOWFLAKES (*snöblomma*): The word has several connotations here. The Swedish word translates three ways: 1) the flower which is called "snowflake" in English (a flowering bulbous plant, genus Leucojum); 2) literal snowflakes (though this is not the common Swedish term); and 3) other flower-like structures which form in the snow, perhaps more correctly translated at "snow-flowers." SNOWDROPS (*snödroppe*): Another flowering bulbous plant (Galanthus nivalis), native to Eurasia, and has single, white nodding flowers. When the Daughter says, "And the snow drop is a snow star," she brings us back both to the idea of *stars* and of snow formations. SIRIUS . . . NARCISSUS: The bright star Sirius, when visible low on the horizon, is often yellow and red, as is the second crown of the Narcissus flower. Thus ends one of the most complex—albeit short—series of plays-on-words in modern drama. Strindberg has applied Swedenborg's teaching of *correspondences* between things of the spirit and things in nature, making it a poetic device of startling precision. All these different things reflect one another: it's one simple idea—in multiplicity. Dramatically, the Student and Daughter are bound together by the miraculous "game" of images they are playing.

Page 94   COR IN ÆTHERE: Latin, "Heart in the heavens."

Page 96   SOY (*soya*): As it is used here, was also called "*kolorit*" or "*kulör*" in Swedish; a spiced brown liquid used for food coloring, particularly in soups or sauces, also referred to as soya in the last century, whether it contained actual *soy* or not.

Page 98   FUNERAL STAFF (*prestav*): The Swedish word actually refers to the marshal at a funeral, but originally referred to the staff that he carries bedecked with flowers. (G. Lindström)

Page 99   SURSUM CORDA: Latin, "Lift up your hearts." The phrase introduces the Preface, a prayer of thanks in the Catholic mass. (Ollén) LAMIA: A female vampire from Greek mythology, who steals children or drinks their blood. (G. Lindström)

Page 100   BÖCKLIN'S TOTEN-INSEL: "Isle of the Dead": the famous painting, done in various versions, by the Swiss painter Arnold Böcklin, inspired by the volcanic Italian island of Ischia (Where Ibsen wrote most of *Peer Gynt*).

THE PELICAN

Page 103   PAN COUPÉ: French, "cut corner." Strindberg calls for the balcony door/windows to be only partly visible at one side. CARBOLIC AND SPRUCE (*carbol och granris*): Carbolic acid was injected into the bloodstream of people who were recently deceased to prevent decomposition before the funeral. On spruce twigs at funerals see the note above on page 67. In this case it would be strewn from the deathbed, down the hall and to the front steps.

Page 111   THE PELICAN WHO GIVES HER BLOOD TO HER YOUNG: This was indeed a folk myth, as the Son says later, and seems to have emerged from a confusion with the flamingo, which sometimes feeds its young with a reddish substance from its beak. (Ollén)

Page 112   EXECUTOR (*bouppteckning*): This was an public office which undertook some responsibilities of an executor, including securing the inheritance before the execution of the will. A *bouppteckningsman* is translated "executor." (See also in the text, "assessment," etc.)

Page 119   "*BERCEUSE*" . . . "*JOCELYN*": Composer Benjamin Goddard's opera *Jocelyn* from 1888 contained the piece *Berceuse* (lullaby), which, separately, was Goddard's opus 100. Significantly for this play, *berceuse* also means "rocking-chair." (Ollén)

Page 123   CAMORRA: A secret criminal organization after 1820 in the south of Italy, whose members took a vow of silence.

Page 126   VENDETTA: The original meaning of this term in Corsica was literal "blood revenge."

Page 127   PORRIDGE/OATMEAL/RYE: Swedes and Norwegians eat a wide variety of cereal dishes we translate as "porridge," but there is a wider variety, sometimes a kind of pudding, so it's not always a breakfast food.

Page 129   "*IL ME DISAIT*": "He said to me," a slow waltz by Pierre Ferraris; composed in 1903.

Page 131   BLUE SKIM MILK: Skim milk, something much less common at the time. Thus the change in color when all cream and fat is removed was more curious. The loss of calories in a cold country, at that time, would have been of concern.

Page 134   "AT ELEVEN THIRTY MY CASE IS JUST". . . : This refers to an actual Swedish law, in which an appeal overriding a lower court had to be decided by a certain time on a certain date. Strindberg points to the arbitrary nature of much of the Law that is not "natural Law."

Page 138   SMALL TABLE: Strindberg uses the French word *guéridon*: a narrow high table, decorative.

Page 142   DIP BREAD IN THE COOKING POTS (*doppa i grytan*): The Swedish phrase has no equivalent; a Christmas ritual when the family got to enter the kitchen and dip bread in cooking broth.

CARL XII

Page 145   CARL XII: King of Sweden 1682–1718. He ruled from the year 1697, but began his military campaigns in Europe in 1700. He is considered to be the last king of Sweden's period as a great power in Europe (when it was also ruling Finland and controlled the Baltic). Beginning with his victory against the Russians at Narva in 1700, he remained engaged against the Russians till his defeat at Poltava in 1709. He retreated to Turkey, remaining there until 1714. He returned to Sweden in 1715, and died in the invasion of Norway in 1718. Strindberg thus uses a Shakespearean sort of compression, making the action feel as though it takes place during several weeks.

Page 147   ULRIKA ELEONORA (1688–1741): The King's sister, married to Fredrik of Hesse-Kassel, who was heir to the princedom; she ruled alone as Queen of Sweden 1719–20, and ruled with her husband, King Fredrik I 1720–51, a reign which brought in the so-called "freedom time." GÖRTZ (Georg Heinrich von Goertz, also Baron of *Schlitz*, 1668–1719): Görtz was counsel to the court at Holstein after 1702; after 1709 used his influence in Holstein politics to get Duke Karl Fredrik, Carl XII's nephew, accepted as heir to Sweden's throne; First Minister to Carl XII 1716-18; after the invasion of Norway and his catastrophic economic policies he was executed in 1719. ARVID HORN (1664–1742): Swedish count, Major General in the army in 1700; President of the Chancellery in 1709; later a political leader under the next King, Fredrik I, during the "freedom time," as the new King's rule was called. KARL GYLLENBORG (1679–1746): A count, envoy for the King in 1715; court Chancellor in 1720; also a later leader of a political party. SECRETARY FEIF (Casten Feif, 1662–1739): He began his career as a hatmaker's apprentice; military advisor to the King; made a baron in 1715. HULTMAN (Johan Hultman, 1662–1735 [?]): Served as a lackey for Carl XII from 1694 onward, promoted to *couvreur de table* (or Royal table-setter or headwaiter) after 1711; he kept notes on the King and his undertakings. KATARINA LESZCZYNSKA (Katarina Opalinska, 1680–1749): Married with King Stanislaus I Leszczynski of Poland, 1704-09; after Carl had her husband put out of power, she lived as a refugee with members of her court at Kristandstat 1711–14 [The name is pronounced *Lesh-tjyinj-ska*]. EMERENTIA POLHEM (1703–60): Daughter of Royal inventor and engineer Christopher Polhem. EMANUEL SWEDENBORG (1688–1772): Natural scientist, engineer —collaborating with Polhem on Sweden's technologically advanced mines, for example) and later, philosopher and mystic; he was knighted in 1719; the latter half of his life was spent on writing and publishing his massive works of Christian mysticism—*Coelestia Arcana* (6 volumes), *Heaven, Its Wonders and Hell, Spiritual Journal,* and many others. He remained outside the institutional Church, but was revered throughout northern Europe, and taken quite seriously, for a man who wrote openly about his encounters with angels and spirits. DWARF LUXEM-

BOURG: Court dwarfs, as fools or jesters, were found in various parts of Europe from the medieval times through the Renaissance. In Mantua the court dwarf's quarters in the palace, with extraordinarily low ceilings, are still standing. COUNCILLOR OF THE REALM: He would have been a leader of the interim government during Carl's years away from Sweden. SPEAKERS OF THE FOUR ESTATES: Spokesmen for the four classes with places reserved for them in Sweden's parliament: the nobility, the clerics, the merchant class and the peasants. DÜRING (Johan Christoffer von Düring, 1695–1759): Lieutenant Colonel and later Colonel (1715) in the army. ROSEN (Gustaf Fredrik von Rosen, 1688–1769): An Adjutant General with Carl in 1714, he escorted him from Turkey to Stralsund on his return.

Page 149   PLAGUE OF 1710: The bubonic plague spread from the Baltic states to Stockholm, and to the rest of Sweden, according to some sources claiming 100,000 lives. THE ENEMY BURNED . . .: The Danish army invaded Scania (*Skåne*) in 1709–10. POLTAVA: a city in northwest Ukraine, where Carl XII lost the famous battle of Poltava to Peter the Great.

Page 150   SIBERIA: Large numbers of Carl's soldiers were shipped *en masse* to Siberia after the defeat. STRALSUND: A city on the northern coast of Germany, it was a Swedish possession from 1648 until the Prussians seized it militarily in 1715. "HE FLED FROM A WOMAN": Once Carl XII refused an audience with the famously striking Aurora von Königsmarck. The poem Emerentia Polhem reads to Carl later in the play, is attributed to her, when she tried to gain an audience.

Page 151   KARLSKRONA: As a navy port, the town had built a 300-yard-long ropemakers' track in 1690.

Page 152   SUSPENSION: The parliament was called in 1713–14 against the King's stated wish, and it had been proposed that his sister Ulrika Eleonora should be regent, implying a temporary suspension of the King's duties until his return.

Page 156   "THE CITIES OF SAXONY . . ." etc.: These lines refer to Carl's campaigns in Poland (1701) and Saxony (1706), as well as the Russian war and his good treatment by the Sultan (as recorded by Hultman in his journals).

Page 157   THE BRIG SNAPP-OPP: According to Ollén (citing Anders Fryxell) this was actually the brigantine the King returned on. The "Snare-Sven" was a light Dutch galliot (a merchant ship) whose skipper was executed and crew punished. The reports of these events, according to recent historians, were probably wrong.

Page 158   "THE ONE SHALL BE TAKEN . . .": Luxembourg quotes Jesus in Matthew 24:40, on the Day of Judgment.

Page 162   "IT'S MISSING A BUTTON": It was a popular belief that the King, thought by many to be invulnerable to normal bullets, was shot with a button—in some versions, one of his own buttons—which had been hammered around a piece of lead. Such a bullet was discovered in the 1940s, and a ballistics expert for the Varberg Museum argued in a debate, against a historian, that this was the very button/bullet that killed the King. The coat and button have been displayed at the Varberg Museum. (See Ollén, *Samlade Verk*, 299.)

Page 166   BARON TESSIN (1654–1728): An architect who designed the Palace in Stockholm, and was Chancellor of the University of Lund. PIPER (Carl Piper, 1647–1716): Counsel to the King, died a prisoner in Russia.

Page 168   MACHIAVELLI (Niccolò Machiavelli, 1469–1527): His advice to rulers in his famous work *The Prince*, adopts an ends-justifies-the-means position, but also warns rulers about flattery and dissimulation from the people who seek advancement.

Page 169   HIS NEPHEW: Here the King refers to Karl Fredrik, son of his eldest sister, Hedvig Sofia, who was married to Duke Fredrik IV of Holstein-Gottorp. The Czar's daughter Anna Petrovna did in fact marry him in 1725. AUGUST (King August II of Poland, 1679–1733): Ruled Poland from 1697–1704, but was driven from power and the throne was ceded to Carl's man Stanislaus I Leszczynski. Stanislaus was deposed in 1709, and August, backed by the Russians, retook the throne.

Page 170   STANISLAUS: See note above.

Page 173   "THE CZAR . . . COPENHAGEN": Czar Peter made an alliance with the Danes against Sweden; he brought a fleet to Copenhagen in July 1716.

Page 175   POLHEM: Father of Emerentia (see note above). At this time he was also Commerce Counselor.

Page 177   NORTH BRIDGE (*Norrbro*): It was the tradition to celebrate victories in war with marches over this bridge, leading directly to the Palace in Stockholm. PIPER, REHNSCHIÖLD, LEWENHAUPT: For Piper, see above. Karl Gustav Rehnschiöld (1651–1722), former Governor of Scania, was Field Marshal in the Russian campaign. He came home in an exchange of prisoners nine years later, 1718; Adam Ludvig Lewenhaupt (1659–1719, an army chief, died a prisoner in Russia. STENBOCKEN (Magnus Stenbock, 1665–1717[?]), a Major General, defeated the Danes at Helsingborg in 1710; surrendered at another battle in 1713, and died in a Danish prison after suffering grim humiliations there; the ransom for his return had been set at 100,000 dalers in silver coin. KRASNOKUTSK: A place close to Poltava, where Carl defeated the Russians in a cavalry battle.

Page 180   NATIONAL COAT OF ARMS: At this time the "heart-shield" of the Palatine dynasty was used on a banner, or placed on the flag: blue with a yellow cross. PAYKULL (Otto Arnold Paykull, 1662[?]–1707): A German from the coast ruled by Sweden, served in the Saxon regiments as a high officer, and was an alchemist in his spare time; condemned as a traitor in 1706; he briefly persuaded the Swedish authorities that he could make gold for annual payments in exchange for his life; finally executed in 1707.

Page 181   BOËTHIUS: (Jacob Boëthius, 1647–1718) pastor and deacon of Mora, who was condemned to death in 1697 for writing a criticism of absolutism and Church politics; the sentence was reduced to life in prison, and he was released in 1710; he ended his days as a mental patient.

Page 183   BIELKE (Nils Bielke) : Governor General in Pomerania in 1687, condemned to death for fighting for France against Turkey; later pardoned. PATKULL (Johan Reinhold Patkull): Conspired against Sweden, becoming a Russian officer. Executed in 1707. THE WIDOWS: Little is to be found on these women, except for the information on their husbands, see above. ROSEN, DÜRING ... etc.: The first two were seen in the opening tableau, and now have quickly fallen from favor, as have Horn and Gyllenborg. The rest were more or less loyal commanders in the many campaigns; some committed minor infractions like Cederhielm, working for peace with Russia; others seem to have committed no crimes other than to be taken prisoner, and some no crime at all. Three show up as commanders in the final battle, rehabilitated by Carl: MÖRNER was a general, a field marshal at the end; DE LA GARDIE, a Swedish commander whose forebears came from the south of France in the previous century to serve the Swedish crown; SPARRE was a major general who was with Carl on his retreat to Turkey.

Page 189   LOUIS XIV: The French king had formed an alliance with Sweden, and gave subsidies to the government. As a result of Strindberg's dramatic compression, the time frame is off. Louis died in September 1715, thus it was even before Carl got back to Sweden. "TUESDAY'S SOUP" (*tisdagssoppa*): Ollén gives an example of what this might be: a soup of grain, cabbage, potato, previously served food, cooked in Monday's leftover broth. The Dwarf, of course, is not speaking of soup.

Page 194   "THE MATHEMATICIAN": Carl XII was extremely mathematically inclined, and it's been said that he thought anyone who had not studied math was "half a person" (Ollén, citing Fryxell). TOKEN COINS (*mynttecken*): These are coins of cheap metal, like copper, stamped with a value of a more precious metal; that is, the original monetary "token." One copper coin would represent the same weight in pure silver.

Page 195   "CARL, YOUR STEADFASTNESS O'ERCOMES ...": According to Ollén, Strindberg took this poem from Bernhard von Beskow's book *Carl den tolfte: En minnesbild (Carl XII: A Portrait from Memory)*: "Beskow maintains, with the support of Gustaf Adlerfeldts notes, that the poem was written by Aurora von Königsmarck, 'the most beautiful woman in Europe,' in 1706 when she, in vain, sought to get an audience with the King." Beskow uses the French version (Ollén 297). Emerentia seems to know she has Aurora's poem, given the way she "introduces" it.

Page 202   "THE MOMENTS OF LIFE EBB OUT ...": This comes from the final lines of *The Lay of Ragnar Lodbrok (Lodbrokskvädet)*, which is a Norse saga, written sometime around 1200 C.E. In a battle Lodbrok was taken prisoner and thrown in the snake pit. The skald (poet) Snorri says that the battle was the "Hjadning-striden" in the Orkney islands, a mythical eternal battle: "It was from this saga the skald Brage drew the tale of the death of Ragnar Lodbrok." Snorre Sturlason, *Den Yngre Edda* (Oslo: Det Norske samlaget, 1978).

Page 203   TAUBE (Hans Henric Taube): Not the Taube who commanded the Dragoons, mentioned in the play. General adjutant to the Viscount of Hesse; later Chamberlain to the Queen and King.

Page 206   CORPS OF ENGINEERS: Swedenborg's task was to implement Polhem's plan to transport several ships by road, using rollers, about 18 miles from Strömstad to Idefjord. He succeeded. NASIR: In the Old Testament, this refers to "pure" holy men, who gave up many things, including drinking wine; they were bound by a special pledge to Yahweh.

Page 211   MASKING (*skanskorgar*): These were small cylindrical structures or "basket forts" made by weaving flexible branches through heavy piling set in the ground.

Page 212   FRÖLICH, MÜLLERN . . . etc.: All the men named, other than Görtz, were commanders.

Page 216   THE SABBATH: There was a customary cease-fire during the Sabbath, which was from Saturday afternoon till Sunday afternoon.

Page 217   "NATURE MAKES NO LEAPS": Attributed to Aristotle, the phrase was also used by the famous Swedish botanist Linnaeus in *Philosophica Botanica*, though Linnaeus was a child during the events of the play.

[The notes on *Carl XII* are based to a great extent on Ollén, *SV*, vol. 47.]

THE DANCE OF DEATH

Page 221   DANCE OF DEATH (*Dödsdansen*): The origins of this term are found in the medieval *danse macabre*, in which those chosen to die are often pictured in art or story, being led in a dance out of this life by the figure of death—most often the robed skeleton figure. Strindberg's use of the term is half ironic, to the extent that it refers to love or marriage.

Page 223   QUARANTINE MASTER: An official in charge of quarantine stations off the coastline, where ships carrying infected and contagious passengers or animals must leave them for observation or treatment. BATTERY: Fortifications for artillery.

Page 228   NIMB: A well-known Copenhagen restaurant. ALCAZAR WALTZ: The *Alcazar, Spanischer Walzer*, by Otto Roeder.

Page 230   GUNNERS: In Swedish *konstaplar*: low-ranking officers in charge of firing artillery; also "bombardiers."

Page 231   RENTIER: A person who makes a living solely from investments.

Page 233   END OF THE "ALCAZAR WALTZ": The ending changes to a somber key (C minor). *CHAMPAGNE TROT*: Written in 1845, a piece by the Danish composer H.C. Lumbye.

Page 237   "AN AMERICAN?": The Captain seems to be referring to the American temperance movement, which was widespread at the time.

Page 241   A DEBIT AND CREDIT ACCOUNT (*upp - och avskrivningsräkning*): A forerunner of the checking account, which, at the turn of the century, was a great status symbol.

Page 242   "THE WALLPAPER SMELLS OF POISON": Here Strindberg, as always, combines the metaphor with concrete reality. Just before 1900 a particular dye known as Imperial Green was extremely popular in wallpaper design. It contained arsenic, however, which sometimes brought on cases of poisoning, and so was taken off the market.

Page 245   *MARCH OF THE BOYARS (Bojarernes intåg)*: Literally, "The Boyars' March In"; published by Norwegian composer Johan Halvorsen in 1895.

Page 248   "MELITÁM-TAMTÁ MELITÁ-LIALÁY": A doggerel refrain from the Swedish version of an old song, very frequently performed internationally, called *"The Marlborough Song"* or *"Mellbomvisan"* in Swedish.

Page 254   CALCIFIED HEART (*kalkhjärta*): Not a scientific term, but the *physical* illness here is probably arteriosclerosis, and the danger it brings for heart attack, etc.

Page 278   BLOUSE (*liv*): The Swedish word indicates a woman's garment from throat to waist, or a bit below the waist.

Page 282   *TOUT BEAU!*: French; it implies—"Careful," "Don't go too far!"

Page 292   RIFLES (*fältjägarne*): Soldiers of the infantry who were used for combat in terrain without roads, behind the enemy's front lines. The term in Swedish, literally, is more like "field-hunters."

[Many of these notes are based on Hans Lindström, *SV*, vol. 44.]

PARIAH

Page 323   DUCATS: The *dukat* gold coin was minted in Sweden from 1654–1868, and had a very specific standard—25½ karats, and a specific weight. *RES NULLIUS*: Latin, Swedish legal term for, "Goods without owner."

Page 331   COACHMAN: The Swedish says he is a *statkarl*; someone who takes seasonal work at large estates, often paid in-kind, rather than by wages.

Page 332   "TWO YEARS' HARD LABOR . . .": The terms for both crimes in the Swedish Criminal Code were six months to four years. (Ollén, *SV* 33:381)

Page 336   BERNHEIM'S STUDY ON COMPULSION: Ollén points out that in Hyppolyte Bernheim's actual work, *De la suggestion et de ses applications à la thérapeutique*, there actually is no story of forgery corresponding to Mr Y's.

APPENDIX: TOTEN-INSEL

Page 353   LUR: An S-shaped, Bronze-Age horn, from Scandinavia. "AND GOD SHALL WIPE AWAY . . .": Rev. 21:4.

Page 354   "AND WHEN THEY'VE DONE THEIR BEST . . .": Strindberg paraphrases Ps. 90:10. "THE DAY OF DEATH . . .": Eccles. 7:1.

Page 355   "WHERE YOU'VE SOWN . . .": Paraphrase of Ps. 126:5. "They that sow in tears shall reap in joy."

Page 359   "BECAUSE THOU HAST HEARKENED . . .": Gen. 3:7.

Page 360   "ASSIR SITS AS A SPECTATOR.": This is where Strindberg, for a time, thought to use *The Pelican* as a play-within-a-play; see the *Introduction*, 38-43. The notation in brackets is my own.

First Production/Performance Credits

THE GHOST SONATA

This translation of *The Ghost Sonata* was first produced in Washington D.C. by the Strindberg Festival and American Showcase Theatre (now Metro Stage) April-May 1988: Directed by Joe Martin; original music composed by Anna Larson; scenic and costume design by Nicole Quinqueton Platz; choreography by Cynthia Berkshire; lighting design by John Burgess; music performed by Anna Larson and Thomas Ohrström.

THE STRONGER, PARIAH AND SIMOOM

These translations of *The Stronger, Pariah* and *Simoom* were first produced together as *Three One-Acts*, as part of the Strindberg Festival in Washington D.C. at Source Theatre Company in March-April 1988: Directed by Robert McNamara; set design by John Antone; lighting by John James McCarthy; sound by David Crandall; costume design by Zoe Stofflett.

CARL XII

The translation of Strindberg's *Carl XII* was presented in a public reading April 15, 1988 by the Shakespeare Theatre in Washington D.C., Michael Kahn Artistic Director, in association with the Strindberg Festival: Directed by Derek Jones; Assistant Director, Anna E. Southerington.

■ ■ ■

Joe Martin is a writer, translator, and theatre director residing in Washington, D.C. He has lived in Norway, Sweden, and Canada, where he took his MFA and Ph.D. in comparative literature. His translations and original works have been produced and published in the United States, Canada, and Mexico. Martin is a recipient of numerous arts grants and research awards from sources such as the Rockefeller Foundation, the US-Mexico Cultural Fund, the American Scandinavian Foundation, the Swedish Institute, and the D.C. Commission on the Arts and Humanities. His recent books include *Keeper of the Protocols: The Works of Jens Bjørneboe*; a translation of Bjørneboe's *Semmelweis*; a novel, *Foreigners*; poetry, *The Insomnia Suite*; and a forthcoming volume of his own plays, *Conspiracies: Six Plays*. He is a professorial lecturer in theatre at American University, and is a faculty associate in the Johns Hopkins Masters in Drama Studies program.